SHAMANS, SOFTWARE, AND SPLEENS

JAMES BOYLE

Shamans, Software, and Spleens

LAW AND THE

CONSTRUCTION OF

THE INFORMATION

SOCIETY

Harvard University Press
Cambridge, Massachusetts
London, England

Copyright © 1996 by the President and Fellows
  of Harvard College
All rights reserved
Printed in the United States of America
Third printing, 1997

First Harvard University Press paperback edition, 1997

Library of Congress Cataloging-in-Publication Data

Boyles, James.
    Shamans, software, and spleens : law and the construction
of the information society / James Boyle.
        p.   cm.
    Includes bibliographical references and index.
    ISBN 0-674-80522-4 (cloth)
    ISBN 0-674-80523-2 (pbk.)
    1. Intellectual property.   2. Copyright—Moral rights.
    3. Authors—Legal status, laws, etc.   4. Information society.
    I. Title.
    K1401.B69   1996
    302.2—dc20   95-42433

For Lauren

Contents

Preface

For the last twenty years we have been told that we are shifting from the industrial to the information economy. Sometimes the phrase used is "information society," sometimes the more dynamic "information revolution." Most people take these vague expressions to refer to an electronic (and nerdy) modernity—something to do with computers, the Internet, and possibly Vice President Gore. Those who read the science pages might also mention the manipulation of genetic information. With or without Vice President Gore or the human genome, the information revolution is understood as primarily a *technical* one. Most journalistic coverage of the subject limits itself to breathless accounts of the newest technological wonder, with occasional brief forays into futurism. The characteristic quality of these techno-futures is that social relationships, wealth distribution, and belief systems all stay pretty much the same. Only the gadgets change. But this is just bad science fiction. Right now, behind the visible information revolution in technology and economy, a significant but unexamined process of rhetorical and *interpretive* construction is going on. This process of construction produces justifications, ideologies, and property regimes rather than mainframes, software, or gene splices. Yet it will shape our world as thoroughly as any technical change. To understand this process, one needs more than a modem or a multimedia kit; one needs a social theory of the information society. This book tries to provide one.

Consciously and unconsciously, we are already developing the language of entitlement for a world in which information—genetic, electronic, proprietary—is one of the main sources and forms of wealth. We think about issues of entitlement using the vocabularies of classical liberalism, market, family, and property rights. ("Because it's my right." "Because it's efficient." "Because it protects family values." "Because it's *mine*.") Each of those ways of thinking makes assumptions about the relevance of information—whether to the well-functioning state, the efficient market, or the realm of personal privacy and individual ownership. How might those assumptions influence and in turn be changed by an information economy? If there are no fresh starts in history, if the future is made from fragments of the past, then the discourse of entitlement in an information society will draw on images of information that were produced in a society where information bore a very different relationship to technology, to power, to wealth, a different relationship even to our own bodies. To put it another way, if history is collage, then we need to look at the available pictures, scissors, and paste. That is what I have tried to do here, using law and the surrounding discourses on which legal analysis draws, from aesthetics to economics, as my raw material.

Although law is my starting place, I have tried to go beyond the style of legal writing best described as Jetson's Jurisprudence—a listing of technological marvels in the hope they will make a related set of legal rules alluringly futuristic by association. My main focus is on the way our society conceives of information, and on the paradoxical results that conception may entail. To use the jargon, this is an analysis of the social construction of reality. Unlike many such analyses, however, it has a practical intent. Thus I offer not only analysis and structure, but a conclusion—one much qualified in the pages that follow, but a conclusion nonetheless.

The conclusion is that—for a set of complicated reasons traced out in the pages that follow—we are driven to confer property rights in information on those who come closest to the image of the romantic author, those whose contributions to information production are most easily seen as original and transformative. I argue that this is a bad thing for reasons of both efficiency and justice; it leads us to have *too many* intellectual property rights, to confer them on the *wrong people,* and dramatically to undervalue the interests of both the *sources of* and the *audiences for* the information we commodify. If I am right, this unconscious use of the author paradigm has wide-ranging negative effects, with costs in areas ranging from biodiversity and the production of new drugs to the shape of the international economy and the structure of the computer industry. As one Orwellian case study here reveals, it may even threaten our control over the genetic information in our own bodies.

Why should we believe that the idea of authorship would assume more importance in an information economy, let alone that it might produce the negative consequences I describe here? The argument is a complicated one with a simple conclusion. In law and ideology as in other more prosaic realms, things that seem to "work" tend to be used. Information presents special problems; the idea of authorship seems (wrongly) to solve or at least defer those problems.[1]

But what does it mean to say that information presents special problems? I do not mean that the regulation, ownership, and control of information presents special *technical* or *functional* difficulties, though that is sometimes true. The "problems" I refer to are problems in the realm of ideas, paradoxes, or tensions in our assumptions, brought to the surface when the subject is information. To put it more specifically, as a form of wealth, a focus of production, and a conception of value, information is a problematic category within our most basic ways of thinking about markets, property, politics, and self-definition.

In market terms, information has significant "public good" qualities; it is often expensive to create or generate but cheap to copy. Economic theory tells us that "public goods" will be underproduced because there will be too little incentive to create them. Suppose I spend two years and fifty thousand dollars creating a software program that can be copied for the price of a diskette. Alternatively, to use a nonelectronic example, suppose I spend the same time and money testing a thousand substances to find out which are valuable drugs—drugs that someone else can produce for pennies once the information about their properties is known. I sell one copy of my program, one dose of my drug, and then find the market has disappeared. Who would spend the time to write the program or test the drug in the first place? The obvious answer to these problems is the creation of "intellectual" property rights. Give inventors, scientists, programmers, and genetic engineers some kind of legal monopoly—a protection against copying. But information also has significant "efficiency" qualities; the more costly and restricted the access to information, the more inefficient the market, scientific research community, computer industry, or what have you. Is there a balance between incentive and efficiency? If so, how do we know where to strike it?

Information is problematic in other ways. Liberal political theory sees free access to and transmission of information as the lifeblood of the public sphere. The First Amendment is only the most famous of the many incarnations of this ideal. It is already hard—if not impossible—for us to square this tradition with two others: our strong idea of intellectual property rights on the one hand, and our vision of individual privacy on the other. In a world where "information" was the dominant form of wealth, the problem could only be magnified. I could go on but the basic point is simple. Information presents special problems and the discourse of authorship *seems* to solve those problems. (Actually, it merely assumes them away in a particularly unfortunate manner.) The discourse of authorship premises a grant of a limited monopoly (most familiarly, an intellectual property right) on a transformative originality more often assumed than proved. The author stands between the public and private realms, giving new ideas to the society at large and being granted in return a limited right of private property in the artifact he or she has created—or at least assembled from the parts provided by our common store of ideas, language, and genre. Precisely because of the way it couples romantic appeal and *apparent* efficacy, I would argue that this way of thinking—with its corresponding suppression of the claims of "sources" and "audience"—will be the default mode for dealing with issues of ownership and control of information.

The importance of the structure of thought I outline here goes beyond the negative effects of any particular rule or set of rules. The notion of the author does for information, for the knowledge-value revolution, what the Divine Right of Kings did for the monarchy, what classical economists' notion of the justice of "natural" unregulated markets did for the economic relations of the industrial revolution. This then is the story of the *imperial author* and the role that *the ideology of authorship* might play in an information society.

The author-vision conjures up a new political economy of wealth supported, and reflexively constituted, by a particular ideology of entitlement. At the bottom of the pyramid would be those whose lives, bodies, and natural environments provide the raw materials, or those who themselves are the ultimate "audience," for the products of an information economy. At the top of the pyramid of entitlement claims—at least in theory—would be those who gather and shape information and information products. More important, perhaps, is the fact that the bureaucratic and corporate actors who *employ* the manipulators of information can justify their own, derivative intellectual property rights through the rhetoric of individualism and original genius. In fact, a striking feature of the language of romantic authorship is the way it is used to support sweeping intellectual property rights for large corporate entities. Sony, Pfizer, and Microsoft tend to lack the appeal of Byron and Alexander Fleming.

Actual "authors"—writers, inventors, genetic and software engineers—often lose out under the kind of regime I describe here. It is not merely that they find their work belongs to their employers. There are justifications for such a result, albeit ones that are currently invoked too widely. The true irony comes when we find that large companies can use the idea of the independent entrepreneurial creator to justify intellectual property rights *so* expansive that they make it much harder for future independent creators actually to create. The expansion of intellectual property inhibits the very process on which the expansionists premise their arguments. This irony has not gone entirely unnoticed. For example, recent years have seen the development of a fascinating set of protests in the software industry. People who owe their fame, and in some cases their fortunes, to their status as innovators—Mitch Kapor, creator of Lotus 1-2-3, Richard Stallman, the creator of GNU Emacs—have begun to argue that contemporary intellectual property rights are so broad as to *slow* the rate of innovation.[2]

The structure of thought I describe here does not make an equivalent social pyramid inevitable, anything but. Nor does it mean that struggling authors, inventors, and computer programmers are going to reap the rewards of the information society. How should we understand it then?

I am not imagining a conspiracy of the software designers or the genetic engineers; a real-life revenge of the nerds. Quite the contrary. My claim is that—for a number of reasons—the author vision exercises a strange fascination over our conceptions of the commodification of information, so that it is hard *even to imagine an alternative system*. There is nothing inevitable in all of this, however. No World Spirit stands ready to chide us if we stray from the path I sketch here. No executive committee of the ruling class or unbreakable consortium of multinationals dictates such a result. For one thing, the author paradigm—when played out in the way I describe here—produces effects that are not only unjust, but unprofitable in the long term. As the Bellagio Declaration points out, "At present, drugs drawn from the rain forest or from indigenous pharmacopeias do not economically support the protection of either. Traditional patterns and dances can be taken without permission or recompense, perhaps diminishing the chance that the culture that originated them will survive."[3] Even a conventional economic analysis supports the idea that it is in the interest of those who are exploiting a "commons" to make sure that the commons continues to exist. The author vision blinds us to the importance of the commons—to the importance of the raw material from which information products are constructed. But precisely because of that blindness, there is some space for intervention by scholars, citizens, and activists of various stripes—before the information society's assumptions about entitlement rigidify in an inegalitarian and ultimately self-defeating pattern.

When I began this project, I found I was working largely without maps. There have been few attempts to produce a critical social theory of the information society. Most newspaper coverage has concentrated on a few narrow issues, generally defined by the technology to which they relate—the information superhighway, computer privacy, the Clipper chip. This is useful, but it doesn't get us far. An analogy might help to illustrate the point. Imagine a group of feudal serfs gathered around a newly invented power loom, wondering whether the lord of the manor will now increase the tithes. With the easy arrogance of hindsight, we find the picture ridiculous. How silly it would be to assume that all social arrangements, all hierarchies, all ideologies of entitlement, will remain exactly as they are and only the technology of production will change! Yet this is exactly the assumption made by most discussions of the *information* society.

There are exceptions, of course. Books have proclaimed the dangers of "futureshock" or—more interestingly—have speculated about the "knowledge-value revolution"—the tendency for an increasing proportion of a product's value to be made up of its information content.[4]

Anne Wells Branscomb's book *Who Owns Information?* published in 1994, provides excellent case studies that illustrate the conflicting goals of information policy, and the absence of any holistic perspective.[5] Naysayers have argued persuasively that the fetishization of the computer may drive us to social arrangements, educational theories, and workplace experiences that are neither humane nor desirable, neither efficient nor equitable. At least one excellent book has been written about electronic civil liberties and the demonization of the hacker.[6] These insights are valuable, but much of the literature alternates between a meliorist historicism and a dark but crude economic determinism in which "the big companies" always get the results they want. One is left wanting more—more explanations of exactly whose ox is gored and how the goring is justified, more discussion of the complex reciprocal relationship between our current ideas of politics, justice, efficiency, and entitlement and the variegated set of economic and technological changes that are collectively referred to as the information society.

In my own field—law—there is surprisingly little writing on the impact of "the information society," and most of what there is manages to be both vague and optimistic.[7] More information is, by definition, good. What threats could an information society hold? Occasional articles discuss the relevance of the Fourth Amendment to electronic mail, the remedies for the unauthorized use of someone's genetic information, the trade effects produced by the intellectual property provisions of the GATT (General Agreement on Tariffs and Trade). But the key to these articles is that information issues are considered in isolation, each ingeniously stretched or trimmed to fit the Procrustean bed of the nearest legal category. One looks in vain for a general discussion of how the information economy will affect law, and of how the assumptions embedded in law will affect the information economy.

By and large, the self-consciously academic literature of postmodern theory and cultural studies offers even less than the popular or legal literature.[8] It is hard to understand why, given the philosophical climate of postmodernity. If postmodernism has a material base—a social reality on which it reflects, a set of shared experiences that makes it seem apt and convincing—then that reality is the world of electronic media. Postmodern theories are full of references to computers, hypertext, channel surfing, and the processed image. (And

Madonna, of course.) Postmodernists are also fond of references to the knowledge/power nexus, and it is hard to think of a more promising starting place for the analysis of an information age. Thus, for reasons of both content and form, one would expect postmodern philosophy to have sophisticated and interesting things to say about the ways in which a new political economy of information power is constructed, conceived, and defended.

Sadly, what one finds instead are rather uninformed sweeping statements about American popular culture made by (French) academics whose main source of information seems to be each other's books; there is also an occasional snippet from the Pay TV in the airport hotel or the 1950 B movies that are badly dubbed back home on TeleFrance 1.

In any event, such was my perception of the available work on the subject. If this book strikes some as altogether too analytic and programmatic for the postmodern age it is because the paucity of the critical literature denied me the luxury of constant irony, a tone that flourishes only in conditions of overabundance—theoretical as well as material. I would also add in my own defense that the following pages are entirely free from references to Madonna. Surely this ought to be worth something.

SHAMANS, SOFTWARE, AND SPLEENS

The Information Society

The idea that we are moving toward an "information age" or an "information society" has now passed from iconoclasm through orthodoxy to cliché. Yet the idea is a vague one, even for a cliché, capable of conjuring up radically dissimilar images in different minds. For some, the information age simply means a shift in emphasis in the global economy, a shift from tangible to intangible goods, from things to ideas, from tractors to software. Others imagine that the information age will be the age of direct democracy, as technology gives a global citizenry both the knowledge and the means of control necessary to decide the daily issues of the polity. Ross Perot's promise of the electronic town meeting is only the most recent of such modem-government reveries. For still others, the information age conjures up a science fiction, "cyberpunk," dystopia—a world dominated by large corporations trading equally in genetic and electronic information, a culture in which genetic engineering will become a matter of fashion rather than science, where instead of fake Rolexes or Vuitton bags, the underworld will offer cheap copies of the latest computer program or the trendiest gene-splice technique.

Whatever the information age will ultimately look like, some parts of it are already with us. It is not simply that the market for computers and software is a huge one or that the manipulation of genetic information is a fast-growing area of the economy. It is not even the shift of so many skilled workers into jobs that collect, refine, manipulate, package, and deploy *data,* rather than more tangible things. The *idea* of information has colonized new areas of human activity. Aerodynamics, weather prediction, and traffic patterns have been reconceptualized as problems for information technology, but also as problems to be thought about through the metaphors offered by computer models. Popular magazines write beautifully illustrated articles about the delights of chaos theory, full of mystifying anecdotes about dripping taps and butterfly effects. The scientists interviewed show uncharacteristic enthusiasm for their discoveries. They talk of "patterned randomness" and "familiar haphazard arrangements." Behind the oxymorons, one can sense the missionary zeal of a new paradigm, the excitement of reimagining everything from the performance of the stock market to the behavior of gas-turbine blades as a series of data-packets, clustered in some elegant fractal geometry.

Academics are very fond of talking about the collapse of disciplinary boundaries, a process they seem to imagine as principally involving the creation of a whole new group of readers for *their* work. In information theory right now, one can watch the disciplinary boundaries evaporate in real time. One of my favorite Internet discussion groups—the Biological Information Theory and Chowder Society—spends much of its time discussing Maxwell's demon (which used to be thought of as a thermodynamics thought experiment), the possibility of reversible computing (which used only to concern those who fantasized about nanotechnology), and Shannon's mathematical models of information transmission (originally set out in the context of radio communication). Yet most of the participants are not mathematicians, electronic engineers, physicists, or radio buffs. They are biologists attempting to understand genetic information—combing other disciplines for useful ways of thinking about information transmission, compression, and entropy—and creating a new discipline called bio-informatics in the process.

Information is not merely an organizing concept for the technologies and disciplines of the twenty-first century. It is a central feature of the international economy. Indeed, the protection of information "value-added" in products is one of the key elements in the foreign policy of the developed world. Intellectual property—which stretches beyond "information" conventionally defined—has become a major area of international concern. This is particularly, and ironically, true for the United States, which used to be the biggest pirate of them all.[1] It has been claimed that over one-quarter of the United States' total exports rely on intellectual property rights. The International Trade Commission claims that foreign piracy of U.S. intellectual property costs $40 to $60 *billion* per year. The music industry claims to lose $2.45 billion worldwide. The software industry claims that it lost $15.2 billion in 1994.[2]

The interesting thing about this supposed wave of piracy is not that these huge numbers are absolutely accurate. Indeed, the assumptions on which they are based turn out to be extremely problematic. The interesting thing is the transformation of social and technological conditions that would cause a wave of piracy to exist at all. Why is the software industry losing billions of dollars? Because both the facilities for copying and the market for using information technology have increased in quantum leaps over the last ten years. As the marginal cost of both hardware and copying drops, the "information content" assumes a greater proportion of the product's value. This is as true of the $100 million invested in developing computer architecture or source codes that can be copied for pennies as it is of the $100 million spent in genetically engineering a strain of wheat that grows its own "copies." Unacknowledged by most students of international relations, the "sanctity of intellectual property" has come to play an iconic role in the foreign policy of the developed world similar to the role played by "freedom of the seas," or "prompt, adequate, and effective compensation for expropriation," in an earlier age.

The transformation of information technology has implications in areas closer to home than intellectual property protection and international trade. Another side of the transformation can even be seen in the most mundane domestic situations. Why do supermarkets offer their preferred customers discounts just for running an electronic card though a scanner on their way past the checkout? Because technology now permits the store to keep a precise record of those customers' purchases and to correlate it with demographic information about them. Advertisers will soon know everything from our individual brand-name preferences for toilet paper to the odds that a middle-class family on a particular street will buy Fig Newtons on a Wednesday. If you are what you eat, then manufacturers will soon have the information technology to know exactly what you are. This commercially driven intrusion has not reached Orwellian proportions—at least, not yet. Nevertheless, information technology has the capacity, if not to *end* privacy, then to redefine what we mean by the term. There has been a quantum leap in the ability of both the state and the market to gather, process, and retrieve information about individuals. The best way to understand the change might be to see it as a shift from administration by *actuarial statistics* to administration by *personal biography*. As you apply for your mortgage or file your income taxes, it is not reassuring to imagine the relevant decision makers noting the fact that your consumption of wine is up this year, that you bought two books on depression, or that the videos you rented were violent and escapist. Is freedom inversely related to the efficiency of the available means of surveillance? If so, we have much to fear.[3]

Finally, we should beware of the tendency to equate information with computers, software, and electronics. Information does not need to be stored in ones and zeroes, and those who collect and manipulate information are not confined to the world of computers (though they often use computers to do their work). The most obvious example is the biotech industry. Why are the drug and chemical companies pushing so hard for intellectual property protection for genetic material, or living organisms? Because they are on, or over, the brink of mass-market production based on the manipulation of genetic information.

We have already reached the point where genetic information is thought of primarily *as* information. We look at the informational message—the sequence of As, Gs, Cs, and Ts—not the biological medium.[4] The human genome project is simply a large-scale exercise in cryptography. Like archaeologists with the Rosetta Stone, we have broken the cipher, and can now deal with DNA as a *language to be spoken*, not *an object to be contemplated*. We have not yet been forced to think about the implications of this transformation; only science fiction writers or professional moralists worry about equal rights for clones or ponder the morality of the use by computer companies of biological "wetware" based on human brain tissue. Admittedly, Harvard has patented a mouse with some human genes for use in cancer research. You may be surprised to learn that we already have intellectual property-holding "authors" of living animals, even animals that have had human genetic information spliced into their basic genetic code. Still, the most wrenching dilemmas of transgenic animal species—part human, part chimp for example—are some years down the road. As yet, no genetically engineered lumpenproletariat uses the language of the Thirteenth Amendment to plead for citizenship, but in the judgment of many, that is only a matter of time. It is the ultimate mark of the information society that we will soon have "authors" of living, sapient beings, authors who will presumably assert that they are not slavemasters but creators, and entitled to intellectual property rights as such.

For some, these ideas are too futuristic to be taken seriously. In a truly remarkable example of deliberate self-impoverishment, contemporary intellectuals have convinced themselves that futurism is adolescent (and anyway uncool). Whether or not such bioethical dilemmas will arise, there is something so *strange* in the idea of genetic engineering that it is more comfortable to consign it to the realm of fiction, to worry about the problem only when it is actually presented so squarely as to be undeniable. To be fair, this may not be quite as silly a strategy as it seems. Predictions of technological progress often miss the key twist that transforms the problem. My point is that, even without these futuristic trappings, enough of the information society is *already* with us for it to be irresponsible not to think about it as a whole.

Information Humbug?

There are two powerful objections to this brief account of the information age. The first is that of historical redundancy. Haven't we always lived in an information society? The argument goes something like this: Rome conquered most of the world not because of its legions and its onagers, but because of its superior information technology (the techniques of writing), information class (the scribes of the bureaucracy), information storage (libraries), and information-retrieval mechanisms. In their time, papyrus, the quill pen, double-entry bookkeeping, and the printing press were all revolutions in "information technology." Thus, says the skeptic, either there is no such thing as an information society or we have always had one. The innovators of yesteryear deserve their place in today's pantheon of the pioneers of the information society. Gutenberg equals Türing. Caxton equals Crick and Watson. The examples could be multiplied, but the point is clear. The power to gather, manipulate, retrieve, and commodify information has always been important.

The second objection to my account of the information society is that of incoherence. Barring my labeling of the subjects I discuss here as "information issues," is there really any interesting or useful link to be seen between them? With two exceptions, my list of issues is typical of those produced in discussions of the information society. (This, of course, might mean merely that there are *many* incoherent lists.) The increasing importance of computers, the concepts and models provided by information technology, and the dangers posed to privacy by the accumulation and sale of information—these are standard fare in the news media. The debate about the "National Information Infrastructure" has popularized the Internet and provided a slew of ungainly road metaphors. A few writers have emphasized the issues raised by the technological and conceptual treatment of genetic information *as* information. The increasing prominence of intellectual property in domestic politics and international trade has received little or no attention, though logic would suggest its importance. But is there anything, apart from the *word* information, that holds these issues together? If there is some useful link, is it new to our society?

The historical point is fair but not decisive. Yes, information has always been important, but the scale of the transformation we have already undergone justifies the idea of a tectonic shift. There were machines and there was "industry" before the "industrial revolution," but the phrase is still worth using. What's more, and this also provides my answer to the second question, one of the reasons we can describe our society as an information society is that we *think of it as such.* This argument is not quite as circular as it seems; social self-perceptions are part of the social reality. We already use the concept of an information age in our political arguments, legislative schemes, and industrial proposals. Issues become questions of information policy because we think of them as such. The economic, technological, and policy tools used to deal with those issues change as a result. The metaphors and the technologies of information move forward in reciprocal relationship.

I have another reason for believing that the idea of an information society is an important one, though I can only introduce it obliquely. The denizens of the Internet have a saying, almost a mantra: "information wants to be free." Often the phrase merely connotes a crude but passionate libertarianism, a belief that the spread of information is both inevitable and good. This mantra comes with the accompanying belief that authorities—corporate or governmental—which oppose the spread of information are doomed to extinction, preferably sooner than later. This idea could be criticized as both simplistic and optimistic; I doubt Bill Gates, the chairman of Microsoft, is losing any sleep. But on another level the saying is true, and true in a way that suggests my answer to both kinds of skepticism.

Let's return to my sampler of information age problems. We have a loosely related cluster of issues, linked by several different connotations of the word "information." We have the information technology issues, the genetic information issues, the privacy issues, the dataflow issues, and the intellectual property issues. The justification for treating these together is precisely the *homologization of forms of information,* their liquidity, in the monetary sense of easy conversion from one form into another. The phrase "information wants to be free" has part of its force because it anthropomorphizes this liquidity, this conceptually, technologically, and economically driven tendency to float free of some particular form and context. One might even call it the universalizing logic of the information relation. The tendency is toward the economic and conceptual separation of the informational message from the medium—cells, diskettes, telephone directories, or whatever—and of the progressive devaluation (literally, the diminishing marginal cost) of the medium as compared with the message. As the information content is decontextualized, the location or form of the information comes to seem increasingly irrelevant—as irrelevant as the color of two books would be to a comparison of their arguments. Thus ideas originally applied to one "information area" seem to apply to another, first in metaphor and then in technological reality. The same problems arise in area after area and, increasingly, solutions are borrowed too.

For an example of what I mean, take the human genome project, the attempt to "map" and "sequence" the entire human genome—to plot the location of the 300,000 genes that biologically define a human being and to work out the arrangement of the 1,000 DNA "bases" in each gene—3,000,000,000 in all. Mapping sketches the position of genes on the chromosome, sequencing tells you the order of the Cs, the Gs, the As, and the Ts that spell out our biological destiny.

The human genome project might seem to be one of biology, of medicine. What does it have to do with the information age and with the other issues I named—information technology, privacy, dataflow, and intellectual property? Information technology is vital to the new project, not just in scanning and recording the maps and sequences of DNA, but in conceiving of the project. Earlier I described the rise of bio-informatics, the new science and technology of managing, modeling, and manipulating molecular biological data. Computer science, which lists among its most fertile developing grounds the successful attempt to break the code of the German Enigma cipher machine during the Second World War, is now the indispensable adjunct to the attempt to crack a deeper, fleshier code. Bill Gates, of all people, has endowed a chair at the University of Washington in a molecular biology department devoted to linking robotic technology, mathematical models, and computer storage in the effort to parse the genome. Increasingly, the technology of mapping and sequencing is automated, and the genetic sequences are stored on disk. Presumably, the next step will be the automation of recombinant gene engineering as well. The analogy can go much further. A lot of biologists think that the human genome project will be the eventual key to the genetic medicine of the next century, to a set of techniques that will allow doctors to edit the genetic codes for diseases and predispositions to disease in the same way that a word processor allows you to edit a document onscreen, and to do so *within a living patient.* Biological destiny becomes merely a first draft, subject to spell-checking, editing, and even complete rewrites.

This example shows the way in which the form of the information—genetic, electronic—becomes increasingly irrelevant. But think of the other problems it raises. What about intellectual property rights? As I pointed out earlier, the same tendency that leads to the devaluation of the form of the information also leads information to be a classic public goods problem. It is because the result of a $100 million genetic research project could be stored on a 50-cent diskette, and then copied at 50 cents a time, that intellectual property assumes such incredible importance. This point was raised with particular force when Dr. Craig Ventner of the National Institutes of Health (NIH)—an organization that is one of the principal actors in the U.S. human genome project—attempted to patent 2,750 partial cDNA sequences. Patenting genetically engineered organisms *is* possible. The

Supreme Court decided that issue in 1980.[5] Dr. Ventner's claim was unusual in a number of respects, however. He was patenting sequences of human DNA. He had "discovered" rather than "invented" these sequences, and he didn't know what they actually did (though he did know that they did *something*—that they weren't the so-called junk DNA.) In the end, the NIH patents were rejected, but the trend that they represent continues in force. There is an intellectual land grab going on, the unclaimed frontier "land" in this case being the human genome: " 'This is a quick and dirty grab—like the wild West, where everyone was trying to stake a claim,' complained one geneticist, who spoke on the condition of anonymity because he said he had several friends involved in genome companies. 'It's basically people with a lot of human genome money trying to cash in.' "[6]

American historians have long pointed out the importance of the idea of an "infinite frontier" to the economic and political decisions of the late nineteenth and early twentieth centuries. In the information society, the "frontier" is a conceptual one but, for reasons explained in this book, it depends on the same expansive idea of an infinite landscape available to future arrivals. Locke tells us that, to be legitimate, a set of property claims must leave "enough and as good" for future claimants. If there is always "enough and as good" left, then who can complain about the expansiveness of current grants of intellectual property? The idea of the frontier seems to solve the problem of scarcity. But in important ways, the information frontier is no more infinite than the West was infinite, and the monopoly property rights now being given out to software and biotech companies rival anything given to the railroad or banking "trusts" a hundred years ago.

The appropriate level of intellectual property protection is all the more difficult to identify because a large part of the research behind this land grab was funded by the public purse, by the hundreds of millions of dollars poured into the genome project. If intellectual property is justified by the claim that it is necessary to produce the research investment necessary for progress, then the existence of massive state-supported basic research ought to make *some* difference in the decision over the level of property rights. In practice, however, the (probably well-justified) belief that private industry will produce useful products more quickly is coupled to the erroneous belief that the greater the level of intellectual property protection, the greater the progress.

Walter Gilbert, one of the pioneers in this area of research, believes that private corporations are the ideal institutions to crack the genetic code. " 'Information [the cosmid library map] is the product,' said Gilbert . . . And will Gilbert's private project patent the human genome? He says no. 'I don't think the genome is patentable,' Gilbert said. 'We will copyright the sequence. It just means that if you want to read the sequence, you will have to pay for access rights. Our purpose is to make the information available to everyone, at a price.' "[7]

The conflict between incentives and monopolies, efficiency and property, could not be more starkly posed than by the prospect of a copyrighted genome. What about the question of access? Vice President Gore's plan for the National Information Infrastructure has as its second cardinal principle the idea of universal access. (The first—in classically Clintonesque manner—is the promotion of private investment.) The plan's Agenda for Action declares that the United States must "extend the 'universal service' concept to ensure that information resources are available to all at affordable prices. Because information means empowerment, the government has a duty to ensure that all Americans have access to the resources of the Information Age."

Do these same concerns apply to the fruits of the human genome project? Science fiction authors love to speculate about the hold that gene-splice medicine—protected by intellectual property rights—could give to corporations on their employees or governments on their citizens. "Leave the company and your Prolong®, anti-senescence treatments stop right here." No such futurism is necessary, however, in order to imagine the problems the human genome project could raise. Once the code has been cracked, what then? On the one hand, desires for universal egalitarian access run up against the hard wall of property rights. On the other, they hit our concern for individual privacy. The ability to "read" the genetic code *already* poses nightmarish problems for privacy, particularly in a system where both employers and insurance companies have a strong incentive to deny health insurance to those likely to need it most. Genetic predispositions to heart disease, cancer, or other diseases *already* make insurance more costly—and sometimes unavailable. What happens when genetic mapping is more accurate in its predictions? What statistically accurate generalizations will the state forbid? To turn from the disturbing to the apparently ridiculous, some geneticists even claim that the human genome project will provide the body of knowledge necessary to explore the genetic roots of behavioral tendencies—and to turn that knowledge to commercial use.

> Just as genetic cartography confirms the powerful relationships between our genomes and our physical attributes, researchers are finding there are strong genetic ties to personality attributes as well. Personality appears to be a product of heredity as well as upbringing and environment. There are, of course, a swarm of ethical, legal, and practical considerations arising from gene-based marketing. But if today's marketers are prepared to spend billions on demographic and psychographic data to better sell their wares, should it come as any surprise that tomorrow's marketers may try to use databases based on "genographics"—the gene sequences that help shape people's personalities? If it makes economic sense—and bitter controversy—for today's insurers to want to know about gene markers for disease, there could be equally compelling economics for marketers to better grasp the genetic predispositions of their customers' personalities. "The numbers clearly indicate that the genes influence behavior," says Oliver P. John, an associate professor at the Institute of Personality and Social Research at the University of California at Berkeley. "Genetic influence doesn't mean that personalities are fixed or don't change, but that learning more about genes will give us better insights into behavior."[8]

If the idea of a sociogenetics of junk mail makes you smile, other possibilities may be less amusing. Imagine a political campaign in which gene maps played as big a role as video tapes of clandestine sexual encounters, or tapes of incriminating phone calls. Suppose there *was* a genetic marker that indicates a predisposition to homosexuality; would homophobic candidates disclose their gene maps as proudly as they now do their medical and psychological records, daring their opponents to do the same?

I could go on, piling up the "what if's" like leaves in autumn, but the basic point is a simple one. The same conditions that make it conceptually and technologically attractive to talk of an information age also guarantee the migration of problems from one information area to another. Public goods problems, intellectual property, privacy, the importance of dataflow and processing power, the clash between the values of private property and the public domain—these problems reappear in each new area, and in each new area they are dealt with by using a set of ideas about information that had their roots in a society where information bore a different relation to property and power. This *doesn't* mean that "the-law-needs-to-become-modern-in-order-to-fit-changing-social-conditions." That is the emptiest of legal clichés. Rather, the point is that there will be unintended consequences and political "hangovers" produced by the juxtaposition of the information economy with the ideas of information produced by classical liberalism, neoclassical economics, post-realist property rights and individual privacy. Those unintended consequences might be desirable ones. But we will not know until we look. That is the reason that "the information age" is a useful idea, and it is also the reason that we need a critical social theory to understand it.

Why Look at *Law* to Understand the Information Society?

Very well, then. Let us say you agree at least that we are now in the throes of a transformation of economy and culture in which the production, manipulation, and distribution of information of all kinds are likely to be increasingly important. If we want to have some sense of the contours of that transformation, where should we look? In this book, I argue that we should pay more attention to the legal forms in which information issues are framed, debated, and resolved and to the cultural, economic, and ideological assumptions those legal forms present in fascinatingly stylized and abstract terms.[9]

Think of the changes in international trade I described earlier. These events did not take place in a vacuum of abstract scientific progress. Technological change shapes and is shaped by ideology and legal form. On the simplest level, it is easy to see that intellectual property protection will assume (and has already assumed) greater importance in the international economy.[10] Information products often have significant "public good" qualities; the same unit can supply many additional customers at negligible cost. In more familiar language, it is often both easier and cheaper to copy such products than to buy them. If the international economy is dominated by sales of raw materials, or even finished machinery, the public goods problems are less salient. When one is selling bauxite, the ultimate user can hardly run off 200 copies. When one is selling software, the risk is of copying is high.

Of course, it is hardly surprising to find technological changes shaping both the prominence and the contours of the legal forms within which that technology is developed and exploited. Less obvious, perhaps, is the reverse effect. Sometimes the technologies, art forms, and commercial practices that succeed are those that fit a particular set of legal metaphors. Rules of intellectual property may push research in a particular direction, simply because the likely result would be more easily protected than the result of some other, equally promising line of research.[11] More subtle effects can be perceived if one focuses on the clusters of belief on which legal norms rely for their coherence, or on the legalistic language we use to describe our imaginary political topography. We locate questions of information regulation on the conceptual map—type it as "public" or "private," "intervention" or "the status quo"—thus deciding the issue in the moment it is described. Effects such as these are hard to detect for many reasons. Our interpretive construction of the issue may be so reflexive that it is hard even to imagine an alternative, let alone to tease out its likely implications.

To some, law may seem a quixotic or even a parochial place to begin the inquiry. Scholars from other disciplines often talk as if law were either formalism—proceeding by itself in logical chains of deduction—or functionalism—a mere appendage to economic and social change. Thus, it might seem that the study of law has little to offer in our attempts to imagine the cultural, social, and ideological patterns of an information society. Yet when we turn our gaze backward in time, few would dispute that a critical analysis of legal forms is an important part of any history we might write. If one wants to understand the American economy of the early twentieth century one has to know something about the legal and social arrangements of wage labor and the institutional framework of capital formation. If this is true for the past, is it not likely to be true for the future? To exaggerate the point for emphasis, one could say that *intellectual property and its conceptual neighbors may bear the same relationship to the information society as the wage-labor nexus did to the industrial manufacturing society of the 1900s.* Yet the former relationship remains underanalyzed, if it is analyzed at all. Thus we are left with the paradox that even as the mechanisms of the GATT are used to set up the central legal forms of an international information economy, there is almost no critical writing about the cultural, ideological, and intellectual presuppositions behind those legal forms. It is as if we were trying to understand the development of industrial capital without Marx, Weber, or even Adam Smith or Thorstein Veblen on our shelves. Call me an idealist, but this seems like a bad plan.

There is of course, a danger in this analogy. I said that intellectual property and its neighbors might play the same role for an international information economy that the wage-labor nexus did for industrial capitalism. That kind of analogy could lead one into a dangerous grandiosity of thought. After all, the typical error of large-scale social theory is to imagine that one feature of society or economy determines all of history. Now we have a more chastened vision of theory. Yet it would surely be an equal and opposite mistake to *ignore* the legal form that is likely to be central to an information economy, and the broader discourse of entitlement and justification that a study of the law of information reveals.

How can one avoid the totalizing tendencies of grand social theory or the limitations of functional explanations and yet make use of the profound insights to be found in legal materials, and in the cultural presuppositions and policy discourses that give those legal materials determinacy? Two things about my method seem very different from that used in the great tradition of functional and deterministic studies of law.

First, the vision of law offered here is an expansive one, and the very expansiveness of the vision makes it harder to slip into dogmatic reductionism. I take the position that to understand law fully, one must see it as much more than a collection of rules, or even a collection of social effects. Instead, law should be seen as a complex interpretive activity, a practice of encoding and decoding social meaning that merges imperceptibly with rhetoric, ideology, "common sense," economic argument (of both a highly theoretical and a seat-of-the-pants kind), with social stereotype, narrative cliché and political theory of every level from high abstraction to civics class chant.

Let me offer a simple example. When processed by our legal culture, a mundane dispute over the ownership of some apparently abandoned jewelry is converted into a complicated abstraction that lawyers call a case.[12] We can treat the case as giving rise to a "rule" (itself part prediction, part interpretation, part normative claim) or to an "effect," either particular or more general. If we look at it more broadly, however, we find that the case is dependent on common-sense theories about human behavior, speculative ideas about the effect of legal norms on citizens' actions, economic nostrums about the advantages of keeping property in the market system, and moralistic pronouncements about careless owners and diligent finders (or blameless owners and predatory finders). Legal materials, the arguments used to interpret them, and the scholarly discourses that surround and are sometimes drawn on by such materials are a fertile source of assumptions about our world. They offer a microtomic slice through a complex, socially constructed reality. More than that, they give one a formalized and systematized account of the ideas of justice, desert, and incentive to which particular claims of right and utility must appeal. Functionalist errors aside, it is important to see the lacunae and contentious assumptions involved in a particular society's discourse of entitlement—the language in which entitlement to that particular society's most important resources is both described and justified.

Second, functionalist and determinist accounts of social forces generally offer an account in which one area of social life—the economy, the means and relations of production, the pattern of child-rearing— is the *real* determinant of history. All else is chimera, superstructure, and illusion. The claims I make here are much more modest. The ideas and ideologies I am describing are neither so deeply rooted in the culture that they can never be criticized nor so determinate that they dictate only one solution. At most, I am trying to lay out the normative topography, the geography of assumptions within which issues are framed, possibilities foreclosed, and so on. This geography *matters*, because it excludes some options from consideration (excludes them even from being seen, perhaps), or prompts a hasty leap to judgment, or because it is one of the many forces shaping subsequent political struggles. But the process I describe is neither a giant conspiracy nor a deterministic and inevitable deep structure of thought. Indeed, it is precisely because the process is neither conspiracy nor destiny that the enterprise of criticizing it is worthwhile.

To develop this kind of criticism, I have focused on the communication, manipulation, and commodification of knowledge— whether found in RNA, a typeface, a programmer's code, or a blackmailer's photographs—and on the parties who are seen as the rightful owners of, controllers of, or audiences for that knowledge. This has led me into cognate issues presented by copyright law, even though *Pierre Menard; Author of Don Quixote* and *The Name of the Rose* are not normally seen as "information."[13] Bringing these disparate areas together does have its advantages. Each of these areas deals with issues where tangible control of a single *res* is not enough. A piece of software, a compromising photograph in a blackmailer's hands, a best-selling novel, a genetic program plugged into a vat of energetic, gene-spliced *E. coli* can all produce an infinite number of copies. In each, it is the message rather than the medium that seems central to the analysis. In each, one is forced to confront the division and disaggregation of the property concept. In each, one meets the same tangle of access and privacy, free transmission of ideas and restrictive economic incentives.

To some, this approach may seem doubtful. Literature produced by professional economists has tended to concentrate more on "innovation" than on "information"—particularly in its coverage of intellectual property, but occasionally in its coverage of such issues as insider trading. I chose quite deliberately to move away from this literature and to use a broad and open definition of information as my organizing concept. In part, this choice stems from the belief that there are interesting things to be said about both levels of generality, and information was the conceptual box into which my particular theoretical interests fitted most neatly. My choice was also guided by the fact that those studies which concentrate on "innovation" seem destined to repeat the paradigm of the original transformative genius, rather than subjecting it to critical assessment in each of the new contexts in which it is deployed. Some writers seem to assume that production, whether industrial or literary, is marked by two distinct forms—one representing imitative, organic, normal science; the other, transformative innovation. This is as true of Joseph Schumpeter as it is of William Wordsworth.[14] I am heartened to find that one of the most empirically detailed and historically sensitive *economic* studies of technology and innovation seems to echo my dissatisfaction with this conclusion.[15] By themselves, of course, these explanatory remarks could not *justify* my choices. In the end, it will be the work created from the materials thus assembled that either justifies or discredits the criteria of inclusion. For epistemological reasons, if for no others, the proof of this pudding *is* in the eating.

CHAPTER 2

Four Puzzles

I take my raw material from four puzzles: the repeating pattern of contradictions in the structure of copyright doctrine, the separate but strangely similar attempts to explain why blackmail and insider trading are illegal, and the text of an opinion in a bizarre California Supreme Court case which deals, among other things, with the ownership of one's own genetic information. Each of these issues seems marginal or anomalous in some way. Each deals in some way with a situation where the fact that information can be copied and transmitted with ease is part of the problem. In each, a physicalist, absolute conception of property rights seems to miss the point somehow. Ownership of an individual physical thing is not enough, whether that thing is a lump of tissue, a faded photo of a compromising position, a confidential prospectus for a takeover, or a book like the one you hold in your hand. Each presents us with an attempt to control the flow of information, to restrict access, to delimit control. Yet these examples are also different. We have different types and degrees of sympathy for the claims of the author who wants to prevent copying, the blackmail victim, the company seeking to prevent exploitation of its secrets for profit, and the patient who finds his genetic material used without his consent to develop a new cell line. Each example presents us with a different mixture of our implicit assumptions about information.

A warning is in order, however. The combination of these examples will not give us a "whole" view or "the real picture." This is not like the story of the blind men whose fragmentary impressions combine to capture the reality of the whole elephant. There is no single, pre-existing elephant out there for the blind men to discover. My examples—any set of examples—will present an *argument*, not a *description*.

Copyright

Copyright is the name that lawyers give to a particular type of intellectual property. It is most familiar in the context of books, but it also governs records, statues, computer programs, and a host of other artifacts. As the best-known type of intellectual property, copyright hardly seems anomalous or puzzling. Yet its familiarity conceals rather than enlightens.

To start with, think for a moment about the strangeness of *all* intellectual property. I sell you something that is protected by copyright—it could be a CD, a computer program, or a statue of Elvis, but we will say it is a book. You think the book is yours, your "property." You have paid money for it; you have a receipt. You could burn it if you like, give it to a friend, tear out its pages and shuffle them, leave it in a hotel room. But you may not copy it, or so the inside cover tells you. How can this be? Could you also be enjoined from *mocking* the book, or from telling anyone else about the ending—if it was particularly shocking, say? How about a parody that hewed closely to the original? Copyright (indeed intellectual property in general) forces us to confront the fact that property rights are not absolute, despite the popular—and occasionally the legal—insistence to the contrary. You "own" the book for some purposes and not for others.

Copyright challenges not only our unreflective notions of property but our basic assumptions about the circulation of information. What about free speech and the transmission of ideas, for example? It is all very well to say that copyright provides incentives to authors and thus encourages the production of more ideas and more information for public consumption. Copyright is a fence to keep the public out as well as a scaffolding for the billboards displayed in the marketplace of ideas; it can be used to deny biographers the ability to quote from or to paraphrase letters; to silence parody; to control the packaging, context, and presentation of information. To say that copyright promotes the production and circulation of ideas is to state a conclusion and not an argument. At the very least we might wonder if, *in our particular copyright regime,* the gains outweigh the losses.

The sense of unease is heightened when one turns to the actual legal framework of copyright. The most basic questions continually surface, even in relatively mundane cases. What is the distinction between idea and expression?[1] Are the page numbers in the West Law Reports or the alphabetical compilations of names in a telephone directory actually copyrightable?[2] What are the criteria we would look to in order to decide such cases? The originality of the work? The amount of labor that has gone into it?[3] The potential loss to the original compiler, or the potential profit to the copying party, or to society?[4] Can anyone own "facts"?[5] Does a computer program such as Windows infringe the copyright of the Apple operating system if it has a similar "look" or "feel," regardless of whether that look or feel is produced by lines of computer code which share nothing with the original work?[6] Again, what would the basis for such a decision be? What is the extent of the "fair use" exception to copyright?[7] How far does the "public domain" extend and how are we to conceive of it?[8] The list of questions could be extended almost infinitely. Indeed, in a comment on the state of "fact works" doctrine that could well be applied to the whole field of copyright, one scholar put the point succinctly: "There is ample precedent deciding almost every copyright issue in almost every conceivable direction."[9]

The point here is not merely that copyright doctrine is uncertain or internally contradictory—that is true of every field of legal doctrine to greater or lesser extents. Nor is it merely that copyright is perceived as uncertain; other areas of law are commonly acknowledged to be in flux. It is that in copyright law—to a greater extent than in most other fields of legal doctrine—there is a routine *and acknowledged* breakdown of the simplifying assumptions of the discourse, so that mundane issues force lawyers, judges, and policymakers to return to first principles. It is as if the building of every bridge required us to derive Newtonian physics from the ground up, as if every breakfast demanded a Cartesian refutation of solipsism before it could be consumed. Is there something particular about intellectual property which explains this apparent doctrinal chaos, and if so, is there any connection to the fact that copyright challenges common assumptions about property and about the transmission of information?

Blackmail

Why is blackmail illegal? The crime is defined as "an unlawful demand of money or property under threat to do bodily harm, to injure property, to accuse of a crime, or to expose disgraceful defects." It is easy to understand that the demand of money is unlawful when the accompanying threats are of bodily harm or property damage. After all, these threats themselves are illegal on other grounds. It is also possible to explain why you cannot demand money as the price of refraining from accusing someone of a crime. But what about the case where a private individual asks another private individual for money as the price of not revealing legally obtained information about activities perfectly legal in themselves? "If you do not pay me $100, I will reveal to your boyfriend the fact that I saw you coming out of another man's house at two o'clock in the morning." After all, in this case it would be perfectly legal to carry through with the threat. Clearly the person being blackmailed does not wish to pay, but then many of us do not wish to pay when others ask for money, telling us that if we do not comply with their demands, they will carry out some unpleasant course of action. How is this different from a baseball team "demanding" concessions from a city and local residents (in the form of tax reductions and parking spaces, for example) under threat of moving the team to another city? It does no good to say that the baseball team has a right to do so, whereas the blackmailer does not.[10] That, after all, is exactly the point we are supposed to be explaining.

Scholars have been drawn to blackmail like wasps to a picnic. Posner, Goodhart, Nozick, Coase, and Epstein have all suggested explanations—none terribly convincing.[11] The commodification of this kind of information is generally reviled and legally prohibited, yet no one has explained why.[12] *Is* there a reason?

Insider Trading

Securities law prohibits certain individuals from trading in securities on the basis of certain kinds of material nonpublic information. (One line of legal authority—currently not favored by the Supreme Court—even suggests that *all* individuals should be prohibited from trading on *any* material nonpublic information.) But why should any insider trading be illegal? Despite widespread popular condemnation of insider trading, scholars agree that the reasons are hard to come by. In fact, a recent article *supporting* the prohibition of insider trading began with the following startling admission. "American jurisprudence abhors insider trading with a fervor reserved for those who scoff at motherhood, apple pie, and baseball. *The commonly stated reasons for this reaction to insider trading are many and unpersuasive. The case law barely suggests why insider trading is harmful.*"[13] Needless to say, those arguing *against* the criminalization of insider trading are even less charitable toward the reasons offered. In the ubiquitously cited work on the subject, Henry Manne argued that "prior to the year 1910 no one had ever publicly questioned the morality of corporate officers, directors and employees trading in the shares of corporations." What's more, he claimed that since that time no one has offered a cogent set of reasons to believe that there is actually anything wrong with insider trading on either moral or economic grounds. Most of the commonly cited scholarly critiques of insider trading, he claimed, were "largely statements of conclusions." The Congressional Hearings of 1933 and 1934 were no better. "To say the practice was vicious or unscrupulous was . . . not a reasoned answer. Worse than that, the emotional tone of the arguments probably intimidated anyone who tried to defend the practice or even make cogent inquiries."[14]

At first blush, it would seem that Manne has a point. We live in a society which distributes wealth through a market system built on the inequality of economic power and which normally exalts an individual who is able to convert some temporary advantage of information or economic leverage into a position of market advantage. Why not here? And why is it that, just as with blackmail, so many people share the sense that insider trading is wrong but find it hard to explain the reason?

Spleens

So far, I have given three brief and general descriptions of areas of doctrine. My last example is longer and comes from a single case,[15] the rhetoric and reasoning of which is so extraordinarily revealing that it deserves extended consideration.[16] In 1976, John Moore started treatment for hairy-cell leukemia at the University of California Medical Center. His doctors quickly became aware that some of his blood products and components were potentially of great commercial value. They performed many tests without ever telling him of their commercial interest, and took samples of every conceivable bodily fluid, including sperm, blood, and bone marrow aspirate. Eventually, they also removed Moore's spleen, a procedure for which there was an arguable medical reason, but only after having first made arrangements to have sections of the spleen taken to a research unit. In 1981, a cell line established from Moore's T-lymphocytes was patented by the University of California, with Moore's doctors listed as the inventors. At no time during this process was Moore told anything about the commercial exploitation of his genetic material. The likely commercial value of the cell line is impossible to predict exactly, but by 1990 the market for such products was estimated to be over $3 billion.[17]

This case hinges on issues of information—on at least two levels. On the most obvious level, Moore was not told about his doctors' financial interest in exploiting his genetic material, an interest which might well have conflicted with the demands of responsible medical care. Dealing with this issue, the Supreme Court of California had no difficulty in ruling that Moore had stated a cause of action for breach of fiduciary duty or lack of informed consent. After all, he had been denied information in which he had a legitimate interest and which the doctors had a corresponding duty to provide.

On a slightly more abstract level, this case concerned the ownership and control of another kind of information, genetic information. T-lymphocytes are white blood cells which have, coded into their genetic material, "blueprints" or "programs" for the production of lymphokines, proteins which regulate the immune system. If these genetic "programs" from the T-lymphocytes can be isolated, they can then be used to manufacture large amounts of the valuable lymphokine through a variety of recombinant DNA processes. For example, whole vats full of bacteria can be "told" to manufacture the particular lymphokine just as a computer word-processing file can issue the same commands to any compatible printer. The key issue in the case was whether or not Moore owned the genetic information coded into his cells or, indeed, whether he owned the cells from which that information had been extracted. The court held that he did not own either—at least in this case.

A fascinating array of reasons is offered for this decision. First, the court appears to believe that Moore had "abandoned" his cells when he consented to their removal. (This argument is hard to square with the rest of the decision, where—while ruling on the issue of whether or not he had stated a cause of action in tort—the court did everything but hold as a matter of law that Moore had *not* been given sufficient information to consent to the removal.)[18] Second, the court argued that the cells were not property, anyway, because California's genetic material statute "by restricting how excised cells may be used and requiring their eventual destruction, . . . eliminates so many of the rights ordinarily attaching to property that one cannot simply assume that what is left amounts to 'property' or 'ownership' for the purposes of conversion law."[19] By implication, one cannot assume that property rights exist in exotic and highly regulated substances such as plutonium, which are subject to the exactly the same types of regulation. In fact, since almost every kind of property is regulated, what can the court mean?[20] The court also said that Moore could not piggy-back a conversion suit on the claim that his so-called rights of publicity or of privacy had been violated. These may be rights, the court suggests, but they are not *property* rights, so Moore has no remedy in conversion. Thus though Johnny Carson has an enforceable interest in the phrase "Here's Johnny!" (a phrase uttered by *someone else*), Moore does not have one in his own DNA.[21] In any event, the court argues that since everyone's genetic material contains information for the manufacture of lymphokines, the particular genetic material is "no more unique to Moore than the number of vertebrae in the spine or the chemical formula of hemoglobin."[22]

Finally, in perhaps its most interesting twist, and the one which is most relevant to the subject of this study, the opinion concluded that Moore could not be given a property right in his genetic material because to do so might hinder research. To back up this argument, the court paints a vivid picture of a vigorous, thriving public realm. Communally organized, altruistically motivated, and unhampered by nasty property claims, the world of research is moving dynamically toward new discoveries. "At present, human cell lines are routinely copied and distributed to other researchers for experimental purposes, usually free of charge. This exchange of scientific materials, which still is relatively free and efficient, will surely be compromised if each cell sample becomes the potential subject matter of a lawsuit." This argument is convincing. We cannot bring property rights into this world of research; they would only slow down discovery. Convincing, that is, until one reads in the very next column, the court's conclusion that "the theory of liability that Moore urges us to endorse threatens to destroy the economic incentive to conduct important medical research."[23] On the one hand, property rights given to those whose bodies can be mined for valuable genetic information will hamstring research because property is inimical to the free exchange of information. On the other hand, property rights *must* be given to those who do the mining, because property is an essential incentive to research. Do these assertions contradict each other? Do they tell us anything about the doctrinal chaos of copyright or the anomalies of blackmail and insider trading? Is there a reason that the court is willing to give Moore an entitlement to "decisional," but not to *genetic,* information? Finally, does the decision give us any logical or ideological hints about the future legal regime covering biotechnology? I would say that the answer to each question is yes.

I have presented four puzzles. My claim is that each one is best understood as a conflict over the use of information and that the conflict is structured by a recurring pattern of contradictions. It is to that pattern I now turn.

CHAPTER 3

The Public and Private Realms

The state as a state abolishes *private property* (i.e. man decrees by *political* means the *abolition* of private property) when it abolishes the *property qualification* for electors and representatives, as has been done in many of the North American States ... The *property qualification* is the last *political* form in which property is recognized. But the political suppression of private property not only does not abolish private property; it actually presupposes its existence. The state abolishes, after its fashion, the distinctions established by *birth, social rank, education, occupation,* when it decrees that birth, social rank, education, occupation are *non-political* distinctions; when it proclaims, without regard to these distinctions, that every member of society is an *equal* partner in popular sovereignty ... But the state, none the less, allows private property, education, and occupation to manifest their *particular* nature. Far from abolishing these *effective* differences, it only exists so far as they are presupposed; it is conscious of being a *political state* and it manifests its *universality* only in opposition to these elements.[1]

There are many reasons to doubt the prescience of Karl Marx, quoted above, as a theorist of the modern liberal state. But any American lawyer would have to acknowledge that he got one thing right; the centrality of the public-private distinction to any understanding of the legal system. The liberal state depends on the idea of equality. That, after all, is one of the key differences between the liberal and the feudal idea of politics. Liberalism mandates an end to status distinctions in politics. There can be no restriction of the franchise to a particular social class, no weighting of the votes of the nobility. Thus we have equality, but only inside the public sphere. Citizens are equal, but only in their capacities as citizens, not as private individuals. Each is guaranteed an equal vote, but not equal influence. We draw a line around certain activities—voting, appearing in court, and so on—and guarantee equality within this realm. Outside that line is the private sphere, the world of civil society. It is the private sphere which contains all the real differences between people—differences of wealth, power, education, birth, and social rank. It is this process of conceptual division that allows us to use the language of egalitarianism to defend a society marked precisely by a highly stratified distribution of wealth or power.[2]

The real dilemma of liberal state theory is that it must exalt the virtues of egalitarianism, of each person's voice counting equally and, at the same time, confine that egalitarianism to the public sphere. Our vision of society must be a vision of two separate spheres, with two different governing principles, two theories of justice, and even two different *personae* to go with them. As Marx describes it, the process sounds almost like a kind of religious schizophrenia. "Where the political state has attained to its full development, man leads, not only in thought, in consciousness, but in *reality*, in *life*, a double existence—celestial and terrestrial. He lives in the *political community*, where he regards himself as a *communal being*, and in *civil society* where he acts simply as a *private individual*, treats other men as a means, degrades himself to the role of mere means, and becomes the plaything of alien powers."[3]

The law is implicated in every stage of this process.[4] First of all, the law draws, and in a more complex way depends upon, the line between public and private. The central fear of the liberal political vision is that unrestrained state power will invade the private sphere. And yet the only force available to police the state *is* the state. The rule of law appears to be the answer to this dilemma. By policing the lines between public and private and between citizens and other citizens, the law offers us the hope of a world which is neither the totalitarian state nor the state of nature. In this sense, both the *role* of law and the *rule* of law depend on the public-private division.

On a more mundane level, both lawyers and citizens perceive issues through the lens of the public-private distinction. Controversial political and moral issues often resolve themselves into questions of *placement* in either the public or the private realm.[5] Access to medical professionals, for example, is in the private sphere. It depends upon my resources, my wealth. There is no constitutional guarantee to equal health care, or even minimum health care. Access to legal professionals, however, is at least partly in the public sphere. When I am accused in a serious criminal trial, I have the right to an attorney *whether or not* my private resources will let me pay for one.[6] This example suggests one last important point: our conception of justice differs depending on whether we are dealing with public law or private law. Suppose a driver negligently knocks over a pedestrian and the pedestrian sues. What kind of damages will he get? The answer depends on the condition of the pedestrian *before* the accident. If the victim is poor, homeless, and out of work, the law is likely to put him back in exactly that position. Tort damages, after all, are compensatory. We aim to restore the *status quo ante*. If the victim is a $200,000-a-year investment banker, then the injurer is likely to find himself paying out a lot more, in lost wages among other things. Yet when we turn from private law to public law, to criminal law, the picture changes completely. Should the law punish an assault against an investment banker more seriously than an offense against a homeless person? Our sensibilities are outraged at the thought (even if we suspect that in practice this may frequently be the reality). In the private sphere our ideal of justice is, broadly speaking, to make the parties whole, to restore them to the position they were in before the wrongful act. Obviously, this means treating differently situated people differently. In public law, on the other hand, we aim for equality.[7]

One of the claims of this book is that disputes about property rights in information resolve themselves, in part, into disputes about whether the issue "is" in the public or the private realm. This rhetoric of geographic placement suggests that we are engaged in a factual inquiry about the location of a preexisting entity within a well-charted and well-settled terrain. Nothing could be further from the truth. In fact, the process is one of contentious moral and political decision making about the distribution of wealth, power, and information. The supposedly settled landscape is in fact an ever-changing scene which folds back onto itself like a Möbius strip. The market, for example, is on the public side of the divide when we are talking about commercial exploitation of private information about families, but is on the private side in its dealings with the government over the Freedom of Information Act. If a geography metaphor is appropriate at all, the most likely cartographers would be Dali, Magritte, and Escher.

Because there is, in fact, no intelligible geography of public and private, I suggest that our decisions should focus on a different set of criteria. The first is egalitarian—having to do with the relative powerlessness of the group seeking information access or protection. The second is the familiar radical republican goal of creating and reinforcing a vigorous public sphere of democracy and debate.[8] These two criteria are not neutral or descriptive—they represent a value choice. They do not algorithmically "resolve" the questions I put forward here or banish contradictions from the field of law about information. In fact, apart from the normative attractiveness of the ideas of egalitarianism and democracy, all that could be said for the proposed criteria is that they are conducive to treating all questions of information regulation holistically and that they restate the boundaries of the argument in a way which, for a while, might produce a more fruitful exchange than the hackneyed language of public and private. In the Conclusion, I try to assess the extent to which these values are supported or undermined by our current rhetoric of information regulation. Now, having introduced the public-private split, let me turn to the second part of this conceptual background, the particular role of information.

. . . .

Information plays a central, if not a defining, role in both the public and the private worlds of the liberal political vision. If we are talking about the private world of the family and the home, we define these institutions partly in terms of their right to close their doors to the outside world, shutting off intercourse and controlling the flow of information, particularly information going *out*. "How many times a week do you make love? Do you sleep in the nude? Do the people in your household pick their noses or vote Republican?" The response, if not obscene, is likely to contain the words "that's private"; indeed the very word "privacy" is most commonly defined in informational terms.[9] The right to withhold information is also, as Judge

Frank Easterbrook points out, one of the main forms of protection given to private citizens facing an accusing state.[10] Fourth and Fifth Amendment protections are the classic cases, but the lawyer-client privilege is also a good example.

As I pointed out a moment ago, we also think of the market as "private"—at least when it is counterposed against the state. We talk of private enterprise, the private sector, privatization—again conjuring up the idea of justified freedom from intervention. And when we turn to microeconomic theory, information is again a defining feature. The analytical structure of microeconomics includes "perfect information"—meaning free, complete, instantaneous, and universally available—as one of the defining features of the *structure* of the perfect market. But the perfect market must also treat information in a second way: as a good *within* the perfect market, something that will not be produced without incentives—costly incentives. This dual—and contradictory—incarnation of information reappears in the *actual* market. Our search for efficiency pushes us toward ever freer and less costly information flow at the same time as our understanding of incentives necessary for production tells us that information must be costly, partial, and deliberately restricted in its availability. When I discuss information economics, this apparent paradox will be of central importance.

Finally, in the public world of politics—which is defined in the liberal vision by the information-centered ideas of debate, exchange, and decision—the free flow of information is a prerequisite for atomistic citizens first to form and then to communicate their subjective preferences in the great marketplace of ideas. At the same time, the availability of information to citizens is thought to be as important a check on governmental activity as that provided by the rule of law, a point made most famously by James Madison: "A popular Government, without popular information or the means of acquiring it, is but a Prologue to a Farce or a Tragedy: or perhaps both. Knowledge will ever govern ignorance; And people who mean to be their own Governors must arm themselves with the power which knowledge gives."[11]

So far I have argued that information, loosely defined, is central to our conception of the family, the market, and the democracy. I claimed that there are tensions "between spheres" in the roles we expect information to play. Thus, for example, it is conventionally accepted that the public interest in a sphere of vigorous debate and discussion often clashes with the demands of personal privacy, while claims to own information in the market mix uneasily with the values of the First Amendment.[12] I also have claimed that, within spheres, information is often conceived of in apparently conflicting ways. Looking at the market through the lens of microeconomics, we find that information is both an analytical prerequisite for the model and a commodity to be traded under the model. In First Amendment theory, analysts sometimes talk as if information exchange had its own inevitable tilt toward democratic values and the good life ("the cure for bad speech is more speech"); at other times they present the First Amendment as the jewel in the crown of liberalism, drawing its nobility precisely from the fact that it is value-neutral as to content. ("I loathe what you say but would die for your right to say it.")

To some it might seem that these contradictions are actually the result of the broad definition of information that I have adopted here. An objector might argue that it is only with the broad definition that commodification seems to conflict with the perfect market, copyright with the First Amendment, and so on. With the use of sensible sub-divisions—into copyright issues, First Amendment issues, privacy issues, insider trading issues, commodification issues, efficient capital market issues—these problems would disappear, or at least lose their salience. I am unconvinced by this argument. Given my vision of language and definition, however, I can imagine no "proof" of my method, except its ability to work in a way that the reader finds useful.

Others might ask for reasons. *Why* do we think such different things about information? Part of the answer seems to be that what we have is an overlay of two sets of conflicts. First, there is the matrix of conflicts between the theories of justice that we apply to the family, the market, and the democracy. This could be thought of as the geographical question; in which realm, which paradigm of justice, does this particular question of information control belong? But this matrix is overlaid by another set of conflicts; how should we conceive of information? This could be called the question of *characterization.*

Information is conceived of as both *finite* and *infinite,* product and process. As an infinite good, information seems to be that magical thing: a gift that can be given without making the giver any poorer. I explain Pythagoras' theorem to you, or teach you how to work out the area of the circle. Afterward, I seem no poorer *in the sense that* we both have the knowledge. This is the positive side of the public goods dilemma. The same unit of the good apparently satisfies the needs of an infinite number of consumers. Perhaps this is one of the reasons that in moments of high moral or ideological conflict, we often reach for a solution that involves giving the parties more information. Is the experimental drug dangerous, the factory unhealthy? Is the cost of this refrigerator—sold on disadvantageous terms to recent immigrants—unusually high? Does a purchaser of this investment run a risk more serious than the glowing prospectus would indicate? In each case our tendency is to believe that mandatory information transfer is the answer. We *make* the drug manufacturer, employer, renter, or investment company disclose details they might not wish to disclose, details that would cost the other party a lot to find out. *If* we are thinking of information as a resource that is infinite in this sense, then the distribution of wealth does not seem to have been changed when parties are forced to transfer information. What has really happened is that one party has been forced to transfer a valuable resource to the other. When that resource is money, we think "socialism." When the resource is information, it just seems "fair."

Yet there are occasions when courts and scholars switch perspectives. From being an infinite resource, a good that may be given infinitely without impoverishing the giver, information is reconceived as a finite good, whose production and distribution are subject to the same economic laws as any other commodity. Mandatory information transfer is suddenly viewed as an inefficient forced exchange, rather than a baseline for informed decision making. In economic terms, the positive side of the costlessness of information—that the same unit of the good can satisfy many consumers at little or no additional cost—suddenly becomes the foundation of the public goods problem. Without an ability to commodify, to exclude others and to make information costly, producers will have no incentive to make more information.[13] In political terms, the uncontentious idea that citizens should be able to make informed decisions is suddenly recast as a coercive transfer of property from one individual to another without compensation.

Until now, I have described information's various roles separately and in a rather static and synchronic way. But the historical importance of the connection *between* information, the market, and liberal democracy should not be underestimated. In fact, the writers of the Scottish Enlightenment believed that commerce was desirable largely because it would force people from widely separated areas to talk to each other, to obtain information about the beliefs and practices of others, and inexorably to question the basis for their own. Thus the invisible hand would subject social practices and traditions to the test of reason. *Doux commerce* would be the crucible in which superstition and myth were burnt away and the rationalism of the Enlightenment brought to the provinces. In later years, Scottish philosophers changed their minds and began to worry that commerce would produce enormous disparities in wealth and power (including power over information) and that these disparities would subvert the republican form of government. Sadly, although this change of heart had some sympathizers in the United States, it never received the same attention as the original optimistic message.[14] One of the implicit claims of this book is that it should have.

. . . .

It is time to sum up. If the concept of information has potentially conflicting roles to play in family, market, and state and if information itself is sometimes conceived of as infinite and sometimes as finite, how are social problems involving information decided? A lot of the time, the answer is, "By drawing lines." We "type" certain situations or conflicts as "public" or "private" and then act as if we have solved the problem. Unfortunately, we have merely restated it: the notion of "private" can be defined largely by the idea of the justified ability to withhold information, but the same word, with its connotations of "that-with-which-we-cannot-interfere," can conjure up the freedom of the market from state intervention. The fact that we think of the private sphere as encompassing both the market (vis à vis the state) and the family (vis à vis the market *and* the state) produces a Laocoon of ideological and rhetorical contradictions.[15]

For example, many consumers do not wish biographical details, provided to a retailer for another purpose, to be traded in the flourishing direct marketing industry. They might argue that this information was "private" and that the state should step in to prevent the companies involved from passing it on, compiling it into larger databases, or whatever. Others might want the state to protect the private sphere of home and family from information coming in from the outside. The telemarketing phone call interrupting the family dinner is the most frequently used example. In both cases, the classification "private" is supposed to trigger, or at least justify, state protection. Yet the owners of the databases would protest the unfairness of the public world of the state interfering in a *private* disposition of *private* property—in this case, mailing lists or databases of consumer information. The telemarketers might say the same thing. Yet, because information is involved rather some other form of property, they would probably also claim that the issue is one which should be settled by appeal to the constitutional norms that govern the *public* realm.[16] In other words, they might argue both that the government should not interfere because this was a (fundamentally private) activity in the market, and that the government should not interfere because this was a (fundamentally public) matter of free speech— and equal protection, for that matter.[17]

When I first wrote this chapter, I intended these as purely hypothetical examples. Since then, Senator Ernest Hollings introduced and the Congress passed a bill that outlaws most autodialers.[18] "Calling autodialers an 'outrageous invasion' of people's homes, Senator Hollings said 'privacy rights outweigh any concerns about the free speech of the marketing companies.'" The Portland, Oregon, American Civil Liberties Union (ACLU) disagrees. One of their lawyers, Charles Hinkle, is "representing a small business against an Oregon law banning the commercial use of autodialers." His arguments? The ban would interfere with free speech and would violate the constitutional commitment to equality in public life—in this case the equal protection clause—since it distinguishes between commercial and noncommercial speech.[19]

On top of these issues—which present classic examples of what I called "the question of geography"—we have the additional issues raised by the question of characterization. Should we adopt the finite or the infinite vision of information? Are people really "taking" anything from you when they learn of your address, or your consumption patterns, and sell those facts to a thousand databases? You still have all the "goods" that you had before—except, of course, that peculiar good that exists in the *negation* or restriction of information.

If there really was an intelligible geography of public and private and a unitary concept of information, then we might hold out the hope that one set of claims could be proved to be "true" and the other "false." But since the legal realists, that hope has seemed a chimerical one.

The story cannot end here, however. One of the themes of this book is that the implicit frameworks within which the regulation of information is discussed are contradictory—or at least aporetic—and indeterminate in application. As far as the rhetoric of public and private goes, that seems an unexceptionable conclusion.[20] And since that rhetoric dominates popular discussion of information issues, a large part of the groundwork for my theoretical discussion is devoted to the multiple ways in which liberalism portrays information as central to both public and private realms. It is hard to read a public debate on any issue involving information without coming to the conclusion that a great deal of it is an exercise in line drawing or typing, increasingly isolated from the moral and political ideals the lines are supposed to represent. Perhaps this is the best we can do. But then again, perhaps not.

So much for public debate. Is scholarship any different? Increasingly, scholarly discussions of information issues are turning away from liberal constitutionalism and rights theory and toward the language of microeconomics.[21] Whether the issue is copyright,[22] patent,[23] insider trading,[24] blackmail,[25] or simply "valuable information,"[26] some of the most ambitious recent scholarship is informed by some kind of economic approach. A cruder form of economic analysis also surfaces in the discussion of public policy. The developed world has recently engaged in a ferocious intellectual land grab, backed by trade sanctions, and has used the economic need for intellectual property protection as its primary—and supposedly objective—justification. The idea is an attractive one. Yet microeconomics provides no surcease from the paradoxes of information. Those paradoxes are just as central to the discipline of economics as they are to liberal state theory.

Both liberal state theory & econ analysis suffer from info. paradox

CHAPTER 4

Information Economics

In economics, once again, information plays many roles. The analytical structure of microeconomics includes "perfect information"—meaning free, complete, instantaneous, and universally available—as one of the defining features of the perfect market.[1] At the same time, both the perfect and the *actual* market structure of contemporary society depend on information being a commodity—that is to say being costly, partial, and deliberately restricted in its availability. Our concern with market efficiency pushes us toward information flows that are costless, general, and fast. Our concern with incentives for the producers of information pushes us in exactly the opposite direction—toward temporary monopolies that delay the release of information, limit its availability, and raise its price.

When I first wrote on this subject, I tried to summarize the problems of information economics in a single sentence. "Perfect information is a defining conceptual element of the analytical structure used to analyze markets driven by the absence of information in which imperfect information itself is a commodity."[2] I even offered an analogy. Imagine a theology that postulates ubiquitous God-given manna—food from heaven—in its vision of the heavenly city, but otherwise assumes that virtue and hard work are both maximized under conditions of scarcity. Now use that theology to provide the basic theoretical structure for a practical discussion of the ethics of food shortages.[3] Unfortunately, I found that both these devices led readers to misunderstand my position.

My point is *not* that the reality is more complicated than the abstraction, nor is it that the vision of information in the perfect market contradicts the realities of information in an actual market. That would be a critique of all abstractions and models. But abstractions and models are necessary to life. My claim is that information is a problem case for that specific set of abstractions we call economic theory, that—at *each* level of the analysis—information can and must be represented within the theory in two conflicting ways, and that certain concrete problems follow as a result. Some economists believe that these problems can be solved by changing the level of analysis— from perfect to imperfect markets, from imperfect information as commodity to imperfect information as transaction cost to perfect information as a component of the analytical structure—just as Bertrand Russell and Alfred North Whitehead believed that they could banish paradoxes from mathematics by segregating the component parts of a paradox on different levels of analysis. Gödel's Theorem convinced mathematicians of the impossibility of getting rid of this pattern of circularity, recursive definition, and self-swallowing analysis. Sadly, with some notable exceptions that I shall discuss in a moment, economists seem to have avoided any comparable moment of professional modesty.[4]

In practice, economists tend to treat some information issues in their "efficiency–perfect information" mode, in which case the answer will probably (but not always) be that the commodification or restriction of information is bad.[5] They treat other information issues in their "incentives for future producers–solve public goods problems" mode, in which case the answer will probably be that information *must* be commodified. Yet they have no master principle or algorithm to explain when to be in the first mode and when to be in the second. It is possible, with eminent formal correctness, to reverse the polarity and switch the categories. Copyright *could* be portrayed as an intolerable monopoly over information production and legalized insider trading as a necessary incentive to bring information to market. Both portrayals would have as much conceptual and empirical backing as is normally provided in this kind of economic sleight of hand. This basic theoretical aporia explains the weakness of much economic analysis of information regimes.[6]

The first manifestation of this aporia in information economics is the fact that the requirements of "motivation" and those of "efficiency" seem contradictory.[7] For example, if markets are to be efficient, the prices must perfectly reflect available information. Yet information is costly to obtain. If prices perfectly reflect available information, with no part of the price going to the producer of the information, then there is no incentive to produce more information. To postulate efficiency in the production of information we must assume away the incentive necessary to produce. To postulate the incentive is to make efficiency impossible. It looks like a classic paradox. This is not an observation confined to those skeptical of information economics. Some of the most sophisticated economists writing in the area have acknowledged this problem: "There is a fundamental conflict between the efficiency with which markets spread information and the incentives to acquire information."[8] Are property rights in information a transaction cost that impedes the full and efficient circulation of information? It might seem obvious that they are. After all, perfect information is one of the elements of the perfect market. If information can be commodified, then a host of transaction costs are introduced into information flow and a limited monopoly is granted in the midst of a system supposedly based on competition.[9]

Yet the picture changes when information is viewed not as an element within the theoretical structure of the economic system, but rather as a commodity produced and distributed according to the rules of that system. In fact, most economic analysis of information takes this "commodity perspective."[10] From that perspective, the goal of the analysis is to discover the level of property rights that will produce the optimal level of production. Take the classic case of International News Service v. Associated Press.[11] Associated Press (AP) operated a news-gathering service. An international network of correspondents and wire services provided news which was printed in AP papers. Unfortunately for AP, International News Service (INS), which operated a far less expansive news-gathering apparatus, made a practice of free-riding on AP's efforts. INS employees would gather news from AP's noticeboards and from early editions of its East Coast newspapers and would then reprint the news, often taking advantage of the time difference between the East and West Coasts. AP sued, claiming that INS was engaging in unfair competition.

This case raises a difficult question for economic analysis. One line

[margin note: Acquisition v. Efficient Spread]

[margin note: But isnt this possible at times]

of rhetoric and analysis indicates that we should secure to producers the fruits of their labors, and thus induce them to produce more. Without some legally protected interest in the news it gathers, AP will presumably be under a competitive disadvantage. News will become a "public goods problem." Unable to exclude its competitors from the fruits of its efforts, AP will be driven to cut back its news-gathering activities—as will all the other newspapers. Thus though consumers might be willing to pay for a higher level of news gathering, it will be impractical for any individual newspaper to provide such a service. Put this way, the actual outcome in the case, a judicially created, legally protected interest in freedom from unfair competition in news gathering, is the perfect solution to the public goods problem. By allowing commodification, it ensures continued production and avoids the prisoner's dilemmas set up by the alternative regime.

Yet one cannot solve the problems of economic analysis merely by adopting the commodity perspective—leaving perfect competition and information efficiency concerns aside. The problem of the free flow of information reappears. For example, should we approach the question of "fair use" in copyright through the lens of the commodity perspective? If we do so, will we only tolerate limitations on intellectual property rights when those limitations are necessary to minimize transaction costs or accomplish well-defined public goals? The most sophisticated scholarly analysis takes this approach.[12] Consequently, it tries to preserve incentives for creators, even establishing a typology of "fair uses"—assigning or denying property rights in part according to whether those uses would tend to reduce the reward available to the author.[13] Yet the analysis largely ignores the opposite perspective, that of the efficient flow of information. If we switch the perspective, we see that one important purpose of "fair use" law is to make sure that future creators have available to them an adequate supply of raw materials. From this perspective, too many "incentives" could convert the public domain into a fallow landscape of private plots.

To their credit, some economic analysts have attempted to reconcile the two perspectives. Thus, for example, William Landes and Richard Posner describe copyright as constructed by the tension between the need to grant legally protected interests to authors in order to motivate them and the need to limit the rights of authors so as to allow future creators legal access to the raw materials they need.[14] This seems reasonable enough, but it also leaves them dangerously close to the mushy "balancing" analysis from which economics was supposed to provide surcease. At the same time, the aporia reappears in the question of classification *within* the theory. For instance, how are we to classify a telephone directory of agents and publishing houses or an index price measure of a futures market in books? Is the former—the information necessary to make the market run—something that should be freely available? Is the latter a commodity in which the creators must be able to claim a legitimate intellectual property right if we are to encourage continued production of information? Or is it exactly the other way around?[15]

My argument is not merely that analysts are concentrating too much on motivating creators and not enough on the free flow of information (although that is certainly sometimes true). I am claiming that a change in the focus of the analysis does not dispose of these difficulties; it merely reverses their "polarity." There *are* issues which economists tend to analyze by thinking of information *as information* rather than as a commodity—for example, in the discussion of the efficient capital market hypothesis. Yet, as some economists have pointed out, unless the questions of commodification and incentive are worked into the analysis, the theory ends in paradox as soon as the slightest costs or imperfections are introduced into it. The best example comes from Sanford Grossman and Joseph Stiglitz's description of the self-destructing futures market.

> Whenever there are differences in beliefs that are not completely arbitraged, there is an incentive to create a market. (Grossman, 1977, analyzed a model of a storable commodity whose spot price did not reveal all information because of the presence of noise. Thus traders were left with differences in beliefs about the future price of the commodity. This led to the opening of a futures market. But then uninformed traders had two prices revealing information to them, implying the elimination of noise.) But, because differences in beliefs are themselves endogenous, arising out of expenditure on information and the informativeness of the price system, *the creation of markets eliminates the differences of beliefs which gave rise to them, and thus causes those markets to disappear* . . . Thus, we could argue as soon as the assumptions of conventional perfect capital markets model are modified to allow even a slight amount of information imperfection and a slight cost of information the traditional

theory becomes untenable . . . [Precisely] because information is costly, prices cannot perfectly reflect the information which is available, since if it did, those who spent resources to obtain it would receive no compensation.[16]

Commodification could be the answer. A futures market produces information—in the form of the price of futures contracts. We do not normally think of price as a public good—but it seems to fit all of the criteria. In this case, it is a valuable commodity costing considerable transactional effort to create, available thereafter at a marginal cost near zero.[17] If we wish to eliminate the public goods problem, the answer might be to commodify the price measure—to assert an intellectual property right in the price output of the market, in order to prevent others from gaining free access to the information it offers. We would have to pay to get the prices in the "secret stock market." Yet if there is one thing that microeconomics cannot justify treating as a public good, surely it is price!

If all of this seems like an Alice-in-Wonderland conclusion, it is worth considering the case of Board of Trade of City of Chicago v. Dow Jones & Co., Inc., in which the court recognized that Dow Jones has a "proprietary interest in its indexes and averages which vests it with the exclusive right to license their use for trading in stock index futures contracts." The court does point out, however, that "the extent of the defendant's monopoly would be limited, for as defendant points out, there are an infinite number of stock market indexes which could be devised."[18] This case does not go as far as the "secret stock market" I proposed half-jokingly, but it *does* give eloquent testimony to the ineradicable tension between the idea of perfect information and frictionless markets and the idea of commodification and property rights.

This internal tension in the analysis always leaves open the question whether a particular issue is to be classed as a public goods problem, for which the remedy is commodification,[19] or a monopoly of information problem, for which the remedy is unfettered competition.[20] The problem is not merely an empirical one. Even the existence of precise empirical evidence (of a kind currently unavailable for any area of information regulation except, arguably, stock market prices) would not, alone, tell us which was the right answer unless we had also decided on what level of generality the analysis was to be carried out.

In Feist Publications, Inc. v. Rural Telephone Service Co., Inc., case, for example, the Supreme Court denied copyright protection to the compilers of a white pages phone directory.[21] The logic of the analysis I just applied to the *INS* case might seem to indicate that it was necessary to give the compilers of the directory some protection. After all, directories raise classic "public goods problems." The cost of creation is high, yet it is possible at minimal extra cost for additional users to enjoy the same unit of the "good" thus created. (In other words, the directory is expensive to make and cheap to copy.) The Court was not disposed to agree. Partly by means of doctrinal linedrawing (copyright rather than unfair competition) and partly by means of definitional fiat (telephone directories are not original, so in *that* sense nothing truly new is being created), the Court moved away from the "sweat of the brow" theory, and denied the compilers the possibility of protecting their directory through copyright.

At first, it appears that the opinion has nothing to tell us about economic analysis. On closer inspection, it becomes apparent that the Court is not so much rejecting the commodity perspective, as it is changing the level of generality of the analysis. From Justice O'Connor's perspective, it is the structure of copyright law *as a whole* that strikes the right balance between the need to reward producers and the need to maintain competition and the free flow of information. Since copyright law *as a whole* allows the commodification of expression but not of the ideas or facts which that expression contains, and since the Court finds this particular arrangement of facts to be "unoriginal," no legally protected interest can be recognized. It is only once this prior decision about the level of generality has been made that the questions of efficiency and incentive can intelligibly be posed.

For all these reasons, economic analysis of information regimes is extraordinarily indeterminate. A person reading the confident-sounding statements of legal scholars about the superior efficiency of the patent regime over the copyright regime,[22] or the economic inefficiency of the regulation of insider trading, or the law of fraud,[23] would be surprised to find that economists cannot even agree over the absolutely basic question of whether, in the absence of commodification, there will be underinvestment or overinvestment in the production of information. Kenneth Arrow takes a position that seems to support the Court's result in the *INS* case, arguing that,

[handwritten margin notes: sweat of brow doesn't seem to be a strike / not p. goods problems w/ timing issue of getting product together quickly to compete / of a public good that you only need 1 of.]

[handwritten note at bottom: O'Connor says its about whether it is an expression of info or info]

without property rights, too little information will be produced because producers of information will not be able to capture its true value.[24] Eugene Fama and Arthur Laffer, by contrast, argue that too *much* information will be generated, because some information will be produced only in order to gain some temporary advantage in trading, thus redistributing wealth but not achieving greater allocative efficiency.[25] In other words, in the absence of information property rights, there may be inefficient investment of social resources in activities that merely slice the pie up differently, rather than making it bigger. Jack Hirshleifer gives a similar analysis of patent law, ending up with the conclusion that patent law may be *either* a necessary incentive for the production of inventions *or* an unnecessary legal monopoly in information that overcompensates an inventor who has already had the opportunity to trade on the information implied by his or her discovery.[26] It is hard to think of a more fundamental disagreement.[27]

It is my argument in this book that much contemporary economic analysis conceals these tensions, aporias, and empirically unverifiable assumptions by relying unconsciously on the notion of the romantic author. I have tried to show that most issues in information economics could be portrayed (in the absence of more detailed empirical information) as *either* public goods problems for which the state has wisely chosen the remedy of commodification in order to avoid underproduction *or* as potential monopolies in which intolerable transaction costs are introduced into the free flow of information. In later chapters, I will argue that this choice is often concealed by an implicit reliance on the notion of the author, a reliance that tends to push the analysis toward the incentives-commodity vision of information. This could have serious negative consequences since it will lead analysts (and governments) to support a greater commodification of information than is actually warranted. Such a discourse could also be used cynically to protect existing information monopolies. Economists would be mainly concerned by the possible efficiency losses implicit in such a result. In the Conclusion, I argue that there are also profound distributional issues which should concern us—particularly if we believe that information is becoming one of the primary resources in the international economy.

So much for the theory. What about the facts? The empirical evidence, of which there is surprisingly little, seems to justify these conclusions, or at least to cast doubt on current assumptions about the level of international intellectual property protection necessary to promote research and innovation. A historical statistical study of the effect of patent protection on the development of drugs in both developed and developing countries from 1950 to 1989 found that

> The existence of a patenting system is not a prerequisite for inventions ... The relationship between patent systems and their influence on the inventive capacity of developed countries was also tested. Two different tests using Yule's coefficient showed conclusively that, for those countries in which nearly all inventions are made, the relationship is not significant ... The hypothesis that the number of inventions would increase along with the world-wide increase in patent systems was also considered, but it was concluded that there is no significant relationship between these two variables, either in the United States or in the world at large.[28]

The certainty of these conclusions warrants some skepticism. A small correlation (Yule's association coefficient = 0.15) between patent protection and invention was observed in developed countries. There was a much more significant correlation between economic development and invention (Yule's association coefficient = 0.94).[29] Yet when the question is what level of intellectual property rights to maintain domestically, the latter correlation is of dubious relevance — at least for developed countries. Still, the absence of a strong correlation between patent and invention is significant, and the study certainly tends to undermine the claims made by the developed world that a stronger international regime of intellectual property is necessary to encourage innovation.

Finally, while all such studies warrant methodological skepticism, the studies that support intellectual property protection seem even more problematic. One study estimated that without patent protection 65 percent of new drugs produced by the U.S. pharmaceutical industry would not have reached the market.[30] The analysis was based, however, on data supplied by the pharmaceutical industry in response to a questionnaire on the impact of patent protection on research and development. The problems with such a method are obvious.

In another context, the paradoxes and empirical uncertainties of economic analysis might be of mainly theoretical interest. In discussions of information, they are of immediate practical relevance to almost every issue. In part this is so because economists—to their great credit—have been in the forefront of attempts to treat information holistically. Another reason may lie in the perception that information issues are somehow more "intangible." Escaping more easily from the absolutist, formalist, and physicalist notions of tangible property, information has historically seemed more amenable to a utilitarian calculus.[31] Consequently, these issues are often debated in economic terms—both inside and outside the academy. When the U.S. Trade Representative argued that the General Agreement on Trade and Tariffs (GATT) should be used to pressure other countries to increase their levels of intellectual property protection, she turned to the language of necessary economic incentives, rather than to the labor theory of property or the language of natural rights.[32] Once again, we meet the simplistic claim that more protection of intellectual property means more innovation and invention.

There is another reason that economics shapes the debate on information issues. Neoclassical price theory is not only the most sophisticated utilitarian language available, but also the one whose disciplinary assumptions—consumer sovereignty, exogenous preferences, and so on—best reflect a liberal vision of the production, distribution, and exchange of information.[33] The "marketplace of ideas" is more than just a random metaphor: it is an accurate summation of many of the assumptions that our society brings to the discussion of information issues. In a moment, I will argue that this metaphor brings still more problems in its wake.

If microeconomics has become one of the most attractive languages in which to discuss questions of information regulation, then it is almost inevitable that the specific blindnesses[34] of economic analysis will be replicated in information policy. Thus, to the particular difficulties of the economic analysis of information are added the more general difficulties of the economic analysis of law in general—baseline problems, wealth effects, and so on. These have been analyzed elsewhere, so I will not dwell on them here.

To sum up, there are at least two types of theoretical problems in microeconomic analysis of information issues. The first stems from the cluster of contradictory roles that information has to play in the market and in microeconomic theory—information as both perfect and imperfect, property rights in information as both necessary incentive and dubious transaction cost. The second type of problem stems from the conflict between the assumptions of microeconomic analysis and actual social behavior. For example, when poor school-children are convinced by relentless advertising and peer pressure that they "need" hugely expensive basketball shoes, even a staunch liberal may begin to doubt both the descriptive accuracy and the prescriptive fairness of an unswerving application of the norms of "consumer sovereignty" and "exogenous preferences."[35]

What conclusions do we draw from the combination of these two theoretical problems? One conclusion would be that one of the most influential ways we have to discuss issues of information is a theory so indeterminate that it frequently functions as a Rorschach blot for dominant social beliefs and the prejudices of the analyst. At the same time, this theory tends structurally to undervalue issues of power and inequality.

Call that the pessimistic conclusion. Is there an optimistic one? My answer would be a guarded "maybe." It is a good idea to focus on incentives to production, on transaction costs, and on the problems created by the presence or absence of legally protected interests. It is certainly a good idea to try to discover actual effects of a particular regime of information regulation. (Economists have not done this as much as one would have hoped, but at least *they have talked about it a lot*.) The tendency of economic analysis to go at least one layer below reified doctrinal concepts is also to be welcomed. One could imagine a type of information economics that was sensitive to base-line errors, offer-asking problems, and wealth effects, that questioned the reality of exogenous preferences, and that openly acknowledged the tension between the efficiency and incentive views of information problems. If this economics also paid more attention than is currently fashionable to the diminishing marginal utility of wealth, I, for one, would be pleased.

If all of these things were done, what epistemological *status* and practical *effect* would information economics have? It would be a little less imperial, a lot more modest, and much more empirical. Its con-clusions would be more carefully hedged than they are now, and it would openly declare its partiality—the inherent prejudices of any utilitarian, efficiency, or welfare-maximizing calculus and the politi-cal consequences of the distinction between allocation and distribu-tion.

To some, this judgment may seem strange in light of my claims that information economics is beset by a basic paradox or aporia. If the discipline is truly paradoxical, isn't it useless—no matter how chastened its conclusions? The answer, I think, is that economics is only useless if one makes particular positivist and scientistic assumptions about the kind of knowledge a theory has to provide in order to qualify as "a theory." Admittedly, both professional economists and economic analysts of law—not merely those from the Chicago School—sound in their more expansive moments as if they subscribe to those scientistic assumptions. But that is no reason for the rest of us to do so. Neoclassical price theory is a way of thinking which enriches our understanding of the world. Like all theoretical systems, it has blind spots and moments of formal "undecidability." Used with an awareness of its paradoxes and its blind spots, an awareness of the unconscious process of interpretive construction that conceals its indeterminacy, it would nevertheless be a valuable theoretical tool. Seen this way, economics would be a spur to concentrate on incentives and information flow, to worry about perverse motivations and unintended consequences. It would, in short, be more a rough-and-ready set of analytical techniques and checklists than a Newtonian science.

Whether or not this is the economics we should have, it is not the economics we have at the moment. With a few significant exceptions, we have an economics more like my pessimistic picture: an aporetic discipline which, as I hope to show in the rest of this book, often conceals its indeterminacy through romance. To understand the origins of that romance, we must first look at the liberal conception of property.

CHAPTER 5

Intellectual Property and the Liberal State

L ike information, property plays a vital role in liberal state theory. That role imposes certain conflicting requirements on the concept of property itself.[1] Legal realism, Lockean political theory, critical legal thought, and law and economics have all stressed—each in its own vocabulary—the idea that property is perhaps the most important mechanism we use in our attempt to reconcile our desire for freedom and our desire for security.[2] How can we be free and yet secure from other people's freedom, secure and yet free to do what we want to do?[3] The most obvious way to deal with this apparent contradiction is to conceive rights of security "in a manner that both makes them appear to be absolute and negates the proposition that they restrict the legitimate freedom of action of others. Thus if we define liberty as free actions that do not affect others at all, and rights as absolute protections from harm, the contradiction vanishes."[4] The traditional Blackstonian definition of property does just that. But there are irresoluble conceptual tensions in any such formulation, a point which has considerable relevance to intellectual property law, as we will see later. Kenneth Vandevelde states the problem in the following way:

> At the beginning of the nineteenth century, property was ideally defined as absolute dominion over things. Exceptions to this definition suffused

property law: instances in which the law declared property to exist even though no "thing" was involved or the owner's dominion over the thing was not absolute. Each of these exceptions, however, was explained away. Where no "thing" existed, one was fictionalized. Where dominion was not absolute, limitations could be camouflaged by resorting to fictions, or rationalized as inherent in the nature of the thing or the owner ... As the nineteenth century progressed, increased exceptions to both the physicalist and the absolutist elements of Blackstone's conception of property were incorporated into the law ... This dephysicalization was a development that threatened to place the entire corpus of American law in the category of property. Such conceptual imperialism created severe problems for the courts. First, if every valuable interest constituted property, then practically any act would result in either a trespass on or a taking of, someone's property, especially if property was still regarded as absolute. Second, once property had swallowed the rest of American law, its meaningfulness as a separate category would disappear. On the other hand, if certain valuable interests were not considered property, finding and justifying the criteria for separating property from non-property would be difficult.[5]

To the extent that there was a replacement for this Blackstonian conception, it was the familiar "bundle of rights" notion of modern property law, a vulgarization of Wesley Hohfeld's analytic scheme of jural correlates and opposites, loosely justified by a rough and ready utilitarianism and applied in widely varying ways to legal interests of every kind. The euphonious case of LeRoy Fibre Co. v. Chicago, Milwaukee & St. Paul Ry. is used in many a first-year law school class to illustrate the conceptual shift.[6] Could a flax maker be found guilty of contributory negligence for piling his stacks of flax too close to the tracks? The majority bridled at the very thought. The flax maker was piling his flax on his own property, after all. "The rights of one man in the use of his property cannot be limited by the wrongs of another ... The legal conception of property is of rights. When you attempt to limit them by wrongs, you venture a solecism." Though the majority's circular reasoning carried the day, it is Oliver Wendell Holmes's (partial) concurrence that pointed to the future.[7] Rather than imagining an absolute sphere of rights surrounding the property lines like a glass bubble, Holmes was happy to remove the flax-piling entitlement from the bundle of property rights for whatever swathe of the property was "so near to the track as to be in danger from a prudently managed engine." He also directed a few sanguine, if vaguely crocodilian, comments toward the majority on the subject of their concern about the apparent relativism of his concept of property: "I do not think we need trouble ourselves with the thought that my view depends upon differences of degree. The whole law does so as soon as it is civilized. Negligence is all degree—that of the defendant here degree of the nicest sort; and between the variations according to distance that I suppose to exist and the simple universality of the rules in the Twelve Tables or the Leges Barbarorum, there lies the culture of two thousand years."[8]

Presumably, the majority consoled itself with the fact that its concern with absolutism and universality was two thousand years out of date. In any event, the writing was on the wall. Property was no longer conceived of as absolute, no longer a guaranteed trump against the interests of the majority or the state, no longer related to any physical thing. Indeed, so thoroughly had the conception been relativized that courts were willing to admit that there could be property rights restricted to particular interests, to be asserted against one person, rather than another, and only in some situations and moments. But if this is the case, where is our shield against other people or the state? If the flax-piling entitlement can be stripped from seventy yards of the LeRoy Fibre Company merely because there would be utilitarian benefits to letting the railroad run unmolested, then why not from one hundred yards, or from the whole thing? Instead of an absolute, unchanging, and universal shield against the world, property is now merely a bundle of assorted entitlements that changes from moment to moment as the balance of utilities changes. It seems that the modern concept of property has given us a system that works on the day-to-day level, but only at the price of giving up the very role that property was supposed to play in the liberal vision.

Thus when we turn to *intellectual* property, an area which throughout its history has been less able to rely on the physicalist and absolutist fictions which kept the traditional concept of property going, we will see an attempt not only to clothe a newly invented romantic author in robes of juridical protection, but to struggle with, mediate, or repress one of the central contradictions in the liberal world view. This, then, is the redoubled contradiction of which I spoke earlier. If it is to protect the legitimacy and intellectual suasion of the liberal world view, intellectual property law (and indeed, all law that deals with information) must accomplish a number of tasks simultaneously. It must provide a conceptual apparatus which appears to mediate the various tensions associated with the role of information in liberal society. Thus, for example, it must give some convincing explanation as to why a person who recombines informational material from the public sphere is not merely engaging in the private appropriation of public wealth. It must explain how it is that we can motivate individuals—who are sometimes postulated to be essentially self-serving, and sometimes to be noble, idealistic souls—to produce information. If the answer is, "by giving them property rights," it must also explain why this will not diminish the common pool, or public domain, so greatly that a net decrease in the production of information will result. (Think of overfishing.) It must reassure us that a realm of guarded privacy will be carved out for the private sphere and at the same time explain how it is that we can have a vigorous sphere of public debate and ample information about a potentially oppressive state. It must do all of this within a vision of justice that expects formal equality within the public sphere, but respect for existing disparities in wealth, status, and power in the private. And all of these things must be accomplished while we are using a concept of property which must avoid the conceptual impossibilities of the physicalist, absolutist conception, but which at the same time is not too obviously relativist, partial, and utilitarian.

CHAPTER 6

Copyright and the Invention of Authorship

So far I have argued that, because of the contradictions and tensions described here, there are certain structural pressures on the way that a liberal society deals with information. When we turn to the area of law conventionally recognized as dealing with information—intellectual property law, and in this case copyright law—I claim that we will find a pattern, a conceptual strategy which attempts to resolve the tensions and contradictions in the liberal view of information. On one level, understanding this pattern will help us to make sense (if not coherence) of the otherwise apparently chaotic world of copyright. On another level, I claim that the conceptual strategy developed in copyright is important to understand, because parts of it can also be found in most, if not all, of the areas where we deal with information—even if those areas are conventionally understood to have nothing to do with copyright.

From what I have argued previously, it should be apparent that although intellectual property has long been said to present insuperable conceptual difficulties, it actually presents exactly the same problems as the liberal concept of property generally. It merely does so in a more obvious way and in a way which is given a particular spin by our fascination with information. All systems of property are both rights-oriented and utilitarian, rely on antinomian conceptions of public and private, present insuperable conceptual difficulties when reduced to mere physicalist relations but when conceived of in a more abstract and technically sophisticated way, immediately begin to dissolve back into the conflicting policies to which they give a temporary and unstable form. In personal or real property, however, one can at least point to a pair of sneakers or a house, say "I own that," and have some sense of confidence that the statement means something. As *LeRoy Fibre* case shows, of course, it is not at all clear that such confidence is justified, but at least property presents itself as an *apparently* coherent feature of social reality, and this is a fact of considerable ideological and political significance. In intellectual property, the response to the claim "I own that" might be "what do you mean?"

As Martha Woodmansee discovered, this point was made with startling clarity in the debates over copyright in Germany in the eighteenth century. Encouraged by an enormous reading public, several apocryphal tales of writers who were household names, yet still living in poverty, and a new, more romantic vision of authorship, writers began to demand greater economic returns from their labors. One obvious strategy was to lobby for some kind of legal right in the text—the right that we would call copyright. To many participants in the debate, the idea was ludicrous. Christian Sigmund Krause, writing in 1783, expressed the point pungently.

> "But the ideas, the content! that which actually constitutes a book! which only the author can sell or communicate!"—Once expressed, it is impossible for it to remain the author's property . . . It is precisely for the purpose of using the ideas that most people buy books—pepper dealers, fishwives, and the like and literary pirates excepted . . . Over and over again it comes back to the same question: I can read the contents of a book, learn, abridge, expand, teach, and translate it, write about it, laugh over it, find fault with it, deride it, use it poorly or well—in short, do with it whatever I will. But the one thing I should be prohibited from doing is copying or reprinting it? . . . A published book is a secret divulged. With what justification would a preacher forbid the printing of his homilies, since he cannot prevent any of his listeners from transcribing his sermons? Would it not be just as ludicrous for a professor to demand that his students refrain from using some new proposition he had taught them as for him to demand the same of book dealers with regard to a new book? *No, no it is too obvious that the concept of intellectual property is useless. My property must be exclusively mine; I must be able to dispose of it and retrieve it unconditionally.* Let someone explain to me how that is possible in the present case. Just let someone try taking back the

true but if you have no incentive to copy - $ you wont either

ideas he has originated once they have been communicated so that they are, as before, nowhere to be found. All the money in the world could not make that possible.[1]

Along with this problem go two other, more fundamental ones. The first is the recurrent question of how we can give property rights in intellectual products and yet still have the inventiveness and free flow of information which liberal social theory demands. I shall return to this question in a moment. The second problem is the more fundamental one. On what grounds should we give the author this kind of unprecedented property right at all, even if the conceptual problems could be overcome? We do not think it is necessary to give car workers residual property rights in the cars that they produce—wage labor is thought to work perfectly well. Surely, an author is merely taking public goods—language, ideas, culture, humor, genre—and converting them to his or her own use? Where is the moral or utilitarian justification for the existence of this property right in the first place? The most obvious answer is that authors are special, but why? And since when?

Even the most cursory historical study reveals that our notion of "authorship" is a concept of relatively recent provenance. Medieval church writers actively disapproved of the elements of originality and creativeness which we think of as an essential component of authorship: "They valued extant old books more highly than any recent elucubrations *and they put the work of the scribe and the copyist above that of the authors.* The real task of the scholar was not the vain excogitation of novelties but a discovery of great old books, their multiplication and the placing of copies where they would be accessible to future generations of readers."[2]

Martha Woodmansee quotes a wonderful definition of "Book" from a mid-eighteenth-century dictionary that merely lists the writer as one mouth among many—"the scholar, . . . the paper-maker, the type-founder and setter, the proof-reader, the publisher and bookbinder, sometimes even the gilder and brass worker"—all of whom are "fed by this branch of manufacture."[3] Other studies show that authors seen as craftsmen—an appellation which Shakespeare might not have rejected—or at their most exalted, as the crossroads where learned tradition met external divine inspiration.[4] But since the tradition was mere craft and the glory of the divine inspiration should be offered to God rather than to the vessel he had chosen,[5] where was the justification for preferential treatment in the creation of property rights? As authors ceased to think of themselves as either craftsmen, gentlemen,[6] or amanuenses for the Divine spirit, a recognizably different, more romantic vision of authorship began to emerge. At first, it was found mainly in self-serving tracts, but little by little it spread through the culture so that by the middle of the eighteenth century it had come to be seen as a "universal truth about art."[7]

Woodmansee explains how the decline of the craft-inspiration model of writing and the elevation of the romantic author both presented and seemed to solve the question of property rights in intellectual products: "Eighteenth-century theorists departed from this compound model of writing in two significant ways. They minimized the element of craftsmanship (in some instances they simply discarded it) in favor of the element of inspiration, and they internalized the source of that inspiration. That is, inspiration came to be regarded as emanating not from outside or above, but from within the writer himself. 'Inspiration' came to be explicated in terms of *original genius* with the consequence that the inspired work was made peculiarly and distinctively the product—and the property—of the writer."[8]

In this vision, the author was not the journeyman who learned a craft and then hoped to be well paid for it. The romantic author was defined not by the mastery of a prior set of rules, but instead by the transformation of genre, the revision of form. Originality became the watchword of artistry and the warrant for property rights. To see how complete a revision this is, one need only examine Shakespeare's wholesale lifting of plot, scene, and language from other writers, both ancient and contemporary. To an Elizabethan playwright, the phrase "imitation is the sincerest form of flattery" might have seemed entirely without irony. "Not only were Englishmen from 1500 to 1625 without any feeling analogous to the modern attitude toward plagiarism; they even lacked the word until the very end of that period."[9] To the theorists and polemicists of romantic authorship, however, the reproduction of orthodoxy would have been proof they were not the unique and transcendent spirits they imagined themselves to be.

It is the *originality* of the author, the novelty which he or she adds to the raw materials provided by culture and the common pool, which "justifies" the property right and at the same time offers a strategy for resolving the basic conceptual problem pointed out by

is it not also the innovation.

Krause—what concept of property would allow the author to retain some property rights in the work but not others? In the German debates, the best answer was provided by the great idealist Fichte. In a manner that is now familiar to lawyers trained in legal realism and Hohfeldian analysis, but that must have seemed remarkable at the time, Fichte disaggregated the concept of property in books. The buyer gets the physical thing and the ideas contained in it. *Precisely because the originality of his spirit was converted into an originality of form,* the author retains the right to the form in which those ideas were expressed: "Each writer must give his own thoughts a certain form, and he can give them no other form than his own because he has no other. But neither can he be willing to hand over this form in making his thoughts public, for no one can *appropriate* his thoughts without thereby *altering their form.* This latter thus remains forever his exclusive property."[10]

A similar theme is struck in American copyright law. In the famous case of Bleistein v. Donaldson Lithographing Company,[11] concerning the copyrightability of a circus poster, Oliver Wendell Holmes was still determined to claim that the work could become the subject of an intellectual property right because it was the original creation of a unique individual spirit. Holmes's opinion shows us both the advantages and the disadvantages of a rhetoric which bases property rights on "originality." As a hook on which to hang a property right, "originality" seems to have at least a promise of formal realizability. It connects nicely to the romantic vision of authorship which I described earlier and to which I will return. It also seems to limit a potentially expansive principle, the principle that those who create may be entitled to retain some legally protected interest in the objects they make—even after those objects have been conveyed through the marketplace. But while the idea that an original spirit conveys its uniqueness to worked matter seems intuitively plausible when applied to Shakespeare[12] or Dante, it has less obvious relevance to a more humdrum act of creation by a less credibly romantic creator— a commercial artist in a shopping mall, say. The tension between the rhetoric of Wordsworth and the reality of suburban corporate capitalism is one that continues to bedevil intellectual property discourse today. In *Bleistein,* this particular original spirit had only managed to rough out a picture of energetic-looking individuals performing unlikely acts on bicycles, but to Holmes the principle was the same.

"The copy is the personal reaction of an individual upon nature. *Personality always contains something unique.* It expresses its singularity even in handwriting, and a very modest grade of art has in it something irreducible, which is one man's alone. That something he may copyright."[13]

This quality of "uniqueness," recognized first in great spirits, then in creative spirits, and finally in advertising executives, expresses itself in originality of form, of expression.[14] Earlier I quoted a passage from Jessica Litman which bears repeating here: "Why is it that copyright does not protect ideas? Some writers have echoed the justification for failing to protect facts by suggesting that ideas have their origin in the public domain. Others have implied that 'mere ideas' may not be worthy of the status of private property. Some authors have suggested that ideas are not protected because of the strictures imposed on copyright by the first amendment. The task of distinguishing ideas from expression in order to explain why private ownership is inappropriate for one but desirable for the other, however, remains elusive."[15]

I would say that we find the answer to this question in the romantic vision of authorship, of the genius whose style forever expresses a single unique persona. The rise of this powerful (and historically contingent) stereotype provided the necessary raw material to fashion some convincing mediation of the tension between the imagery of "public" and "private" in information production.

To sum up, then, if our starting place is the romantic idea of authorship, then the idea/expression division which has so fascinated and puzzled copyright scholars apparently manages, at a stroke, to do four things:

First, it provides a *conceptual basis* for partial, limited property rights, without completely collapsing the notion of property into the idea of a temporary, limited, utilitarian state grant, revocable at will. The property right still seems to be based on something real—on a distinction which sounds formally realizable, even if, on closer analysis, it turns out to be impossible to maintain.

Second, this division provides a *moral and philosophical justification* for fencing in the commons, giving the author property in something built from the resources of the public domain—language, culture, genre, scientific community, or what have you. If one makes originality of spirit the assumed feature of authorship and the touchstone for property rights, one can see the author as creating something entirely *new*—not recombining the resources of the commons.[16] Thus we reassure ourselves both that the grant to the author is justifiable *and* that it will not have the effect of diminishing the commons for *future* creators. After all, if a work of authorship is original—by definition—we believe that it only adds to our cultural supply. With originality first defended and then routinely assumed, intellectual property no longer looks like a zero sum game. There is always "enough and as good" left over—by definition. The distinguished intellectual property scholar Paul Goldstein captures both the power and the inevitable limitations of this view very well. "Copyright, in a word, is about authorship. Copyright is about sustaining the conditions of creativity that enable an individual to craft *out of thin air* an *Appalachian Spring*, a *Sun Also Rises*, a *Citizen Kane*."[17] But of course, even these—remarkable and "original"—works are *not* crafted out of thin air. As Northrop Frye put it in 1957, when Michel Foucault's work on authorship was only a gleam in the eye of the episteme, "Poetry can only be made out of other poems; novels out of other novels. All of this was much clearer before the assimilation of literature to private enterprise."[18]

Third, the idea/expression division circumscribes the ambit of a labor theory of property. At times, it seems that the argument is almost like Locke's labor theory; one gains property by mixing one's labor with an object. But where Locke's theory, if applied to a modern economy, might have a disturbingly socialist ring to it, Fichte's theory bases the property right on the originality of every spirit as expressed through words. Every author gets the right—the writer of the roman à clef as well as Goethe—but because of the concentration on originality of expression, the residual property right is only for the workers of the word and the image, not the workers of the world. Even after that right is extended by analogy to sculpture and painting, software and music, it will still have an attractively circumscribed domain.

Fourth, the idea/expression division resolves (or at least conceals) the *tension between public and private*. In the double life which Marx described, information is both the life blood of the noble disinterested citizens of the public world and a commodity in the private sphere to which we must attach property rights if we wish our self-interested producers to continue to produce. By disaggregating the book into "idea" and "expression," we can give the idea (and the facts on which it is based) to the public world and the expression to the writer, thus apparently mediating the contradiction between public good and private need (or greed).

Thus the combination of the romantic vision of authorship and the distinction between idea and expression appeared to provide a conceptual basis and a moral justification for intellectual property, to do so in a way which did not threaten to spread dangerous notions of entitlement to other kinds of workers, and to mediate the tension between the schizophrenic halves of the liberal world view. Small wonder that it was a success. Small wonder that, as I hope to show in this book, the language of romantic, original authorship tends to reappear in discussion of subjects far removed from the ones Fichte had in mind. Like insider trading. Or spleens.

A final question remains before I can proceed. Has the structure I have just described been rendered superfluous by economic analysis and public goods theory? An economist might say that the difference between the author and the laborer is that the author is producing a public good and the laborer is (generally) producing a good that can be satisfactorily commodified and alienated using only the traditional lexicon of property. The distinctions drawn from the idea of romantic authorship might appear to be surplus—unnecessary remnants of a conceptualist age.

It is certainly true that there are articles that decry the language of "idea" and "expression" and that offer the prediction that those terms will be used as mere summations of the underlying economic analysis[19]—in the same way that "proximate cause" is used as a way of expressing a conclusion about the desirable reach of liability. But this kind of response mistakes both the popular and the esoteric power of the language of romantic authorship. As the rest of this book will show, the romantic vision of authorship continues to influence public debate on issues of information—far beyond the traditional ambit of intellectual property. I tried to show earlier that the language of economic analysis provides no neat solutions to the problems of information regulation—precisely because economic analysis is marked by the same aporias as the rest of public discourse. In this situation of indeterminacy and contradiction, it is the romantic vision of authorship that frequently structures technical or scholarly economic analysis—providing the vital initial choices that give the analysis its subsequent appearance of determinacy and "commonsense" plausibility. Scholars may criticize the distinctions that flow from the romantic vision, but they should not imagine themselves to be free from its influence. This point will be particularly obvious when we get to the unlikely—and distinctly unromantic—subject of insider trading.

....

Before I go on, I would like to separate my project here from other critiques of the idea of authorship. Poststructuralist philosophy has produced a fair amount of author bashing. Literary criticism has been particularly hard on the idea of authorial intent. (Cynics would say that this is because the author's intentions are the last threat to the author-ity of the critic as the imperial interpreter of the text. Actually the truth is a little more complex.) Strange as it may seem, I would like to differentiate my project from full-court author bashing. I have no particular stake in the question of whether literary authors are being presented as coherent, omniscient individual subjects; if they are, I wish them well. It's nice work if you can get it. I do not believe that authorship is a patriarchal, phallocentric plot; indeed, I am willing to agree that, as an abstract idea, it has great liberating potential. How could someone of even mildly pinko sensibilities fail to be attracted by a system in which workers get property rights in the objects they create, or by a property system built on originality, where iconoclasm is actually the warrant for ownership? The irony about many of the critics of the author is that they fix on qualities to revile—defiant individuality, transformation, noncommodifiable moral rights—which under a slightly different set of historical and social circumstances they would have been the first to celebrate.

The historical work on the actual development of authorship as both an interpretive construct and a repository for property rights has been much more important to me—indeed, I have tried in a small way to add to it. But nothing in my argument turns on whether authorship is something that law has unwisely borrowed from literature, something that literature has unwisely borrowed from law, or something in between, as seems most likely.

Finally, this book is not written out of hostility or condescension toward the authorial ideal or its adherents. Attachment to the idea of the individual transformative authorship is not a silly "mistake."

First, it has a clear element of existential truth—our experience of authors, inventors, and artists who *do* transform their fields and our world, together with the belief (one I hold deeply myself) that the ability to remake the conditions of individual life and collective existence is to be cherished and rewarded. Second, as a basis for an intellectual property system, it seems to *work*, precisely because it makes a series of wrenching and difficult conflicts disappear—largely by defining them out of existence rather than solving them, however. It is possible to portray the fixation on originality and the neglect of sources and audience as a technical error made by the rational guardians of the legal system or as a deep plot by the multinationals. Instead, my argument has been that we need to see the romantic vision of authorship as the solution to a series of ideological problems. For those who do not like the word "ideology," at least as applied to any group of which *they* might be a part, we could call these problems deep-seated conceptual conflicts in our ideas of property and polity. The romantic idea of authorship is no more a "mistake" than classical economics was a mistake. It is both something more and something less than that. If one is critical of a system built on its presuppositions, one must begin by understanding both its authentic appeal and the deep conceptual itches it manages to scratch. Only then can one begin the critique.

. . . .

In the next chapter I turn to the question of blackmail. My aim in this book was to pick examples each of which illustrated a different aspect of the structure of information regulation I describe. Copyright offers the idea of romantic authorship as a way of reconciling the demands of private property and the public realm. By contrast, I argue, blackmail presents a situation in which the state *forbids* the commodification of information, precisely because it concerns the private sphere of home, hearth, and personal self-definition.

CHAPTER 7

Blackmail

B lackmail is of academic interest primarily as a proving ground.
Each new generation of scholars comes to it, as to some muddy
and treacherous test track, to try out their new theories.[1] The test is
an apparently simple one: to find out whether their approach will
answer the question "why is blackmail illegal?" Before we plunge
headlong into the morass, it is worth focusing for a moment on the
qualities that make blackmail a problematic case in the first place.
When scholars talk about the difficulties of explaining blackmail,
they are generally referring to a restricted subsection of the law of
blackmail. It is easy to explain attempts to extort money by threats
that would be illegal to carry out—to do physical damage, say. It is
also easy to explain why a blackmailer cannot ask money as the price
of keeping silent about some violation of the law by the victim. The
hard case to explain is the situation in which one person asks another
person for money as the price of not revealing legally obtained information about activities perfectly legal in themselves. The example
I gave earlier was "if you do not pay me $100, I will reveal to your
boyfriend the fact that I saw you coming out of another man's house
at two o'clock in the morning." The information was legal to acquire
and would be legal to reveal; the conduct was legal to engage in; yet
it is illegal to demand money for keeping quiet.[2] In Hohfeldian terms,
the sale of a privilege has been criminalized but the privilege itself

has been retained. How is this different from any other situation in which one economic actor makes a bargain with another to forgo a legal course of action that the second party wishes to avoid? To put it another way, what is the qualitative difference between a blackmailer's demands for money and a baseball team's demands for tax breaks, rezoning, and direct grants as the price of not moving to another a city?

There is something else in the blackmail question that makes it an irresistible puzzle for legal scholars, but a matter of little concern for courts, practicing lawyers, or citizens. Blackmail just *seems* so undeniably bad. It is the combination of the rule's intuitive moral sense and the lack of an obvious theoretical justification that leads scholars to believe that there is an answer out there if only they think hard enough about it. In that sense, blackmail is like other jurisprudential puzzles, such as the definition of law, which intrigue the novice and tantalize the professional by their apparent simplicity—only to confound and confuse when any theory is proposed.[3]

The attempts to explain the criminalization of blackmail point in very different directions, and I could not begin to cover the full range of explanations here. Instead, I will give examples of three kinds of attempted explanations—economic theories, libertarian theories, and third-party theories. I will argue that all three fail to explain blackmail and that we need a theory that focuses on the various roles that information is expected to play within our society. Admittedly, such a theory gives an answer of a different type than the ones sought by the theorists I cite here. To me, however, that answer seems both more credible and more useful than the answers other theorists provide.

Economic Theories

William Landes and Richard Posner believe that the prohibition of blackmail springs from the state's attempt to prevent (inefficient) examples of the private enforcement of the law. In other words, prohibiting blackmail is supposed to help the state keep its monopoly in law enforcement. "Were blackmail, a form of private enforcement, lawful, the public monopoly of enforcement would be undermined. Overenforcement of the law would result if the blackmailer were able to extract the full fine from the offenders . . . Alternatively, the blackmailer might sell his incriminating information to the offender for a price lower than the statutory cost of punishment to the criminal, which would reduce the effective cost of punishment to the criminal below the level set by the legislature."[4]

The first problem with this argument is its assumption that exactly the right level of activity had been chosen by legislators. Surely that assumption is made problematic by an economic approach. What mechanism would operate to make self-interested legislators, concerned mainly with reelection, choose the correct level of an activity?[5] This argument appears to presume too easily the existence of a "perfect market for legislation." The second problem with the argument is that it is weakest precisely at the point where blackmail most needs to be explained—where both revelation and silence on the part of the blackmailer and the act on the part of the victim would be entirely legal. If George Bernard Shaw is secretly eating rack of lamb, despite his publicly announced vegetarianism, his butcher may not make him pay for the privilege of silence. At the beginning of their discussion of blackmail, Landes and Posner note that blackmail appears at first sight to be an efficient way of enforcing the law, "the moral as well as the positive law."[6] This leaves open the idea that the analysis quoted above could somehow be transplanted to the Shaw hypothetical. Yet (rightly or wrongly) Shaw is not assumed by most people in this society to be violating a moral law—thus the idea of over- or underenforcement does not seem to arise.

Perhaps realizing these difficulties, Landes and Posner then offer a slightly different explanation for the criminalizing of the sale of humiliating, as well as incriminating, information. "The social decision not to regulate a particular activity is a judgment that the expenditure of resources on trying to discover it and punish it would be socially wasted. That judgment is undermined if blackmailers are encouraged to expend substantial resources on attempting to apprehend and punish people engaged in the activity."[7]

This is an ingenious suggestion, but there are a number of problems with it. First of all, the implications Landes and Posner draw from "the decision not to regulate" seem problematic in the extreme. All over the United States there are parents trying to find out if their children—whether infant or adult—are eating their vegetables, doing their homework, smoking cigarettes, or dating "the wrong people." The idea that the legal system ought to step in to prevent them from investing time in checking up on any legal activity does not survive prolonged scrutiny—no matter how attractive it might be to the children involved. To put it another way, it is already stretching a point to claim that criminal statutes are accurate judgments of the efficient level of an activity. It is going altogether too far to claim also that the *absence* of criminal statutes represents a measured judgment by the legislature that "research" on such behavior would be inefficient.

The second problem with the argument is its leap to deduction from negative evidence. The idea that "noncriminalization" of some form of behavior is equivalent to a judgment that information should not be gathered about it for trading purposes simply does not follow. One can imagine all sorts of reasons we might have for failing to criminalize behavior that would not prevent us from wanting to have news gathered and spread. A politician makes repeated sexist or racist jokes, an air force officer in charge of nuclear weapons is a moody alcoholic, a candidate for a teaching position has awful teaching evaluations at a prior school—in each case, we can acknowledge some social value to the information despite the fact that the behavior concerned is perfectly legal. Landes and Posner would need to show *both* (1) that noncriminalization was a conclusive judgment that the information was not worth the investment of social resources and (2) that forbidding citizens to trade in it would be a sufficient deterrent to have a meaningful effect on its acquisition. Yet the second idea seems empirically doubtful in the extreme, while the first seems to be just plain wrong.

One response to these problems might be that Landes and Posner object only to *monetary* incentives to engage in this kind of research. Where affection and sentiment, public or private interest supply the motive, we might hope that all is for the best—my examples notwithstanding. Of course if there are enough nonmonetary incentives to investigate legal behavior, the prohibition of monetary incentives would be irrational—an invocation of the state's cumbersome and expensive machinery in the service of a goal that is already unreachable. But even if the empirical question was dealt with adequately (and Landes and Posner do not deal with it at all), such a response brings a whole new school of problems in its wake. If we concentrate only on occasions involving monetary incentives to gather information, the theory as stated seems unable rationally to distinguish between paid concealment and paid revelation. If adultery is not criminal in a particular state, does that represent a judgment that we do not want resources devoted to the discovery of adultery? Thinking of the blackmailer, Landes and Posner would presumably say "yes." Does this logically require that we prohibit newspaper reporters from following Gary Hart, or one spouse from hiring private detectives to check on the other?

Just at this point in their discussion, Landes and Posner reverse their tack, apparently without realizing it. "We therefore predict that in areas where there is a public monopoly of enforcement, bribery, like blackmail, will be prohibited, while in areas where there is no public monopoly, it will be permitted. And so we observe."[8] This may seem to deal with the spouse example. But it completely undercuts their idea that the decision not to regulate implies a judgment that resources should not be spent trying to acquire the information. There is no public monopoly of enforcement of George Bernard Shaw's vegetarianism, yet "private enforcement"—through blackmail—is illegal. In many states there is no public monopoly of enforcement of prohibitions against adultery, certain types of plagiarism, or violation of the individual's professed creed; yet blackmail would not be permitted.

Perhaps what Landes and Posner meant was that where the state does not criminalize an activity, and private parties have no rights to restrain it, *but* still act censoriously toward it, we should minimize the gathering of information about it. If that is the idea, then they seem again to be ignoring the fact that blackmail may well be one of the least important motives for gathering information. Prurience, moral disapproval, or simple curiosity may lead citizens to pry, as can the desire to help another human being, gain status as a gossip, or achieve political power. Surely if we wished to avoid this kind of wasteful "research," the solution would be to criminalize it, or at least to allow the injured party to bring suit under an enormously expanded tort of intrusion upon seclusion. Under Landes and Posner's plan, the only person who will be deterred will be the person who wants to sell directly to the individual concerned. Sales to other parties—for example, the tabloids—are untouched, as are all the other nonmarket incentives for engaging in investigation. If this is an attempt to prevent the socially wasteful investment of resources, then it is a signally ineffective one.[9] Though thought-provoking, Landes and Posner's theory focuses on probably the least important market and on only one motive for information gathering. It also neglects empirical considerations that might rob it of any significance, deploys the concept of monopoly enforcement in apparently contradictory ways, and ignores the case in which the information gathering is paid for up front rather than after the fact.

A more promising economic approach is taken by Douglas Ginsburg and Ronald Coase.[10] Both focus on the fact that if blackmail is allowed there will be incentives for potential blackmailers to invest in discovering information that could be used to blackmail others. "Blackmail involves the expenditure of resources in the collection of information which on payment of blackmail, will be suppressed. It would be better if this information were not collected and the resources were used to produce something of value."[11] This is, in fact, an ingenious explanation of blackmail. But a number of problems with it remain.

The first is, as James Lindgren points out, that it does not explain the prohibition of "accidental blackmail" (the clergyman seen in flagrante delicto through a wind-fluttered curtain).[12] Let us assume the response to this critique is, as I suggested earlier, that of formal realizability. Drawing the boundaries this way will make it easier to enforce. The second problem is that the argument appears to rest on an unacknowledged empirical assumption about the *prevalence* of accidental blackmail as opposed to "deliberate blackmail" (the individual who sets out to "get the dirt on someone"). *If* the information necessary for deliberate blackmail is costly relative to the likely benefits to be gained, rational actors would be deterred anyway. Thus even when the practice is legalized, most blackmailers would be of the accidental type. Yet the accidental blackmailer's discovery of the information is unaffected by the rule change. Thus we might be forbidding a potentially productive exchange, leaving the accidental blackmailer, who would rather have been paid off than gossip, but would rather gossip than keep quiet, to spill the beans. To make the argument with any confidence, we would need to figure out the proportion of accidental blackmail to deliberate blackmail, under both rule systems, and the relative utility functions of gossip for both types of blackmailers. In our attempt to prevent the socially wasteful investment of resources, we could be blocking mutually beneficial transactions between eager victims and accidental blackmailers who place a low value on gossip.

The second difficulty is the quick move to judgment that "nothing of value" has been produced. The measure being used here is not the subjective willingness to pay of the parties concerned. Intuitively, because of blackmail's moral repulsiveness, it seems believable that nothing of value has been produced. But is this really the case? What measure of social value is being used? On the part of a victim, the blackmail payment represents "the avoidance of a loss," rather than a "gain," but we are surely not saying that all situations where parties pay to avoid losses are criminal. Consider the behavior of the baseball team, negotiating with its host city for a better deal. As Coase himself admits, "The problem is that all trade involves threatening not to do something unless certain demands are met. Furthermore, negotiations about the terms of trade are likely to involve the making of threats which it would be better if they were not made (and in this Pigou is right). But it is only certain threats in certain situations which cause harm on balance and in which the harm is sufficiently great as to make it desirable that those making them should be prosecuted and punished."[13]

Having implicitly pointed out that no theory can be put forward that would not also criminalize transactions understood to be perfectly legal, Coase concludes by wondering whether the British system, with its broad grant of discretion to judge and jury, represents the best answer. This seems a perfectly sensible response on the level of policy. Yet it also represents an abandonment of the rationalist project in this case, with no consideration of the more general questions that such a rejection seems to raise.

The criticisms I have made so far by no means exhaust the list. We could turn Landes and Posner on their head and argue that blackmail would function, by and large, as an effective way to police social norms, coupled with a relatively efficient buyout provision. If the victim was willing to pay more for the information than the public would, whether through tabloid bounty or indirect celebrity, the blackmailer would sell silence. On its face, a resource has been moved to its highest use-value. Only Landes and Posner's rather dubious assumption about the efficiency of both positive and negative judgments by legislatures allows them to avoid this interpretation. If one views blackmail as a secondary method of social control, it is not entirely clear how one can both stay within the strange world of economic assumptions and yet declare that the information "has no value."

For all the reasons listed, the economic theories of blackmail seem to fail according to their own standard. This is a point that Coase, at least, seems almost to acknowledge at the end of his discussion. Perhaps the central problem with all such theories from my perspective, however, is that they seem so far from the *social* understanding of blackmail. Would social judgments about the normative status of blackmail turn on empirical issues about the relative frequency and costliness of its accidental versus its deliberate varieties? Of course, explanations of the law do not have to assume that social actors understand their own institutions. Yet in the case of blackmail, the goad to answer the puzzle came partly from the juxtaposition of the almost universal sense that the practice is wrong with the difficulty of distinguishing it from "lawful" transactions. To discard the importance of social perceptions is also to challenge a large part of the motive for undertaking the theoretical inquiry in the first place. Finally, as I will point out later, there seems to be a particular problem here for economic analysts. How do we move from a picture of relentlessly rational actors, consumer sovereignty, and exogenous preferences to a world in which we assert that citizens think blackmail has nothing to do with information costs, *but they are deluded?* For me at least, that is a puzzle. It looks like a theory of false consciousness, but that is exactly the kind of theory which most economic analysts of law claim to be avoiding.

Libertarian Theories

Blackmail is also a very troublesome topic for libertarians. If contract is the central metaphor in your understanding of mutually beneficial social relationships, and government intervention in free exchanges is your paradigmatic evil, how can you consistently believe that blackmail is wrong? Some libertarians do not,[14] but it is interesting to note that two of the most prominent libertarians, Robert Nozick and Richard Epstein, do believe blackmail should be criminalized. It is also interesting to note that each gives a different explanation for this apparent exception to their principles.

Epstein, in his article "Blackmail, Inc.," argues that if blackmail was legal it might lead to further crimes as the victim sought money to pay off his blackmailer.[15] This idea seems extremely implausible, being both logically unrequired and subject to some obvious practical difficulties. Why should we suddenly start assuming that this particular monetary pressure would drive the victim to crime? Consider the entirely legal forms of "pressure" that can be put on individuals in our society—ranging from the advertising that encourages us to define our self-worth in terms of consumer goods not all of us have the money to buy to the action of a company in laying off workers, many of whom have mortgages or medical bills that place an intolerable financial burden on them. Each of these might conceivably lead to crime. Yet somehow it seems doubtful that Epstein would criminalize the advertising of Air Jordans or the practice of plant closings. Besides, as Lindgren points out, it would be in "Blackmail, Inc.'s" interests to set the payments at a level not likely to provoke rash criminal activity.[16] An incarcerated victim is an unpromising target for blackmail.

Epstein also speculates that the blackmail victim, unlike other persons needing money, would probably not be able to get a loan because of the difficulty of specifying the reason for needing the money. Again, this seems implausible. In my—admittedly limited—experience, providers of consumer credit, credit cards, and home equity loans care only about the borrower's ability to pay. The liberal state may or may not be indifferent as to "ends" but lenders certainly seem to be. There also seems to be a familiar baseline error here: imagining a hypothetical change of rule, but failing to adjust behavior to conform to the new rule. If blackmail were *legal*, surely lenders would find it an acceptable investment? Imagine a lender contemplating a further loan to a borrower who already owes the lender money. If paying off Blackmail, Inc., will allow the borrower to keep a lucrative job or social position, a blackmail loan would seem like a better investment than a loan for a new car. If lenders are supposed to be irrational, presumably Blackmail, Inc., would be smart enough to develop a good credit division. Rather than exploring either of these possibilities, Epstein imagines that Blackmail, Inc., will stupidly encourage the victim's slide into crime. Thus not only will it open itself to suit and to criminal charges for conspiracy, but it will also forfeit the advantages Epstein has just conferred on it by legalization. Admittedly, a firm this stupid doesn't deserve a break, but why assume such irrationality on the part of all concerned?

Finally, as Epstein himself notes, it would seem intuitively plausible that a rational blackmail industry would pick rich victims—victims who might not *need* credit. Blackmailers would prefer rich victims because of the diminishing marginal utility of wealth[17] and because there would probably be a statistically significant correlation between those who have something to lose in terms of reputation and association and those who have money. The street person is an unlikely victim of blackmail, the minimum wage worker scarcely more likely, and *if there are any costs of investigation at all,* we would need some empirical evidence of the break-even point before we could say whether those who are most likely to be blackmailed would not also be likely to have substantial resources or access to credit on demand. Epstein's conclusion that, unlike kindred transactions, "only blackmail breeds fraud" seems, like religious encyclicals about the depraving effects of rock music, to have little in the way of logic to recommend it.

Epstein has another string to his bow. Working from libertarian assumptions, he views most nonphysical crimes as grounded in fraud or deceit. Thus, for him, "the puzzle is somewhat transformed, as the question might be better asked, why is it that [the victim] escapes criminal punishment for deception, not why is [the defendant] punished for blackmail." In the end, he cannot entirely solve this problem so he pushes it to one side, confident that the blackmail problem, at least, has been resolved. "Blackmail should be a criminal offense even under the narrow theory of criminal activities because it is the hand-maiden to corruption and deceit."[18] I have already dealt with the corruption argument. What about deceit? The trouble here is that this answer seems to avoid the question. The blackmail puzzle is exactly the fact that the law does allow citizens to keep secrets, and to reveal secrets, but not to make others pay for the keeping of secrets. To say that secret-keeping in some wider sense should be illegal, and then to use this as an explanation of blackmail's illegality, is hardly likely to satisfy those who have been seeking a solution to the problem. For someone like Lindgren, this is similar to "solving" Epimenides' paradox ("All Cretans are liars," Epimenides being from Crete) by suggesting that Epimenides was actually from Ios.

In another interesting libertarian analysis, Robert Nozick has argued that blackmail should be illegal because it is an unproductive exchange. The proof of its "unproductivity" comes, for Nozick, from his belief that one party to the exchange would be no worse off if it were prohibited. "Though people value a blackmailer's silence, and pay for it, his being silent is not a productive activity. His victims would be as well off if the blackmailer did not exist at all, and so wasn't threatening them. And they would be no worse off if the exchange were known to be absolutely impossible."[19] This idea is an interesting one, but it collapses as soon as it is exposed to the world of legal powers, privileges, and immunities. There are many cases in which—in some sense—I would be better off if the other party did not exist at all. The neighboring landowner wishes to build a structure which will deprive my courtyard of sunlight, but is willing to forgo building for payment. Perhaps Nozick would respond that even if this landowner did not exist, some landowner must exist and thus—at least potentially—I would face the same problem. But even this kind of confession and avoidance does not solve the problem.

Nozick seems to be relying on an implicit, but indefensible, baseline. The alternative to blackmail is silence, and thus the victim is better off if blackmail is illegal. But the alternative to blackmail may be not silence, but revelation. This is a point that those libertarians who believe blackmail should not be criminalized have made loudly and often.[20] To put it another way, Nozick is making a category error, confusing the *person* with the legally protected interest. The victim might be better off if the blackmailer did not exist, but Nozick instead is arguing for the disappearance of one of the blackmailer's legally protected interests, leaving intact exactly the ones that can do the victim harm. It is true that all those with secrets to hide would be better off if no one ever discovered them. But the law of blackmail cannot get rid of the person who discovers a secret—it merely makes it impossible for him to sell silence. Nozick has stripped the blackmailer not of the privilege of disclosure, but merely of the ability to commodify his decision not to disclose. He is therefore wrong to say that victims "would be no worse off if the exchange were known to be absolutely impossible." In such a situation, a whole range of potential blackmailers who put a low value on the celebrity of being a gossip, but who would instead have accepted a small payment for silence, will now disclose. In such cases, victims might justifiably conclude that they would have been better off if *Nozick* had never existed!

Nozick might choose to reformulate his position by combining the incentives point discussed by Coase with his own definition of unproductive exchanges. The idea here would be that prohibiting blackmail would discourage rational actors from investing resources in trying to "get the dirt on someone" and thus minimize the number of "unproductive exchanges." Such a response, however, faces two major problems. First, and most fundamentally, there is the difficulty of crafting a noncircular definition of unproductive exchanges, a definition that does not also criminalize hosts of other transactions. So far, this is something that Nozick has been unable to do. Second, this response appears to rest on the same unacknowledged empirical assumption about the prevalence of accidental blackmail as opposed to deliberate blackmail. Thus Nozick might be forbidding a potentially productive exchange, leaving the accidental blackmailer who would rather have been paid off than gossip, but would rather gossip than keep quiet, to spill the beans. To make the argument with any confidence, we would need to know how much accidental blackmail and how much deliberate blackmail there would be in both the current system and the system in which blackmail is legalized. We would also need to know how much value would be put on gossip in both systems, for both types of blackmailers. Neither Nozick nor Epstein can know these things and the unacknowledged and unwarranted empirical assumption subverts their arguments.

Third-Party Arguments

Lindgren offers to resolve the paradox of blackmail by reference to third-party interests.

> My own view is that the key to the wrongfulness of the blackmail transaction is in its triangular structure . . . The transaction implicitly involves not only the blackmailer and his victim but always a third party as well. This third party may be, for example, the victim's spouse or employer, the authorities, or even the public at large. When a blackmailer tries to use his right to release damaging information, he is threatening to tell others. To get what he wants, the blackmailer uses leverage that is less his than someone else's. Selling the right to go to the police involves suppressing the state's interests. And selling the right to inform others of embarrassing (but legal) behavior involves suppressing the interests of those other people. Why should this threatener be able to gain personal advantages by coercing others, using leverage that is not really his?[21]

In one sense, I think that Lindgren is on the right track here. Certainly he conducts an impressive survey and critique of other theories, and the structure of his theory at least asks us to look at the reaction of other individuals in the society. But the analysis seems to be flawed by a series of errors based on conceptual "slippage" in the definition of key terms. In what sense, exactly, is the leverage that the blackmailer uses "less his than someone else's"? In what sense is the blackmailer "suppressing the interests of . . . other people"? First of all, note the vagueness of the terms. Is a legally protected interest being asserted here, or merely an "interest" in the same sense that many people have an interest in seeing pictures of Princess Di sunbathing? At times, Lindgren seems to be moving from the latter to the former, thus presuming the point he is obliged to prove. Second, if Lindgren is asserting that the blackmailer has "no right" to capitalize on the latter kind of interest, he seems to be restating the very problem he has set himself to solve. Third, whatever kind of "interest" this is, Lindgren is mistaken if he believes that one may not sell access to something one does not own. Many bargains involve one party using access to a resource or market he does not own as leverage to persuade another party to sign a contract. For the realist scholars of the 1920s, the slippage from "no right to control" to "no privilege to exclude" represents a prototypical Hohfeldian error. In fact, the ability to analyze such issues clearly is exactly the thing that distinguishes post- from pre-Hohfeldian analysis.[22]

For example, if I sell a popcorn concession in my baseball stadium to you, you will be interested only because you know this will give you access to a group of potential consumers. You would never pay me merely for refraining from exercising my right to deny you access to the physical space that I own. Without the crowd, sale of this right would be worthless to you, just as the blackmailer's promise not to exercise the privilege of revelation would be worthless without third parties who will otherwise be told of the secret. I do not own those consumers, or their appetites, but I do control access to them while they are at the game. Is this transaction somehow despicable because the economic leverage I use is access to someone else's appetite, whether for popcorn or for gossip? I will probably lease the stand to the person who pays the most, thus increasing the cost of popcorn to those who attend the game. In some sense, therefore, I sell my right of exclusion, use the "interests" of others as my economic leverage, and yet am not forced to incorporate their interests fully into my calculation.[23]

When we renegotiate, I may threaten to give the lease to someone else. As far as I can tell, Lindgren's analysis is unable to distinguish this case from blackmail. "Why should this threatener be able to gain personal advantages by coercing others, using leverage that is not really his?"[24] But as this analogy should make clear, the phrase "not really his" contains a fatal ambiguity. The leverage is not really mine, in the sense that I do not own the baseball fans and their appetites, or the audience for gossip, but it is "really mine" in the sense that I have legally protected interests that allow me to grant or withhold physical *or informational* access. If we ignore the judgmental possessive "mine," with its associated connotation of the absolute concept of property, the legal relationships become much clearer, and Lindgren's theory—at least in any strong form—fails to distinguish blackmail from innumerable legal transactions.

....

Before I finish the critical part of my coverage of blackmail, I would like to point out three characteristics of the views I have discussed so far. The first is best exemplified by the world of Nozick, Posner, Coase, and Epstein. Their arguments show an interesting willingness to relinquish, or at least modify, a principle they normally hold dear. That principle is the principle of consumer sovereignty, or personal definition of self-interest. Why is blackmail such a difficult case for them? Seeing that the law prohibits a transaction, seeing that the transaction is apparently dependent only on the coercion involved in the relinquishment of a legal privilege, and yet finding the transaction indefensible, they are placed in an agonizing position. To suggest, as the legal realists did, that coercion is inherent in the legal system, that the core of a consensual laissez-faire system is completely dependent on institutionalized coercion, is not a solution that appeals to them.[25] Besides, it is not clear that even that admission would solve the puzzle of blackmail. (In formal terms, it should merely put other transactions on the same level as blackmail—hardly an attractive solution in either theoretical or practical terms.) At the same time, all three wish to put the law of blackmail within the class of "rational social institutions," and thus they must find some logical explanation of its wrongfulness. The explanation must contain some principle to distinguish between this state interference in a "consensual transaction" and all the other state interferences in "consensual transactions." Otherwise, they might be seen to have accepted the premise of liberals and radicals: that paternalist intervention is frequently necessary in the economic system in order to mitigate the effects of unequal power.[26]

Second, it is also noticeable that even in combination all the theories—but particularly the economic and libertarian ones—fail to grasp the *social meaning* of blackmail. Put another way, I doubt that one could find anyone—even on the streets of Cambridge—who would respond to the question "why is blackmail illegal?" by appealing to notions of inefficient incentives for information production, or unproductive exchanges. Of course, there is nothing wrong with giving an explanation for a body of law that conflicts with the explanations of those in the society governed by such laws. But Nozick, Epstein, Posner, and Coase are increasingly forced toward theories that diverge so widely from popular ideas that the only explanation for the discrepancy seems to be the false consciousness of those concerned. For theorists in other traditions this would be unexceptionable. Yet for libertarians and economic analysts to accept that idea of false consciousness is to throw their theories—strongly dependent on a particular version of rational choice—into doubt.

A third observation could be made about all of the writers I have discussed, but it is most clearly at work in Lindgren's scholarship. We could call it "Kantian anthropology." At times, Lindgren seems to assume that the combination of the fact that there is a rule prohibiting blackmail and that the practice seems intuitively bad means that there is a general principle underlying both prohibition and revulsion. The task that he sets himself, and that he (rightly) sees as the basic goal of other studies of blackmail, is to find this missing principle if it exists. This is certainly one way to understand legal institutions. Its premise is that social institutions should have a rational basis, expressible in terms of general principles, and those that do not should disappear from the earth. Its descriptive, rationalist anthropology dovetails nicely with its prescriptive principled critique. As a method of legal studies, its premises are so widely shared that they are not often subject to question. Its weapons also have undeniable critical bite, particularly when deployed against someone who is working within the same genre of scholarship. Indeed, my ability to be understood as criticizing other blackmail theorists, whether well or badly, depends on both author and reader presupposing the background conventions of this idea of the project. But just as information questions make more apparent the weaknesses in the liberal vision of property, and in the conceptual structure of efficiency and incentive discourse in economics, so they highlight the contentious quality of this vision of legal scholarship.

....

I think we should reject Kantian anthropology as a method, at least in this case. We cannot understand why blackmail seems so bad to us unless we look at it in the context of the ideology and institutions of a liberal society, a society that often presupposes different theories of justice and methods of treating people in the realms of the family, the market, and the state. We get a different picture if we look at legal institutions and moral beliefs in the light of the history, social arrangements, and ideology of this actual society, rather than viewing them in an unspecified and featureless world of legal hypotheticals and pure rationality.

Let me use a nonblackmail hypothetical for a moment. Consider the contract rules about penalty clauses and liquidated damages. We could come up with a rationalistic explanation of the difference, based perhaps on allocative efficiency or the Rawlsian original position. But although such an explanation would be useful, it would also ignore the absolute terror that liberal social theory in general and classical legal thought in particular has of private law's assuming a redistributive function. This concern is built on moral ideals and ideas of political theory, but it is also built on concerns of legitimacy and of the apparent soundness of an entire ideological view of the world. The difficulty that any study of legal ideology would point out is that the two conclusions deduced from the supposedly non-redistributive nature of contract law are (1) that the court should merely interpret the wills of the parties, because to go further would be to move from being an instrument of the parties' bargain to being an independent redistributive actor; and (2) that punitive damages are inappropriate in contract law, which functions only to achieve the results the contract would have reached. The obvious conflict comes when the wills of the parties apparently *specify* punitive damages. If the court shares the legal ideology I have just described (which it may do to various degrees in different times and places), it is faced with a contradiction. And that, we might say, is a vitally important part of the explanation of the confused and confusing morass of doctrine surrounding the distinction between illegitimate "punitive damages" and legitimate, and mutually agreed upon, "liquidated damages." Merely to take the perspective of rational managers of the legal system dealing with one technical problem of doctrine at a time is to underestimate the extent to which these answers fit into a world already structured by history, ideology, and political vision.[27]

How does this insight help us to understand blackmail? To answer that question, I must return to my discussion of public and private. My thesis is that one of the main reasons that blackmail is illegal (and is strongly perceived to be wrong) is that there is a strong social belief, sometimes consciously articulated and sometimes unconsciously held, that not everything should be reduced to "the universalizing logic of the money relation." In particular, the private realm of home and hearth should be protected from the relentless instrumentalism of market transactions. This belief is given a particular spin by the fact that within the private sphere we define the norm of justified protection largely by reference to the right to withhold and control information. Intuitively, blackmail seems like the intrusion of market logic into the realm that should be most "private." To put it another way, we do not think that we should commodify relationships in the private realm. To commodify could itself be seen as a violation of the private realm. To commodify a violation of privacy, then, is *doubly* reprehensible.

Two features of blackmail doctrine seem to me to support this interpretation. First, by and large, we allow the victim (and the blackmailer's assessment of the victim's subjective beliefs) to determine whether or not particular information involves a "disgraceful defect." A vision of blackmail that did not focus on privacy, but instead wanted to prohibit the commodification of information about a particular menu of behavior and practices, could have resorted either to *listing* topics about which individuals could not be blackmailed or to appealing to an objective, or community, standard. In fact, we choose to protect George Bernard Shaw's secret carnivorousness to exactly the same extent that we protect secret marital infidelity, despite the different tolerance for such practices in society as a whole. The comparison to the law of libel is instructive.

Second, we find coercive, and therefore prohibit, only the "threat" to reveal unless paid. This, I think, is a point that reinforces the arguments I made earlier about the multiple contradictory stereotypes about information. Unless I have gone so far as to commit an additional tort such as intrusion upon seclusion, I am allowed to *reveal* all the information I discover—without penalty. The privilege is retained, but the sale of the privilege is criminalized. When freely revealed, *or sold direct to a news outlet*, information—even relatively private information—fits readily into the public, First Amendment stereotype. Information is the life blood of the public realm, that which we must not regulate if we wish to maintain the free flow of ideas. The willingness to keep quiet for money, however, undermines the First Amendment stereotype, allowing the privacy vision to take over. It is the privacy vision of information that makes blackmail seem like a *"threat,"* and the baseball team's demands seem like an "offer." In the chapter on insider trading, I will argue that the reverse mechanism operates to explain the prohibition of trading on material, nonpublic information. There, the "public" view of information, the idea of presumptive equality in this resource alone, operates to give insider trading law a powerful rationale.

Seen this way, blackmail is analogous to a different set of crimes. To understand blackmail, we would not compare it to the robber's demand for a wallet. Instead, we would compare it to other situations where commodification of something "private" is made illegal, despite the fact that, at a slightly greater level of abstraction, the transaction looks like an ordinary market exchange. Thus the analogies would be to the voidability of contracts for sexual services or to the prohibition of baby-selling. I can give sexual favors, but not enforce a contract for them. I have a power to arrange a private adoption of my child, yet I cannot sell that power, or the child.[28]

To many scholars this kind of response is unsatisfying. Even if there are "irrational" or "sentimental" or "romantic" reasons behind a legal institution, should we not work to complete the Enlightenment project—to bring institutions to account in the court of reason? I have a fancy philosophical and a mundane practical response to this suggestion. The fancy philosophical point is that there *is* no pretheoretical, preclassified reality from which we can begin to analyze our institutions. *This* context or *that* context may not be inevitable, but there will be some context, some prior social construction of reality. Wittgenstein's analysis of language games, Kuhn and Feyerabend's (very different) work on the scientific method, Richard Rorty's neo-pragmatism—all seem to cast doubt on the idea of a world not already socially constructed, while leaving open the question of consequences that flow from exploring the limits of the particular, overlapping contexts in which we find ourselves.

My more mundane claim is that it is important to understand the limitations of a system that "decides" issues by typing them as public or private. To say that, however, is not to hold up the possibility of a pure analysis that would treat the issue of blackmail in a "neutral" framework. No such framework is available. On a local basis, I still believe in arguments about whether or not the prohibition of blackmail is good or bad—arguments based on judgments about consequences, on analogies to other kinds of behavior, even on the idea of incentives to engage in particular kinds of information gathering. Those arguments, however, will not discover some universalizable principle that underpins both the institution of blackmail and its social support. Instead, they will be both over- and underinclusive. They will point toward the prohibition of acts that we allow while not explaining our prohibition of other transactions. The goal of the blackmail theorists, to provide *the* single rational explanation, is not only unmet but—I would argue—unreachable.

What then is the benefit of the analysis I offer here? What does it profit us to understand that information issues are resolved partly by the typing of issues into "public" or "private" categories? How does it help us to understand that blackmail prevents the commodification of silence about private information partly because of a romantic notion of privacy, home, and hearth and an associated belief that we must keep the market away from that realm if we hope to maintain it? First, I think it is descriptively useful. To understand how information issues should be resolved, we need first to understand how they *are* resolved. Second, the analysis gives us a very limited ability to prognosticate about the future. In the Conclusion, I point out that any analysis of an "information society" has to deal with the conflicting valences of our various visions of information as public, as private, as commodity, and as "that which must never be commodified." Blackmail doctrine points out the lengths to which we are prepared to go to give individuals sovereignty over information pertaining to them. This surely is an important idea in any society in which the collection, manipulation, distribution, and use of information plays a significant role. Third, dealing specifically with the blackmail puzzle, the analysis points out a reason for the problems I noted with the existing blackmail literature. The very notion of "reason," "theory," and "principle" adopted by the blackmail theorists makes it almost impossible for them to find such a reason, theory, or principle underlying blackmail. There is an old joke about a drunk looking for his car keys under a street light, even though he had dropped them several hundred feet away. When asked to explain his behavior, he pointed out that while the keys might not be there, this was the only place he could see anything. To a certain extent, the Kantian anthropology of the blackmail theorists has the same problem. They wish both to engage and to ignore the socially constructed nature of market, coercion, and privacy. To put it another way, the society in which the kind of principle for which they are looking could be found would be the society in which social forms were already transparent to rational analysis: that is to say, the society for which it was not necessary.

Finally, and not unimportantly, the persistent mistakes that are made by the most sophisticated of analysts in trying to analyze blackmail—the category and baseline errors, the failure to take into account changes in behavior if a new rule is presumed, the conflation of different legally protected interests into an undifferentiated "right" concept—all of these turn out to be mistakes that are instructive, if not canonical, for the remainder of the literature on law and information. The analysis of insider trading doctrine in the next chapter will reveal the persistence of such errors in a case in which the commodification of information is apparently prohibited because of the *public* rather than the private stereotype of information. At the same time, examination of the germinal critique of insider trading doctrine will show that the language of romantic authorship can appear where least expected.

CHAPTER 8

Insider Trading and the Romantic Entrepreneur

O ur era aptly has been styled, and well may be remembered as, the 'age of information.' Francis Bacon recognized nearly four hundred years ago that 'knowledge is power,' but only in the last generation has it risen to the equivalent of the coin of the realm. Nowhere is this commodity more valuable or volatile than in the world of high finance, where facts worth fortunes while secret may be rendered worthless once revealed."[1] This quotation comes from an insider trading case. Anthony Materia worked as a copyholder for the financial printer Bowne of New York City, Inc. One of his duties involved reading documents aloud to a proofreader who checked their accuracy. In this case, the documents were concerned with a forthcoming tender offer. Although the names of the companies had been erased, Materia—whom the circuit court referred to as an "avid market watcher"—was able to work out the intended target. He did this by checking the details revealed in the tender offer documents against a variety of publicly available types of information, including the date of incorporation of the target company, the number of shares outstanding, and so on. In another context, one could imagine Materia's wit, hard work, and eye for an opportunity being held up as exemplary American entrepreneurial virtues. In the context of this case, however, with its persistent overtones of fraud and deceit, the court of appeals found little admirable in Materia's conduct, and sounded disapproving about the enthusiasm with which he pursued his extracurricular interests. At one point, Judge Kaufman noted drily, "If copyholding was Materia's vocation, the stock market appears to have been equally consuming." Having worked out the identity of the target company (displaying, in the process, considerable ingenuity), Materia invested heavily. "Within hours of each discovery, he purchased stock, and within days—after the offer had been made public—he sold his holdings at substantial gains."[2]

In the broadest possible terms, we could say that the question presented by the *Materia* case is: "When can an individual profit from access to material, nonpublic information?" In an earlier case called *Chiarella*, which had strikingly similar facts, the same court had held that "*anyone*—corporate insider or not—who regularly receives material nonpublic information may not use that information to trade in securities without incurring an affirmative duty to disclose."[3] The Supreme Court did not agree. To Justice Powell, writing for the majority, the court of appeal's decision was too concerned with one particular goal of the Securities and Exchange Act. "Its decision ... rested solely upon its belief that the federal securities laws have 'created a system providing equal access to information necessary for reasoned and intelligent investment decisions.' The use by anyone of material information not generally available is fraudulent, this theory suggests, because such information gives certain buyers and sellers an unfair advantage over less informed buyers and sellers."[4] Justice Powell was not inclined to see the Securities and Exchange Act as a document with such relentlessly egalitarian aims or such a broad reach to effect them. "Formulation of such a broad duty, which departs radically from the established doctrine that duty arises from a specific relationship between two parties should not be undertaken absent some explicit evidence of congressional intent."[5]

In *Materia* the court of appeals tried again. Having seen its idea of a general duty to "disclose regularly received material nonpublic information" rejected by the Supreme Court, it recast the issue in terms of misappropriation.[6] Seen this way, Materia's offense was that he had "misappropriat[ed] nonpublic information in breach of a fiduciary duty and [traded] on that information to his own advantage."[7] It was this action which violated Section 10(b) of the 1934 Securities Exchange Act and Rule 10(b)-5. This time, with the issue framed not in terms of formally equal public access to information, but instead in terms of the protection of private information from something the court called "misappropriation" (and one of the headnotes simply called "theft"),[8] the Supreme Court was inclined to agree.[9] From my earlier discussion of tensions in the regulation of information, this choice between an equal access view and a quasi–property rights view should not be surprising.[10]

The conflicts between the court of appeals and the Supreme Court in the *Materia* and *Chiarella* cases are variations on a deeper thematic conflict. Why should insider trading be illegal at all? Earlier, I pointed out that we live in a society which distributes wealth through a market system built on the inequality of economic power and which normally exalts an individual who is able to convert some temporary advantage into a position of market gain. Even those who think insider trading should be criminalized agree that "the case law barely suggests why insider trading is harmful."[11] Critics of the current law argue that insider trading is consistent with norms found elsewhere in society,[12] that it injures no one,[13] that insider trading is impossible in an efficient capital market,[14] and that corporations would regulate it themselves if they believed it to be harmful.[15]

My attitude to these criticisms is a somewhat unusual one. I think that critics of insider trading regulation could rightly claim that it is inconsistent with many of the norms that we apply to market behavior. There *is* something strange in the discovery of a statutory island of egalitarianism at the very heart of capitalism. This island is far from being the only manifestation of egalitarian ideals in the rules defining market transactions. The law of fraud and mistake, the rule against perpetuities, the doctrine of unconscionability, and (the populist understanding of) antitrust could all be seen as having egalitarian components.[16] Nor are all of these rules concerned with *informational* egalitarianism. Nevertheless, there is something undeniably counter-intuitive about the prohibition of insider trading. One might expect that those who are normally skeptical of egalitarian regulation of market transactions would make much of this apparent anomaly, while those more hospitable to egalitarian notions would be keen to explore the dynamics of this egalitarian theme in the treatment of information. The former group might be expected to defend inequality in this particular context in straightforward normative terms—much in the way that Ayn Rand or Friedrich Hayek do, for example.[17]

The latter group might be expected to investigate this apparent "information exception" to our tolerance for market inequality. Does the structure of public and private which I described earlier mean that it is easier to argue for egalitarian results with issues that are presented in terms of inequalities of information rather than straightforward inequalities of wealth or power?

In fact (and from my perspective, sadly), the actual scholarship on insider trading is often very different. In particular, the area is dominated by economic analysis that exemplifies in a rather unreflective way the paradoxes of information economics that I described earlier. To its credit, economic analysis that relies on the efficient capital markets hypothesis is at least backed by empirical research on the actual behavior of stock prices—although, as I will show later, interpretations of those data vary, and the conceptual structure of the analysis runs into the kind of paradoxes pointed out by Sanford Grossman and Joseph Stiglitz.[18]

Economic Analysis of Information Disparities

The more expansive law and economics literature on insider trading treats it as a case study in the regulation of the disclosure of valuable information. To the skeptical outsider, the outstanding features of this analysis—whether supporting or opposing the prohibition of insider trading—seem to be (1) persistent baseline errors, (2) the use of ad hoc claims about behavior in order to give a spurious determinacy to the analysis, and (3) the tendency to ignore contradictions within the economic literature itself at the moment when policymaking conclusions are to be drawn.

Baseline Errors

The best examples of baseline errors in discussions of insider trading probably come from cases.[19] But the law and economics literature runs a close second. Consider the following analysis of the economics of disclosure requirements, drawn from Saul Levmore's "Securities and Secrets: Insider Trading and the Law of Contracts," the article in which Levmore invented the happy phrase "optimal dishonesty."[20] Levmore's argument rests on an exploration of the intersections and analogies between insider trading and the more general rules of disclosure in contract law. According to Levmore, legal rules forcing a mining corporation to disclose discovery of a large ore deposit on a farmer's land would "hurt both present and future shareholders and, in some instances, society as a whole." But the shareholders are "hurt" only if we assume that they should have an entitlement to the amount of profit to be made in nondisclosing situations. And that is the very thing we are trying to decide. Are the Chicago Bears' shareholders "hurt" by the criminal law rules which prohibit the employment of their linebackers as muggers after the game is over? The assumptions about the regime of rules dictate *which* advantages (in strength, knowledge, information) may be exploited and which may not. Either Levmore's comment is redundant (any change of entitlements will hurt those who lose protection and help those who gain it) or it is circular (we assume the current rule is right, use that as the baseline to measure losses—but not gains—and thus find our choice of rule mysteriously confirmed).[21]

Frank Easterbrook uses exactly the same example, and makes a similar baseline error, although in his case it leads him to overgeneralization and non sequitur. "Is it unfair of the geologist, after studying the attributes of farmland, to buy the land without revealing that the land likely covers rich mineral deposits? If the answer is yes, then fairness means that no one may appropriate the value of the information he has created."[22] But this simply is not true. Imagine an argument that if we prohibit an athlete from using his strength to take my money by force, "fairness means" that we must also prohibit him from using his strength to get a job on a football team. Again, the assumptions about the regime of rules dictate which advantages may be exploited and which may not. To say that a particular advantage may not be exploited in one area does not commit us to the view that it may not be exploited in another.

A similar mistake can be found in Easterbrook's argument that an attack on insider trading is an attack on the division of labor itself:

> People do not have or lack "access" in some absolute sense. There are, instead, different costs of obtaining information. An outsider's costs are high; he might have to purchase the information from the firm. Managers have lower costs (the amount of salary foregone); brokers have relatively low costs (the value of the time they spent investigating); Sherlock Holmes also may be able to infer extraordinary facts from ordinary occurrences at low cost. The different costs of access are simply a function of the division of labor. A manager (or a physician) always knows

more than a shareholder (or patient) in some respects, but unless there is something unethical about the division of labor, the difference is not unfair.[23]

Again, the conclusion simply does not follow. Easterbrook seems to be operating on two assumptions. The first is that anyone in a position of power has some kind of natural right to the advantages he would be able to wring from that position if unrestrained by rules. The football player example sufficiently demonstrates the flaws in this argument. Alternatively, perhaps the assumption is that a market comes with an automatic set of default positions and one of them is "allow trading on superior information." It would be hard to find any lawyer since the legal realists who would defend this position. Easterbrook's second assumption seems to be that if we prohibit any person from profiting from any position of inequality, we are logically committed to a root and branch attack on all inequalities everywhere. But this would be obviously incoherent. If the assumption is the narrower one that forbidding citizens to profit from a single one of the advantages conveyed by the division of labor implies we must forbid anyone to profit from any advantage from the distribution of labor, then Easterbrook is making a category mistake. Dogs have four legs and cats have four legs, but that does not imply that cats are dogs, or that rules affecting cats must be applied to dogs—unless, of course, we have previously committed ourselves to treating all four-legged animals alike.

Another typical baseline problem in discussions of trading on superior information occurs at the moment when the analyst imagines a change in the rules, but fails to modify the rest of the analysis. For example, when Levmore does think of shifting the baseline to a different pattern of entitlements, he assumes either irrational behavior or failure to adjust behavior to the new regime. Thus, later in his argument about mineral exploration, he claims that farmers would ask ridiculously high prices, holding up the sale or stopping exploration altogether (because no company would prospect if it had to disclose the fruits of its efforts to sellers). He offers no reasons why rational parties would suddenly begin to engage in holdout behavior after the change in rules. He also seems to ignore the fact that changes in rules produce changes in behavior. Under the new regime, surely we would expect extensive use of pre-exploration option contracts on likely pieces of land. Such contracts would allow companies to factor in estimates of exploration costs, potential profits discounted by the likelihood of a find, and so on. Farmers would simply do the same type of calculation in reverse.

By ignoring this kind of possibility, Levmore can premise his examination of a new rule on the continuation of the pattern of dealing that would have been produced by the old rule. Needless to say, the new rule looks irrational. None of this should be taken to imply that it is wrong to worry about the level of reward necessary to produce information. One could imagine a situation *not* constructed with baseline fallacies, circular definitions of "damage," and inconsistent assumptions of irrational behavior, in which a society would be hurt by contracts which are made on the basis of fuller disclosure.[24] But to have any impact on policy, the analysis would have to show that the hypothetical situation, was actually *our* situation and this is exactly what Levmore does not do.

Ad Hoc Claims about Behavior

Levmore's article also offers a fine example of ad hoc claims about the behavior of different parties under different sets of rules. Levmore sets himself the task of deciding whether disclosure rules are necessary for sellers of termite-infested houses and farmers and mineral companies. "Homeowners . . . need not be offered an incentive [by a rule which allows sellers to withhold information] to inspect for termites. As soon as there is a fleeting rumor of a termite infestation in the neighborhood, every sensible owner calls in the experts and prepares to take corrective measures." Thus Levmore argues that if we do not compel revelation, both buyers and sellers will inspect, leading to a waste of resources. "The efficiency-based distinction is most compelling in the case of the ore discovery. Unlike the owner of an infested house, the farmer is not likely to drill in his fields for minerals. There will be a net societal loss if we do not encourage exploration, and there is no reason to think that the farmer will be inclined to explore unless he is privy to the buyer's information. *The buyer, of course, will not explore if he must disclose the fruits of his efforts.*"[25]

No proof is offered of any of these generalizations. The first two *seem* to rest on class-biased assumptions about the relative foresight and sophistication of home buyers and farmers, as well as on the absence of a well-functioning secondary market in geology experts or mining options. The last statement, that no mineral exploration will ever take place if the explorer has to pay the (post-disclosure) market price for mineral-bearing land, is simply false. Gathering information does have costs, but we cannot stipulate a priori that they must always be so high that concealment is necessary to protect them.[26] The claim is also analytically incoherent for the reasons I explored in my discussion of baseline errors.[27]

Ignoring Contradictions in the Literature

For an example of the ingenious use of contradictory economic analysis *and* baseline errors *at the same time* we must turn our gaze to Christopher Saari's influential Note, in the *Stanford Law Review*, The Efficient Capital Market Hypothesis, Economic Theory, and the Regulation of the Securities Industry, which admits that "unregulated" markets "may or may not" lead to optimal production of information and cites two learned economists (both already discussed in this book) to prove it.[28] Saari points out that the first, Kenneth Arrow, argues that production of information will be "*less* than optimal because producers of information will not be able to capture its true value due to inability to acquire property rights" in the information they produce.[29] The second economist, Arthur Laffer, cited in the same footnote, argues that "production of information will be *greater* than optimal because some information will be produced solely for trading advantages that produce wealth distribution rather than for allocational purposes."[30] These two charmingly contradictory arguments do not lead Saari to question the determinacy of the analysis, but instead lead him to cite yet another economist, Harold Demsetz, for the proposition that "production of information in unregulated markets may not be strictly optimal, but it will lead to better resource allocation than any alternative."[31] That is, we cannot agree what happens in "unregulated" markets, but "regulated" ones are bound to be worse.

This is political dogma masquerading as analysis. In fact, given economists' acknowledgment that "public goods" may require regulation in order to avoid free rider problems, and their frequent claim that information is a public good, this is the *worst* place to make such a claim. It doesn't help that Arrow and Laffer agree that "unregulated" markets will not produce the right amount of information, but can't agree whether they will produce too much or too little. Worse still, if one continues reading Arrow's analysis of markets for the production of information, one finds that he believes that—even allowing for commodification of information—"unregulated" markets will underproduce and that some major form of state intervention is probably necessary. This is hardly consistent with the invocation of his authority for the proposition that "production of information in unregulated markets . . . will lead to better resource allocation than any alternative."

This claim is not only analytically unsupported. It is conceptually incoherent, depending as it does on a completely untenable set of assumptions about the ground rules in a "natural" market. Would those rules require, or not require, disclosure? The question has no answer, in part because there *is* no "natural," unregulated state of affairs. Without the rules of contract, tort, and property there would not *be* a market. Barring a belief in classical legal thought, how could we claim that the particular set of (common law?) rules found in this country at this time is any more natural, neutral, or nonregulatory than the rules imposed by the Securities and Exchange Commission (SEC)? As I pointed out before, reading much of the economic literature, one might imagine that the legal system came with preset, default positions. "Protect owners against physical invasion of land, allow formation of contracts when information is concealed, nullify contracts where lies are told . . ."[32] But this is silly. The choice is not between "regulated" and "unregulated" but between different kinds of regulation.[33] If, as Richard Posner has claimed, economic analysis is the true heir of legal realism, then this really is "the case of the murdering heir."

From Economics to Romance

For my purposes, the interesting thing about insider trading law is that it represents a commitment to a far-reaching, publicly popular, egalitarian program of regulation, a commitment which is valued despite the fact that the program is expensive to administer and difficult to police. What is more, the prohibition of insider trading is merely the capstone of a larger structure which places affirmative obligations to reveal information on companies involved in the securities market, a structure which is defended by broad-reaching appeals to egalitarian norms.

The SEC imposes relatively onerous reporting requirements on both companies and individuals, and even attempts to police the information revealed to make sure that it is not misleading. Thus, for example, income projections which might gull an unsuspecting investor are forbidden, and the form of disclosure required is designed explicitly to put the novice, so far as is possible, on the same par as the experienced investor. (Richard Epstein would probably argue that such disclosure was an uncompensated taking of the latter's hard-won expertise.)[34] Courts, administrators, and scholars say things about the evils of disparate access to information which they would never say about disparate access to wealth, or to other forms of power or property. They even worry about the evils of structural disparities in access, and not merely cases where one individual has mistreated another. This is hardly a popular concern nowadays, even in a presumably hospitable field such as civil rights.[35] And they do all this in the securities market, in the very heart of capitalism, and in the face of practical difficulties of administration and sustained academic criticism (albeit criticism of variable quality). Why?

Examination of the internal structure of the debate over insider trading, with its competing circular arguments and its self-swallowing definitions, shows that the debate reproduces once again the matrix of ideological tensions in the liberal theory of justice that I identified earlier: public versus private, free flow of information versus property, the norm of equality versus the norm of return to the status quo, and so on. Using this framework, I argue that it is precisely the fact that insider trading is trading *on information* which helps us to understand why it is ideologically feasible to subject it to egalitarian regulation. After all, this is a market transaction. In the repetitive and contradictory division of the world into public and private, the market is supposed to be exactly the place which stands outside the norm of equality. Rich and poor both get one vote. Leaving the voting booth as formally equal citizens, they turn instantaneously into members of civil society. One returns to the stock exchange, the other to the unemployment line. The writ of equality does not run to the marketplace. Yet the nonrational association of information with the public sphere, with the world of debate and discussion, makes it easier to talk about insider trading using the language of equality and fairness.

What is more, we are dealing with something commonly thought of as "market information." As I pointed out earlier, the basic model of the perfect market in microeconomics depends on the idea that all parties are "informationally equal," in that they all possess *perfect information*. It does not, needless to say, depend on all parties being equal in wealth or equal in their legally protected interests. Thus, at first blush, it might seem that one would be "arguing downhill" in claiming that a party should not be able to trade on the basis of undisclosed, nonpublic material information.[36] At the very least, it would seem that microeconomic discourse would be more hospitable to this precise form of egalitarian regulation. As we will see, things are actually much more complicated, but the unreflective first plotting of information as a "public" matter, and (to a lesser extent) the *apparent* congeniality of economic theory to ideas of informational egalitarianism, are vitally important to the political acceptability of the insider trading laws.[37] One thesis of this book is that our intuitive ideological mapping matters, whatever the outcome of more prolonged reflection.

If my analysis so far is correct, some idea akin to "authorship" ought to be offered as a device to mediate these tensions between public and private, between the norm of equality and the norm of return to the status quo, between imperfect information as property *in* a market and perfect information as *a* property *of* a market. What would an author figure look like in insider trading, and what would be its most important characteristic? From my perspective, the key feature of authorship as a mediating device lies in its *romance,* by which I mean both the homage to imagination, originality, and the unique spirit which are typical of the Romantic movement in literature, and the actual *romanticization* of the character of this original creator and destroyer—this Faustian figure.

In the stereotyped story line which goes with this construct, the romantic author spurns convention and loathes routine. (He may even violate social *mores!*) Nevertheless, society gains so much from the original creations he throws off, that these matters can be overlooked or perhaps even cherished. If the theme of originality supplies the conceptual basis on which to rest the claim to property, the romanticization of the author supplies both the emotional justification for the normative claim and the device by which it can be limited where necessary. Who can resist the argument, "Senator, you're no Van Gogh" (although, as the *Bleistein* case shows, the same rhetoric allows even the humblest contributions to be conclusively presumed "unique").

Now, insider trading scholarship is the last place one would expect to find odes to romantic authorship. And yet my claim has been that the author device is almost irresistible because of the conceptual neatness and emotional appeal of the way in which it mediates the contradictions in the regulation of information. If we do indeed find the language of romantic authorship incongruously used to defend insider trading, I would say that my argument is strengthened.

The germinal defense of insider trading comes from Henry Manne in *Insider Trading and the Stock Market*.[38] His supporters claim that all subsequent discussions of the criminalization of insider trading "raise, without acknowledging it, the questions first raised by Henry Manne."[39] Manne's book begins with a lengthy economic analysis of insider trading and a consideration of the effects of various insider trading rules. But after a hundred and ten pages of such analysis, he has this to say:

> This somewhat laborious discussion of what happens in the stock market does not constitute a strong argument *against* a proposal to bar all insider trading. Indeed, it is not intended for that purpose at all, but merely to point out that no strong arguments along these lines are available in *defense* of such a proposal . . . But the debate is far from over . . . The argument developed in the following three chapters is that a rule allowing insiders to trade freely may be fundamental to the survival of our corporate system. People pressing for the rule barring insider trading may inadvertently be tampering with one of the wellsprings of American prosperity.[40]

The wellspring to which he is referring is entrepreneurship. Manne begins his normative argument with a reprise of Joseph Schumpeter on the role of entrepreneurship and its likely demise under the rigid and routinized conditions of modern organizational life—conditions which might seem inimical to the entrepreneurial spirit.[41]

Schumpeter's basic argument is that without dynamic innovation from inventors and entrepreneurs, competition will lead to diminishing returns on capital—as more capital goods are added to a market in which the supply of labor is (at least relatively) fixed.[42] Eventually such a process can lead to the point where no further capital accumulation takes place. Inventions and recombinations of productive factors make capital more productive, shifting the factor-price frontier to the right. Yet as soon as a great innovator arises, competitors will imitate the innovation, returns on capital will be driven down once again, and the process will repeat itself. Thus, for both Manne and Schumpeter, originality, iconoclasm, and innovation are simultaneously the keys to economic development and the identifying characteristics of the entrepreneur.[43] Manne takes pains to point out that this innovation is crucial even though the entrepreneur seems (like the author) merely to be recombining elements that already exist; information and productive factors in the former case, language, genre, and perhaps even plot in the latter. "For Schumpeter the entrepreneur's function is to make new combinations of productive factors, that is, to bring them together in a new way. Routine business management is a critical function in the successful operation of a corporation, but it will characterize the work of corporate executives *only after* productive factors have been successfully combined for the first time."[44]

Entrepreneurs have been identified as the agents of development and creative originality has been identified as the mark of the entrepreneur.[45] Manne now turns to the question of incentives. Following Berle and Means, he believes that ownership and control are separated in the modern corporation. Diverging from them, he argues that entrepreneurs will probably seek positions within firms and make their money from stock trading rather than stock ownership. In doing so, he also diverges from Schumpeter, who did not believe that large returns were necessary to motivate the entrepreneur; for him the satisfaction gained from innovational, creative activity was sufficient.[46]

> At first, Schumpeter's point that large returns are not a necessary incentive for entrepreneurial effort seems correct. The supply would appear to be determined solely by personal, psychological forces. Entrepreneurs do appear in government and in salaried positions, and the temperament for innovation may turn up in such nonentrepreneurial professions as the clergy or teaching.[!] But surely these are the exceptions, and, though data would be difficult to obtain, the indications are that entrepreneurial talent tends to concentrate in those industries, professions, and positions providing the greatest potential for very substantial profits.[47]

Thus where Schumpeter saw the rigidity of modern bureaucratized capitalism and the swings of the business cycle as the major enemy of entrepreneurship, Manne sees an absence of reward to the entrepreneur as the biggest problem. In one of his more lyrical and romantic moments, he uses exactly the Faustian imagery I noted earlier to introduce his claim that we need to secure to entrepreneurs the fruits of their labors. "What then is the nature of the return to this upsetter of societies, this creator of disruptive forces?"[48] His answer? Profits from insider trading. The argument here gets a little incoherent: "Certain events or developments lend themselves peculiarly to exploitation by insiders. Not surprisingly, many of these are items that corporate employees or others close to the corporation will have produced. Higher earnings or the concomitant dividend increase are clear examples. New products or inventions, new ore discoveries, oil finds, or successful marketing or management techniques also will generally be known first to those in the company responsible for the development."[49]

The clear implication is that insider trading will be the result of *beneficial changes* produced by innovative "upsetters of societies and creators of disruptive forces." Society benefits by the improved allocation of productive resources and thus should not begrudge the entrepreneur-insider his or her cut.[50] This is nice rhetoric but bad analysis. The insider makes money off information that will cause the future stock price to diverge widely from the current price *in either direction.* Being a lousy manager and selling short before the impending bankruptcy becomes public knowledge will net the same return as being a good manager and recouping part of the increase in stock price. Manne has based his argument on originality and uniqueness, but something can be uniquely *bad* as well as uniquely good. Understandably, Manne does not wish to deal with this fact.

The idea is a little confusing in other ways. The unsupported claims about the placement of entrepreneurs and their stock-trading habits, the category errors inherent in certain of his generalizations, the difficulty in delineating those insider trading opportunities which were the result of entrepreneurial activity—all of these lead us to wonder if something else is going on under the text. My favorite part of the analysis comes at the point when Manne asks himself who should be allowed to trade. Suddenly from the heady language of the creator and destroyer of societies, the relentless romantic innovator, we swoop down to the realities of corporate personnel. The conceptual whiplash is rather like that produced in the *Bleistein* case when the rhetoric of a Van Gogh or a Monet is used to justify intellectual property in an advertising poster.

> The last form of the "person-is-not-entitled" objection to insider trading is that individuals making insider profits are frequently far removed from a time or place or job in which they could perform any entrepreneurial service for the company. It is, however, extremely difficult to identify individuals performing the entrepreneurial function or to know the precise moment at which an individual performs an entrepreneurial act ... Directors, large shareholders, executives, lawyers, investment bankers, or many other individuals may, at one time or another, perform an entrepreneurial function. Most of the time, however, they will not be innovating. And for any particular development, many individuals may have made contributions. Who, among the lawyers, bankers, and executives involved can be given full credit, or the correct portions of credit for conceiving the desirability of a merger, searching out the most likely firm and effectuating the desired plan? An entrepreneurial function has been performed, and the individuals involved will have some claim against the subsequent flow of insider information. But any attempt by an outsider to correlate the contributions and the reward on a one-for-one basis will probably fail. The contribution of an individual may be so subtle—so much the result simply of his being there—and yet so critical that we must be very cautious in concluding that no reward is deserved.[51]

This magnaniminity does not extend to more menial workers, whose jobs are deemed incapable of giving rise to original contributions and who thus deserve no share of the reward. Once again, "sources" get a rough break if they do not come close enough to fitting the image of the great author. What is more, the dividing line seems a little arbitrary. Lawyers are author-entrepreneurs, but secretaries are not? Then again, Manne's intended audience is a legal one, so we might understand a certain rose-tinted view of the lawyer's role.

At this point, it is worth reviewing the structure of Manne's argument again. After having spent half of his book in economic analysis of the market in information, he concludes that "this somewhat laborious discussion of what happens in the stock market does not constitute a strong argument *against* a proposal to bar all insider trading. Indeed, it is not intended for that purpose at all, but merely to point out that no strong arguments are available in *defense* of such a proposal."[52] Harking back to my discussion of information economics, I would agree—at least so far as the skeptical judgment about the determinacy of economic analysis. Some moral or theoretical a priori is required in order to ground the analysis. Ultimately, Manne pins his hopes on a Faustian vision of entrepreneurship, a vision which puts innovation (and not mere labor) at the heart of the issue and which seeks to reconcile society to the granting of a monopoly rent by promising it the spin-off profits from the great innovator's actions. In all significant respects, this is the romantic theory of authorship all over again.

Manne's theory fails, I think. It fails because it cannot separate "bad" originality from "good" originality. It fails because it can neither justify nor limit the class of people entitled to cash in on insider information. It fails because he has only the most tenuous argument to connect insiders and entrepreneurs in the first place. For these reasons, and others, Manne's book has proved more influential in raising the topic of the regulation of insider trading than in its actual approach to that topic. But though the opponents of insider trading regulation may claim that they have gone far beyond his approach, they fail to grasp the crucial moment in Manne's analysis—the moment when an indefinite body of economic ideas about information is given normative content by *romance*.[53] In this case, the romance is attached to the dynamic innovator, the person who is put at the center of all economic development. Though Manne's theory fails to convince, it nevertheless offers a revealing picture of the role of romantic authorship in discussions of information regulation. In the next chapter, that same romance is used to endow the manipulators, rather than the sources, of genetic information with the right to profit from its development.

CHAPTER 9

Spleens

I have been arguing that issues of information will tend to revolve around a set of tensions—between public and private, the norm of equality and the norm of the return to the status quo, between the expansive public domain and the costive world of private rights, between the idea of property as an absolute shield against potentially oppressive others and the idea of property as a bundle of rights, utilitarian in both derivation and application. Public discourse in general and legal discourse in particular must appear to mediate these tensions; otherwise particular regimes of information regulation will seem "ungrounded," "contrary to institutional logic," "dangerous in their precedential implications," or simply "wrong."

For example, we might have a normative theory which argues that any individual who mixes her labor with information should thereby acquire a legally protected interest in it.[1] But to do so would seem an unexplained curtailing of the principle not to endorse the labor theory of value for all property rights and not merely *intellectual* property rights.

At the same time, we would have to give a moral justification of the fact that the individual is being granted a private monopoly rent for recombining language, genre, and ideas that were harvested free of charge from the public domain. Coupled to this moral argument we would need a prudential argument that this particular *level* of property rights will not lead to the privatization of the fertile fields of the public domain—converting it to a patchwork of inaccessible, and increasingly barren, private estates.[2] To give an extreme example, think of granting Shakespeare's heirs a property right in perpetuity over *Romeo and Juliet*'s plot, (though it was derivative even when Shakespeare got it, of course), or Alan Turing's estate a property right in all computer technology.[3] How likely would future Turings or Shakespeares be under such a regime?

Finally, since information property is more obviously dephysicalized than other property rights, we would need some hook on which to hang the legally protected interest. In other words, we need some convincing and apparently firm set of attributes that we can identify as the property that the author, inventor, or artist could own, even after the *particular* book, machine, or print has been sold. If property is to fulfill its ideological function of apparently securing the individual from the dubious affections of the state and other parties, this set of attributes would have to be something a little more reified than whatever today's utilitarian calculation indicates that we should protect.

In the chapter on copyright law, I argued that the figure which is used to "solve" these problems is the romantic author, and that the conceptual device the romantic author makes credible is the division between idea and expression. I argued that the romantic author stands with one foot in civil society and the other in the public domain of political, artistic, and scientific interchange. The author takes facts, genre, and language from the public domain, works on them, adds the originality of spirit presumptively conferred on him by the themes of romanticism, and produces a finished work. The ideas (and the facts on which they are based) return to the public domain, thus enriching it for future use. But because the author's originality has marked the form of the work as "unique," the form or expression becomes his alone. Together, the *figure* of the romantic author, the *theme* of originality, and the *conceptual distinction* between idea and expression seem to offer one of the most convincing mediations of the tensions I described earlier. This assemblage of mediating devices is so convincing, in fact, that I argued we would expect to find it well beyond the familiar realm of copyright. The case of Moore v. The Regents of the University of California seems to support that thesis.[4]

Earlier in the book, I described some of the bizarre features of the opinion in *Moore.* John Moore's doctors fail to disclose that they are engaged in potentially profit-making research and that their interest in his cell line goes beyond the therapeutic. At times, the lower court's description of the facts in the case makes them sound like high-tech vampires, sampling Moore's blood and bodily fluids for their own, hidden, purposes. They cure Moore, but they also use *his* cell line as the template for *their* genetically engineered, cell line. The court must decide whether or not Moore owns his body, but also whether he owns his own genetic code.

At first sight, the case looks as though it has been deliberately constructed to provide a foil for law professors' lectures on bad legal reasoning. The court bumbles and pontificates, apparently at random. The reader is left to make the transitions as best she can. What connects *this* confused discussion of the difference between the right of publicity and the right of property to *that* claim that limited property rights are not really property rights at all? What, if any, relevance does the question-begging discussion of whether or not John Moore's cells were unique have to the idyllic picture the court paints of research carried on free from the dead hand of property rights? How is the idyllic picture reconciled with the court's later claim that the researchers themselves must be given property rights in order to provide the vital incentives necessary for their work? In fact, these apparently random shifts of topic, inconsistent jurisprudences of property, and ostensibly conflicting claims about originality and incentives can best be read as a manifestation of exactly the structure I described in the chapter on copyright.

Worrying about Property

The court in *Moore* worries about the classification, limitation, and relativization *of* property. It also worries about the utilitarian justification *for* property. Despite the surface variety, these strands of the opinion express the same concerns in different words.

Limitations on Property

The best place to begin the argument is at the moment that the court confronts these issues head on, in its discussion of regulatory limitations on property. In this case, the limitations which concern the court come not from the law of copyright, but instead from a statute that regulates the use and disposal of human tissue: "By restricting how excised cells may be used and requiring their eventual destruction, the statute eliminates so many of the rights ordinarily attached to property that one cannot simply assume that what is left amounts to 'property' or 'ownership' for purposes of conversion law."[5]

This is not as extreme as the claim presented in the eighteenth century by Christian Edmund Krause in his attack on the very notion of intellectual property. "No, no it is too obvious that the concept of intellectual property is useless. My property must be exclusively mine; I must be able to dispose of it and retrieve it unconditionally."[6] Nevertheless, there is something peculiar in seeing a late twentieth-century California court talk about the implications we can draw from "elimination" of the "rights ordinarily attached to property." From a practical point of view, such comments invite counter-examples. Most countries put extensive restrictions on the use, reproduction, transfer, and disposal of banknotes without prompting any soul searching about property rights in money.[7] To a greater or lesser extent, similar types of restrictions can be found for cars, plutonium, motor oil, beachfront houses, and air conditioners.

From a slightly more theoretical perspective, this comment also seems strange. After all, in contemporary legal discourse the most common conception of property is the bundle of legally protected interests, held together by competing and conflicting policy goals. The removal of one or more sticks from the bundle should have no particular implications for the legally protected interests that remain. This point should be more, rather than less, obvious in questions of intellectual property. The author claims a right in the work that is severable from the material object bought by the reader. An author cannot prohibit the reader from burning the book, or telling acquaintances about it, or stealing the ideas. Even the jokes may be fair game, if retold under the right circumstances. The one prohibited act is the copying of expression—and even in that case there are exceptions. Thus it seems that to reason from the "normal incidents of ownership" in a case like this is to adopt a formalistic and absolutist vision of property like that of Krause, and to do so in the one area least suited to it.

The Utilitarian Justification for Property

The court does not see itself as formalist, of course. The majority says explicitly that "when the proposed application of a very general theory of liability in a new context raises important policy concerns, it is especially important to face those concerns and address them openly."[8] When the court does address them, it does something very curious. First, the majority opinion describes the existing state of affairs: a world in which "sources" have no property rights over the products developed from their body fluids, tissues, or genetic information. "At present, human cell lines are routinely copied and distributed to other researchers for experimental purposes, usually free of charge. This exchange of scientific materials, which still is relatively free and efficient, will surely be compromised if each cell sample becomes the potential subject matter of a lawsuit."[9] This is a fine example of the rhetoric of the public domain. The property rights of "sources" are portrayed as impediments to innovation, as an unnecessary drag on research.

This principle is potentially an imperialistic one. One could imagine just the same argument being made *against* copyright or in *favor* of the legalization of insider trading. As I pointed out at the beginning of this book, commodification of information can always be portrayed as *either* a time-consuming and unjust impediment to, *or* a necessary prerequisite for, the free circulation of information.[10] Indeed, only moments later the court concludes that "the theory of liability that Moore urges us to endorse threatens to destroy the economic incentive to conduct important medical research."[11] Property rights given to those whose bodies can be mined for valuable genetic information will hamstring research because property is inimical to the free exchange of information. Yet property rights *must* be given to those who do the mining, because property is an essential incentive to research. How can the court tell when property rights will have the effect of stopping the flow of information and when they will be necessary to start that flow?

Characterization as Property

The court also worries about the characterization of certain legally protected interests as "property" rights. The plaintiff and the court of appeal had relied strongly on analogies from privacy right cases dealing with the antinomially named "right of publicity." When the California Supreme Court addressed the cases cited by the plaintiff,[12] its main concern was whether or not the right of publicity is "really" a property right: "These opinions hold that every person has a proprietary interest in his own likeness and that unauthorized, business use of a likeness is redressable as a tort. But in neither opinion did the authoring court expressly base its holding on property law. Each court stated, following Prosser, that it was 'pointless' to debate the proper characterization of the proprietary interest in a likeness."[13]

From the perspective of a legal realist view of legally protected interests, the question is indeed pointless. From the realist point of view, the question of classification of the legally protected interest is anterior to the *purpose* the interest has to serve. Thus rather than staring at the legally protected interest in an attempt to divine whether it was "really" property,[14] one would decide the goals of this particular interest and would then discuss whether the remedies attached to a "property" right would be sufficient to achieve them. The court, however, having tipped its hat to Dean Prosser, was not willing to follow him: "For purposes of determining whether the tort of conversion lies, however, the characterization of the right in question is far from pointless. Only property can be converted."[15]

Nevertheless, having said that the question of classification is vital, the court did not answer it. Instead, the majority simply assumed that the "right of publicity" is not a property right, in part because of its classification as a right that protects privacy. This is a shame because, if seen a little less formalistically, the publicity rights cases themselves present a fascinating example of the tensions discussed in this book.

Publicity and Privacy

In a famous article that formed the basis of much of the law of privacy, Louis Brandeis and Samuel Warren made a great deal of effort to ground the right to exclude others in a person's privacy interest— the legitimate desire to keep certain information from the eyes of the public.[16] Their article implies that the interest is more than just a property right in information about oneself. The vision they invoke is the cozy private sphere of the home, not the bustling private sphere of the market. Indeed, to allow the market to commodify one's privacy might be to accelerate exactly the trends that Warren and Brandeis found so disturbing. If one understands the concern that animates this area of the law to be the protection of privacy, rather than the protection of private property, Moore's analogy might seem to be correspondingly weaker. To a judge, taking someone's genetic information is unlikely to seem intuitively as much of a violation of "privacy" as publishing facts from a diary without the consent of the diarist.

Yet despite their classification under the law of privacy, the publicity rights cases on which the plaintiff relied in *Moore* pay great attention to the importance of commodification, alienation, and transfer of the protected interest, and little or no attention to the concerns that so worried Warren and Brandeis. The *Motsenbacher* case turns on a racing driver's ability to commodify the distinctive image of his car and to control its use in advertising.[17] The *Carson* case spends a great deal of time explaining that Johnny Carson already licenses the phrase "Here's Johnny!" to a chain of clothing stores in which he holds a 20 percent interest. The *Hirsch* case holds that Elroy "Crazylegs" Hirsch should be able to sell the right to use his nickname, and thus that it cannot be used without his consent to promote the sale of products that remove hair from women's legs.[18] The *Lugosi* case allows Bela Lugosi a partial monopoly over the commercial exploitation of a particular image of Dracula.[19]

It is also worth noting that in each case the plaintiffs did not expend great labor, emotion, or even much originality in creating the protectible "mark." It was Ed McMahon's distinctive voice and phrasing that made Carson's introduction more than a pleasantry. Lothar Motsenbacher did not design the car that formed the tangible basis of the image he was allowed to exploit. Crazylegs Hirsch was given his nickname by someone else, and Lugosi's right of publicity protected a figure drawn from a book Lugosi did not write, portrayed in films he did not write, direct, or produce, and based on a historical figure—Vlad the Impaler—who actually did very different (though equally unpleasant) things. To a greater or lesser extent, each case treats fame as a partial public good—something unique and personal which can be gainfully exploited only if it can be commodified and others can be excluded from its use except on pain of payment. This, of course, was exactly what Moore wanted the court to say about his genetic information, and about the cell line developed from his own body. Why did the court refuse? Neither formalism, nor the functional requisites of the biotechnology industry, nor the dictates of economic efficiency seem sufficient to explain the decision.

Perhaps the court was applying an authorship theory after all. Perhaps the deep assumption here is that a celebrity is the author of his of her *fame,* and that the phrases, nicknames, and images that are associated with the fame are, as Judge Anthony Kennedy put it in his dissent in the *Carson* case, actually *expressions* of the essential celebrity. To be famous, after all, is to stand out from the crowd, to be thought unique. There is also a strong popular belief that having labored to create this unique mark, the celebrity is entitled to have it protected. Moore's genetic endowment could certainly be seen as something he got without expending labor.[20] But what about uniqueness and originality? In one of its most surprising passages, the court said Moore's genetic information was not original: "Lymphokines, unlike a name or a face, have the same molecular structure in every human being and the same, important functions in every human being's immune system. Moreover, the particular genetic material which is responsible for the natural production of lymphokines, and which defendants use to manufacture lymphokines in the laboratory, is also the same in every person; it is no more unique to Moore than the number of vertebrae in the spine or the chemical formula of hemoglobin."[21]

This passage is remarkable partly because it is nonsensical. It was precisely the unique properties of Moore's genetic "programs," the fact that his virus-infected cells *over*produced lymphokines, which made his tissue and bodily fluids such an important part of Dr. David Golde's profitable research. If the issue is unique value or unusual ease of extraction, clearly Moore's cells are not like everyone else's. Both sea water and pure gold ore contain gold molecules. That does not stop a cubic foot of gold ore from being more valuable than sea water containing the equivalent amount of gold. If the issue is statistical uniqueness, again it is exactly the unusual degree to which Moore's cells *over*produced lymphokines that made them worth fighting about. The court offered the weak argument in support of its position that "by definition, a gene responsible for producing a protein found in more than one individual will be the same in each."[22] Both Karch Kiraly and I can jump and hit a volleyball. Only one of us, however, will be asked to endorse shoes or to play on the U.S. Olympic team. By the court's logic, since both Karch and I are "playing volleyball" we are both "volleyball players" and are therefore "the same."

But not only is the argument about uniqueness nonsensical, it is also irrelevant to the question of whether or not Moore should have a property right in his cell line; irrelevant that is, unless the issue is once again being restated, whether consciously or unconsciously, in terms of the ideology of authorship.

Thus there are two distinct reasons why Moore's argument goes against the grain of the implicit structure I have described. First, the market has taken from him the most "private" information of all, information about his own genetic structure. Yet our intuitive notions of privacy are constructed around the notion of preventing disclosure of intimate, embarrassing, or simply "personal" *socially constructed facts* about ourselves to others like ourselves. I could stare at my own genetic code all day and not even know it was mine. Even if I could "read" DNA, it is hard to imagine that I would be upset by revelation of my genetic code or, at least, that I would experience the particular complex of anger, shame, and righteous indignation that we associate with "a violation of privacy." For example, I would be less upset if someone chose to reveal that I carry the recessive gene for blue eyes than if someone disclosed my preference in underwear—though neither is unusual or, to the best of my knowledge, aesthetically or socially reprehensible. There is something in the way that our culture has constructed the notion of privacy that makes it more hospitable to the protection of *"social"* facts than *"natural"* facts.[23] Even with the obvious borderline cases—hereditary diseases, for example—revelations are thought to be violative of a person's privacy only when some particular social significance has been given to the genetic coding.

The difficulty with Moore's case is, first, that no one would think worse of him for having a genetic make-up that could be mined for a socially valuable drug and, second, that specialized knowledge would be necessary to make the connection between the "facts revealed" and the "inner life." One mild and reformist conclusion that we could draw from all of this is that our notion of privacy, based as it is on the revelation of intimate social facts comprehensible to a lay audience, does not adequately protect the interests of individuals in genetic information.

Second, if the thesis of this book is correct, decision makers will tend—consciously or unconsciously—to look at questions of information through the lens of the romantic vision of authorship. The publicity rights cases seem to view the protected nicknames, catchphrases, fangs, and cars as the *expression* of some underlying celebrity persona—the marks of a fame that is definitionally original and presumptively the result of hard work. These qualities sound suspiciously like the analytical structure of romantic authorship in copyright. If Moore's claim is not to the protection of his "privacy" *tout court*, but rather to the protection of his ability to commodify the genetic information derived from his cells, then the inquiry shifts from privacy to the "right of publicity," from the home and the secret to the market and the commodity. Once that shift is made, we are led to ask, "Who is the *real* author of the genetic information at issue here?" Reading this case, however, one gets the sense that the court thought that Moore did not exhibit that mixture of arcane labor and dazzling originality that we associate with the romantic author. This sense is deepened when the court moved on to talk about the comparative rights of Moore on the one hand and the doctors and researchers on the other.

The Author and the Source

Having pointed out that Moore does not own the actual cells taken from his own body, the court used the University of California's patent to trump Moore's claim to the cell line developed by Dr. Golde and the other researchers:

> Finally, the subject matter of the Regent's patent—the patented cell line and the products derived from it—cannot be Moore's property. This is because the patented cell line is both factually and legally distinct from the cells taken from Moore's body. Federal law permits the patenting of organisms that represent the product of "human ingenuity," but not naturally occurring organisms. Human cell lines are patentable because "long term adaptation and growth of human tissues and cells in culture is difficult—*often considered an art . . .*" and the probability of success is low. It is this *inventive effort* that patent law rewards, not the discovery of naturally occurring raw materials.[24]

The conceptual structure of patent law contains many of the same oppositions as that of copyright, and in this excerpt the court deployed them to great effect. There is something wonderful in the way that Moore becomes a "naturally occurring raw material" whose "unoriginal" genetic material is rendered unique and valuable by the "inventive effort," "ingenuity," and "artistry" of his doctors. If we look at this case through the lens of the romantic author, then Moore's claim is as ridiculous as if Huey Long had laid claim to ownership rights over *All the King's Men* or the baker of madeleines to *Remembrance of Things Past*. Authorship devalues sources. The fact that this can be accomplished in the face of the strong naturalistic presumption that one owns one's own body, and in the face of the ethically unattractive behavior of Moore's doctors, is a testament to the rhetorical power of the ideas involved.

To a greater extent than the other issues I discuss in this book, the *Moore* case may indicate both the contentious value judgments loaded into the conceptual structure of authorship and the way that discussions of entitlement to control information are carried out through the metaphor of "authorship," even in fields far from copyright. Seen this way, Moore's case almost seems to have been designed to fail the authorship test. The court thought his property was already too limited, that his genetic information was too *natural* to be a creation, that it was neither private enough to be protected by the law of privacy nor original enough to be protected by the rights of publicity. Viewed through the lens of authorship, Moore's claim appears to be a dangerous attempt to privatize the public domain and to inhibit research.[25] The scientists, however, with their transformative, Faustian artistry, fit the model of original, creative, labor. For them, property rights are necessary to *encourage* research. Concern with the public domain fades away as if it had never existed. What should we think about this desire to cast around in every situation until we find the people who most resemble authors, whereupon we confer property rights on them?

There is one last irony in the *Moore* case. The California Supreme Court did not leave Moore entirely without recourse. Indeed, as I mentioned earlier, it acknowledged that doctors have a duty to disclose any financial interests in the treatment of a patient. When the court discussed genetic information, it viewed Moore as a "naturally occurring raw material," a public domain to be mined by inventive geniuses. But when the court turned to his role as a consumer of medical services, it transformed him into a sovereign individual with an unchallengeable entitlement to the facts necessary to make informed decisions. As far as the majority was concerned, Moore was the author of his destiny, but not of his spleen.

CHAPTER 10

Stereotyping Information and Searching for an Author

There are a number of reasons for bringing together under the heading "information" the kinds of issues I have discussed here. One might believe that one had a master theory—a single set of principles capable of resolving all significant conflicts—or simply a single set of functional goals to be rescued from messy doctrinal particularity. Judge Frank Easterbrook, for example was concerned that "if the Court puts information cases in securities law or evidence law pigeonholes, it may overlook the need to consider the way in which the incentive to produce information and the demands of current use conflict."[1] My aim was rather different.

First of all I had a descriptive and analytic goal. I wished to attack from a different angle a series of problems that have puzzled scholars and frustrated courts. The conventional way of addressing these issues is a particularistic one. The legal system commodifies, refuses to commodify, or makes illegal the commodification of certain kinds of information. Scholars then take each issue on its own merits. They ask, "Why is blackmail illegal?" Or, "Why does the state forbid insider trading?" Or even, "Why does copyright doctrine extend protection to expression but deny it to ideas?" Instead, I asked a series of questions about the roles that information is expected to play in the institutions of a liberal state—in the family, in the market, and in the world of politics and public debate. My aim was to remain faithful to the subtlety and complexity of the material by dealing with each issue in some detail and at some length. If I had temporarily to abandon that goal in order to summarize my conclusions here, I would say that the ideology of a liberal society presents different reified visions of information—as the life blood of the disinterested debate in the public world, as the instantaneous omniscience of the actors in the perfect market, as that which must be commodified if we are to encourage more information to be produced, as that potential public manifestation of themselves which individuals must be able to control if we are to protect the cozy world of the home, the persona, and the family. And so on, and so on.

Most analysts start by assuming a certain level of deductive rationality in the construction of our social institutions.[2] They assume that there really *is* some logical reason that blackmail should be prohibited. After all, most of us feel so strongly that blackmail is "wrong," that it is easy to imagine that a little further reflection, a better set of analytical tools, will uncover the principle that distinguishes the blackmail demand from the rent bill or from the baseball stadium's negotiation with its host city. Alternatively, analysts present themselves as critics of the current position, but again assume the deductive rationality of the institutions they analyze. Thus the critics of insider trading regulation seem puzzled by the fact that legislative history, scholarly analysis, and judicial exposition offer little in the way of reasons for prohibiting a practice that, when described in abstract terms, seems to them entirely compatible with the norms of a free-market society. In the place of this fuzzy thinking, they offer economic analyses of secrecy, justifications of "optimal dishonesty," or models of the efficient capital market, confident that their prescriptions are not marred by the analytical flaws of the ideas they criticize.

To me it seems that the reason that blackmail is illegal is that we have a vision of "private-ness" that is constructed in part around the control of *information*[3]—as opposed to, say, control of wealth, health care, or housing.[4] We "romanticize"[5] a notion of subjective control of private information, refusing to allow the blackmailer to demand money for silence. The best analogy to blackmail, then, is not monopoly or monopsony, but something like the "wrongful birth" cases, in which many courts refuse to recognize the costs of raising a child as "damage" flowing from a wrongfully conducted sterilization operation. In both cases, we make a pretheoretical judgment that an activity is "private," and only then do we "deduce" that it must be kept from the ruthless, instrumental logic of the market. The offer to sell silence is pretheoretically classified as a "threat" because of its intrusion into the world of privacy. The decision to sell the disgraceful information to the newspaper, by contrast, fits our public information stereotype; the gossip and the journalist fall on the right, or at least the legal, side of our conflicting images of information.

In insider trading, we are faced with another situation in which someone trades from a superior position in nonpublic information. This is not just any information, but information which by definition will have a profound effect on the world. In blackmail, we pigeonholed the issue into the "private" world of information about home and family. In insider trading, by contrast, there is a strong impetus to type the issue as "public," subject to the norms of equality rather than the norms of the market, precisely because it is material nonpublic *information* and not some other form of wealth or power. Hence, there is a strand in the cases and in the scholarly writings that applies the norm of equality to *all* regular dealings in material nonpublic information. But there is also a strong vision that information should be traded just like every other commodity, a vision that would deny the special public status of information. Thus there is an equally strong—perhaps even a stronger—tendency to see insider trading in terms not of formal public equality, but of private misappropriation and theft.

The disagreements in courtrooms and scholarly journals about the proper characterization of insider trading help to point out the very real limits to my argument. The typing I am describing is neither so deeply rooted in the culture that it can never be criticized nor so determinate that it only dictates one solution. At most, I am trying to lay out the structure within which issues are framed, possibilities foreclosed, and so on. The structure *matters,* because it excludes some options from consideration (excludes them even from being seen, perhaps) or prompts a hasty leap to judgment, or because it is one of the many forces shaping the terrain of political struggle. But the process of typing is neither a giant conspiracy nor a deterministic and inevitable deep structure of thought.

Finally, let me say that this process of typing information issues as public or private—and typing them into conflicting ideas about what public and private *mean*—is not "irrational," in the derogatory sense of that term. There are, to be sure, *reasons* why we think of the control of information about ourselves as fundamental to the preservation of the self. There are *reasons* why a right to control private information will command more support in this society than a right to control some other critical resource—food, for example. There are reasons why the claim that "everyone should trade from a position of roughly equal information" seems merely "fair," whereas "everyone should trade from a position of roughly equal wealth" seems like socialism. Those reasons are a complex of ideology, hip-pocket economic analysis, history, New Deal institutions, class interest, noble ideals, Enlightenment epistemology, and so on. It would take a better philosopher than I to lay them out fully, and one with more hubris to believe that exactly the correct mix could be identified. But it is in the process these "reasons" explain—the process of "typing" information issues that I have described here—more than in the language of microeconomics or Rawlsian rights theory that we would find our answers to the *descriptive* question, "Why are insider trading and blackmail illegal?"

I also draw another, modestly realist, conclusion from this process and the conflicting stereotypes about information on which it relies. During the process of typing issues as public or private, analogies and metaphors play a vital role. Analogies and metaphors are standard fare in legal doctrine; the analogy is used to connect one set of facts, as yet unclassified, to another set of facts which has already been subsumed under some principle. Thus a hoary old case deciding who owned a fox that was first pursued by one hunter and then killed by another might be used to decide a case about natural gas which was being extracted by one company, and which then flowed underground into the spaces under another company's well. The fox is analogized to the gas to make the argument that the owner of the land may have the right to *hunt* some natural resource capable of movement but should not be deemed to *own* it until it is "captured." The legal realists thought that the problem with such a process arose when an analogy for some purposes became the metaphor for all purposes. To go to extremes, imagine that the court ruled against both gas companies because the gas was being mined without a fox-hunting license. Applying a pragmatist theory of language, the realists claimed that this was an example of "reification," or the fallacy of misplaced concreteness; the purpose was being subsumed by the thing which represented it. (Contemporary analyses have pointed out that the "purposes" or "principles" on which the realists relied so confidently were themselves capable of being subject to the same critique.)

While the critique of reification has a long and distinguished history in other areas of legal doctrine, the information field has been curiously immune to it.[6] Take electronic information services. The Prodigy case is a particularly good one.[7] Prodigy has been defending itself from charges that its electronic bulletin boards spent too much time censoring notices critical of Prodigy, and not enough time censoring anti-Semitic speech. The ACLU wanted neither form of restriction; B'nai Brith wanted only the latter. An article from *Network World* offers a series of classic characterizations of an information issue as "public" or "private," shored up by metaphors that hark back to the information technology of yesteryear.

> Prodigy's bulletin board editing policies are, *in essence,* electronic publications, the spokesman added. He said Prodigy has the right to edit or delete material, just as newspapers have a right not to print letters to the editor. Jerry Berman, director of the American Civil Liberties Union's Information Technology Project in Washington, D.C., said the ACLU agrees with Prodigy's assertion that it has the right to edit public bulletin board systems. But he said a Prodigy policy limiting the types of electronic messages users can send is a gray area. Some new rules prohibit users from sending unsolicited messages protesting pricing policies to the Prodigy advertisers. Prodigy developed the rules after kicking about a dozen users off its system for allegedly engaging in that practice. Berman said these restrictions may be justified because Prodigy is a private service, but they could also be seen as an unjustifiable restraint of free speech.[8]

The metaphors are contested, of course. Organizations such as Electronic Frontier compare electronic bulletin boards to public parks. In another article, Berman drew on the shopping mall cases to suggest that "[t]he courts may some day hold that electronic shopping networks like Prodigy are the public forums of the 21st century."[9] The process by which bulletin boards are analogized to shopping malls, which in the past had been analogized to the Roman forums, is a fascinating one. Berman then suggests that Congress should regulate electronic mail under "common carrier principles." The tropes change as the context changes. In libel cases so far, courts have analogized electronic information services to bookshops or for-profit libraries, rather than to newspapers that publish libelous information.[10] The difficulty comes when the analogy alone seems to decide the issue: " 'There is some debate in legal circles on the extent to which video text service providers must screen publicly posted messages,' said Benjamin Wright, a lawyer in Dallas who specializes in electronic communications law. 'If the law sees the provider as more like a newspaper, then the duty to screen is higher. But if the law sees the provider as more like a telephone company, a communications common carrier, then the duty is lower.' "[11]

Parks? The U.S. mails? Federal Express? A telephone company? Community newspaper? Regulated television station? Common carrier? Who is to say? There are advantages—in familiarity, evocativeness, and tradition—to this particular kind of analogical reasoning. Nevertheless, it is hard to repress an occasional wish that the issue be framed as whether a specific type of regulation will help or hinder the creation or reproduction of a particular kind of society, rather than being filtered through an additional layer of simile and metaphor.[12] The difference in the two methods is not the difference between rational analysis and figurative speech[13]—our vision of the good society is, of necessity, an analogical one too. Still, it would be unfortunate if we decided how to regulate the most important technologies of the next century by relying mainly on their formal resemblances to the physical environs or commercial settings in which the public information of the nineteenth century found its home.

. . . .

The second goal of this book was a more complicated one. Recognizing the existence of contradictory pictures of information and the role of the public-private distinction in information issues is only the beginning of the project. At the end of my description of the conceptual elements of information issues—property, the public-private distinction, and information economics—I outlined the ideological and practical prerequisites for the law of intellectual property. Now that I have explored a range of information issues, those prerequisites bear repeating.

If it is to protect the legitimacy and intellectual suasion of the liberal world view, intellectual property law (and indeed, all law that deals with information) must accomplish a number of tasks simultaneously. It must provide a conceptual apparatus which appears to mediate the various tensions associated with the role of information in liberal society. Thus, for example, it must give some convincing explanation as to why a person who recombines informational material from the public sphere is not merely engaging in the private appropriation of public wealth. It must explain how it is that we can motivate individuals, who are sometimes postulated to be essentially self-serving, and sometimes to be noble, idealistic souls, to produce information. If the answer is "by giving them property rights," it must also explain why this will not diminish the common pool, or public domain, so greatly that a net decrease in the production of information will result. (Think of overfishing.) It must reassure us that a realm of costive privacy will be carved out for the private sphere and at the same time explain how it is that we can have a vigorous sphere of public debate and ample information about a potentially oppressive state. It must do all of this within a vision of justice that expects formal equality within the public sphere, but respect for existing disparities in wealth, status, and power in the private. And all of these things must be accomplished while using a concept of property which must avoid the conceptual impossibilities of the physicalist, absolutist conception, but which at the same time is not too obviously relativist, partial, and utilitarian.

The constellation of ideas that seemed most successfully to reduce the salience of these tensions in copyright law was the *figure* of the romantic author, the associated *theme* of originality, and the *conceptual distinction* between idea and expression. This triad manages to make it seem that intellectual property rights are more than just a utilitarian grant by the state, to limit the ambit of something that sounds very much like a labor theory of property rights, and to divide the author's creation so that the idea goes into the world of public exchange while the expression remains the author's. In explaining the history of this constellation of ideas, I tried to show that the idea of authorship is socially constructed and historically contingent. In particular, the romantic vision of authorship plays down the importance of external sources by emphasizing the unique genius of the author and the originality of the work. Since the author gambit is so attractive that it is found far beyond conventional intellectual property law, this fact is of no small importance.

The current trend seems to be to assume that economics is the most appropriate theoretical language in which to discuss questions of the regulation of information. But the turn to microeconomics does not rob the idea of romantic authorship of all significance. In my discussion of information economics, I tried to show that economic analysis of information questions is paradoxical or at least aporetic. I suggested that information offers the same sort of problems to neoclassical economics that rent offered to classical economics. My argument was that these problems could be traced to the fact that perfect information is a defining conceptual element of the analytical structure used to analyze markets driven by the absence of information in which imperfect information itself is a commodity. The implication was that informationally efficient markets are not merely difficult to achieve, but conceptually impossible. The paradoxes of information in liberal state theory reappear in microeconomics. Economists analyze some information from the "commodity" side and other information from the "perfect information" side, but they can neither produce a theoretical meta-principle that justifies their shifts nor completely purge the disfavored aspect from their analysis. It seems perfectly possible to invert the hierarchies, so that the free availability of futures market prices could be analyzed as a public goods problem, or copyright presented convincingly as an intolerable transaction cost.

The most obvious manifestation of this problem is the difficulty that economists have in theorizing about the amount of information that will be produced in an "unregulated" market. Will it be too much, or too little? Despite the fact that many economists say that information is a classic public good and declare as a theoretical a priori about public goods problems that too *little* of the good will be produced, some economists think that the absence of property rights will lead to the production of too *much* information. Thus the use of some general body of "public goods theory" to analyze information issues seems to be impossible.[14] Each information issue needs to be examined on its own in a particularistic, highly empirical way (a style not found very much in the currently available literature). In the absence of such particular, empirical data, and of some convincing aprioristic grounding, economics offers little more than a partial checklist of issues and trade-offs. And that is where the author comes in again. In a strange mixture of Wordsworth and Coase, Byron and Stigler, the values of romantic authorship seem to seep—consciously or unconsciously—into economic analysis. And because the paradigm of authorship tends to fit one side better than the other in most conflicts, this romantic grounding provides economic analysis with at least the illusion of certainty. Authors tend to win.

In the chapters on insider trading and the *Moore* case, I claimed that both scholars and courts have wide recourse to the author gambit. In the *Moore* case, the court finds that John Moore's claims of property rights in his genetic information raise the same concerns that Sigmund Krause felt were raised by the idea of copyright itself, concerns about the limitation and justification of property, the nature of privacy, and so on. Eventually, it is the celebration of original, creative, artistic modification of naturally existing raw material and of the need to motivate society's creators that justifies giving property rights to the doctors but not to Moore.[15] Even the privacy–right of publicity cases seem to reflect this body of ideas, allowing the commodification of the "expressions" of a unique celebrity persona. In both areas, those who do not look like authors find that their property claims are disfavored. Moore presents us with a powerful picture of the unfortunate consequences that can ensue if the court decides you are part of the public domain. Ed McMahon, the World's Foremost Commodian, and the manufacturers of Crazylegs depilatory cream may present less compelling claims to our sympathy, but they all suffer some significant consequence in part because they do not fit the author paradigm.

In the insider trading chapter, the relevance of the romantic author to economic and utilitarian analysis became clearer still. I used as an example the original defense of insider trading by Henry Manne. Manne admits that his economic analysis of insider trading provides no strong reasons to legalize the practice. Again, it is a figure akin to the romantic author who provides the outcome-determinacy the analysis otherwise lacks. Drawing on Joseph Schumpeter's theory of economic development, Manne conjures up a romanticized vision of the entrepreneur-innovator—the creator and destroyer of settled arrangements—and, with the aid of a few category errors, declares that profits from insider trading will function as the entrepreneur's reward, temporary monopoly rents that lie at the heart of capitalism. The parallel to copyright and patent is striking.

In the other writing on insider trading and on the right to withhold valuable information, echoes of the author appear again and again. Saul Levmore's discussion of insider trading and contract law in the context of mineral exploitation styles as "contemptible" the farmer who "to preserve a fraud claim asks specific questions about activities he would otherwise never engage in." Levmore advocates his own proposed doctrine as a way "to deny a windfall to a passive party when to do otherwise might lead to a net social loss."[16]

To me it seems that the judgmental moralism and the preference for the active, dynamic exploring mineral company rather than the "contemptible," "passive" farmer are not required by the economic analysis. Indeed, one could paint a perfectly respectable series of economic vignettes in which the absence of a right to expect disclosure held up transactions and encouraged strategic behavior on the part of farmers, who could never rely on the representations of buyers of their land. Instead, the choice to start the analysis from a preference for the "active," inventive party seems to represent the same romanticization of the innovating, transforming author figure. If one starts from this perspective, then the farmer, like the baker of Proust's madeleines or John Moore, has no *moral* right to the profits the innovator makes from the new object—even though that object was created from raw material supplied by the hapless source. Whatever coating of economics is subsequently put over this pretheoretical orientation, the outcome derives from the initial hidden, and probably unconscious, moment of romance. Easterbrook's arguments about the division of labor seem to be marked by a similar pretheoretical preference for Faust and the individual creator, rather than Job and the public domain.

Am I saying that authors are bad, or that we never need to give property rights to the creators of information in order to encourage further production? By no means. The protection and exaltation of authorship *is* a compelling and attractive idea and the need to reward producers in order to encourage continued production is a real concern (although, of course, the question of just who is a "producer" continues to be a problem). Just as the typing of information issues into public and private may produce felicitous and attractive results, the concern with the motivation of authors may, in any individual case, be exactly what is needed. But I stress the "may." Of the examples I gave above, Proust's baker has no claim to our heart strings or our utilitarian goals, but the farmer and Moore have considerably more. Yet to the extent that we decide information issues by forcing them into a Procrustean concept of authorship, we will tend to ignore countervailing moral and utilitarian concerns—not because we reject them, but because the veil of authorship obscures them. In the next chapter, I will use the international intellectual property regime to give some concrete examples of exactly how this can happen.

CHAPTER 11

The International Political Economy of Authorship

I n this chapter, I turn to the effects of the author paradigm as an international—a worldwide—regime. Using some current intellectual property issues—from both the developing and the developed world—I will now lay out an international authorial *dystopia* to counter the romantic economic, political, and cultural images of the author which currently exercise such a strange fascination over our collective imagination. In the next chapter, I will discuss the political morality of an author-centered regime. In this chapter I deal with its international economic effects. First, I argue that an author-centered regime is distributionally questionable in part *because* it is author-centered—rewarding a narrow set of contributions to world culture and science. More important, perhaps, I show that an author-centered regime is frequently economically irrational. It does not even serve the goals it is supposed to. An author-centered regime can actually *slow down* scientific progress, *diminish* the opportunities for creativity, and *curtail* the availability of new products. Let me stress, my claim is not that these are the only or even the predominant incarnations of an author-centered regime. Rather, these examples are intended to balance a previously one-sided account by showing how an author-centered regime actively encourages us to ignore some of the very issues we ought to focus on if we truly care about the utilitarian effects of intellectual property.

For most people, information issues and intellectual property have little to do with the international economy. Nationalization of foreign holdings, the problems of transnational environmental regulation, capital flight, global reach, the race to the bottom, commodity cartels—these are all issues that come more readily to mind when international trade is mentioned. The prevalent *image* of international economic activity—if news-show videobytes are anything to go by— is of trade in material goods, foreign cars parked in rows along a dock, or huge containers being swung aboard a ship. Analyses of international development, from the right and the left, implicitly adopt a framework that would have been familiar to Lenin. Developed countries take raw materials (and occasionally cheap labor) from the Third World, returning expensive manufactured goods (and thus flattening the boom-bust cycles of consumer spending in domestic markets). Some of the analysts talk despairingly of neocolonialism, others approvingly of comparative advantage. Occasionally the states that control a basic material can form a successful commodity cartel—at least for a while. OPEC, the Organization of Petroleum Exporting Countries, is the best and by some accounts the only example. But in most cases, the advantages are with those who process and shape, rather than those who generate, raw materials. Under such a model, Western countries are principally concerned with the breaking down of commodity cartels and the protection of their corporations and investors from expropriation at the hands of the developing countries. "Free trade" and "prompt, adequate, and effective compensation for nationalization" are the rallying cries of such a regime, OPEC and Castro its bogeymen.

I want to leave open the question of whether this picture of reality was ever accurate. The idea of the Third World as a source of raw materials and a market for the last generation of consumer products has always had to ignore some inconvenient counter-examples. My interest is in a different question. Can a paradigm built around the extraction, processing, and trade of physical raw materials deal adequately with a market in which intellectual property forms an increasing component of Gross National Product (GNP) and in which the creation of information products—broadly defined—makes up a substantial proportion of economic activity? To put it another way, the last fifty years have been marked by the developed countries' insistence on "free trade" and "prompt, adequate, and effective compensation for nationalization." What will be the equivalent set of demands for the next fifty years? Will "piracy" of intellectual property replace nationalization as the main fear of the developed countries? Will there be an intellectual land grab to rival the colonial land grab of the nineteenth century? My answer to both questions would be "yes"; indeed, both processes have already begun.

Reinventing Piracy

When I first studied international law, I was introduced to the topic of crimes under the ius gentium, the law of all peoples. These were crimes so heinous, with such international ramifications, that all states have both jurisdiction and obligation to stop them wherever they are found. They included slavery and genocide and, most memorably to undergraduate eyes, piracy. The professor pointed out jovially that it was only piracy of ships and planes that was condemned in this manner, not piracy of records or computer programs. Nowadays, I would not be so sure. Piracy of intellectual property products has become one of the central concerns in negotiations on world trade, a concern where both the figures for projected losses and the rhetoric of condemnation are surprising to the neophyte.

The Business Software Alliance reports that the software industry sustained losses in excess of $15 billion in 1994.[1] The Recording Industry Association of America claims that in Thailand alone 1992 trade losses to pirates were estimated at $24 million.[2] Its estimate for worldwide losses in 1994 was $2.245 billion.[3] The International Intellectual Property Alliance (IIPA) reports that copyright piracy in 36 countries had resulted in $8 billion in losses to U.S. companies in 1993. The industries under the auspices of the IIPA lost an estimated $15 to $17 billion due to international piracy in 1993.[4] Total estimated losses to the U.S. economy due to intellectual property piracy continue to range from $20 to $40 billion annually.[5]

All of these (somewhat conjectural) losses have prompted an extraordinary shift in the policy of the developed world on intellectual property. For example, the Uruguay round of the GATT built a truly extraordinary range of intellectual property protections into the fabric of the GATT itself. The "Trade Related Aspects of Intellectual Property" section of the GATT establishes the highest level of intellectual property protection in any international agreement—covering trademarks, copyrights, and trade secrets and affecting products ranging from chips and software to drugs and music recordings. The agreement was given effect in U.S. law by the Uruguay Round Agreements Act.[6] It brings the full weight of trade sanctions to bear on those who fail to respect this particular level of intellectual property.

This hard line over intellectual property is a relatively new phenomenon. In recent years, driven by the some very effective lobbying and the specter of the enormous losses to "piracy" that I quoted above, the United States government has dramatically changed its approach. U.S. embassies are now routinely used to monitor the infringement of U.S. trademarks—whether it is Marlboro in Algeria or Mickey Mouse in China. The "Super 301 Regulations" of the United States Trade Act of 1988 establish a "watch list" and a "priority watch list" for nations whose lack of intellectual property safeguards represents a significant trade barrier to U.S. business. Under the 1988 act, a determination that a country should be placed on the "priority watch list" results in a series of steps being taken—six months of bilateral consultations with the U.S. Trade Representative (USTR), followed by trade sanctions if progress is not being made. In 1991, the USTR placed three countries—India, the People's Republic of China (PRC), and Thailand—on the priority watch list. Following that designation, the PRC concluded a bilateral memorandum of understanding with United States, in which it pledged to increase protection of the intellectual property rights of U.S. firms and individuals. (Needless to say, firms from other countries were rather critical of this approach, which, in effect, provides U.S. companies with a significant competitive advantage.)[7] Section 301 was amended by the Act implementing the GATT Uruguay Round Agreement. Now problems are dealt with first by GATT/World Trade Organization mechanisms, and only if those fail does the President have authority to suspend trade benefits.[8]

Apart from these unilateral and bilateral measures, the United States has been using the GATT framework to make intellectual property a significant part of multilateral trade agreements. As I pointed out earlier, by recharacterizing failure to respect even the most expansive Western notions of intellectual property as a "significant barrier to trade" or a "subsidy" conferred upon domestic industries, the United States hopes to be able to use the GATT trade framework as an enforcement mechanism. It is this project that bids fair to shape the future international framework for intellectual property.

What explains this set of changes? At the moment, if one searches academic journals and the popular press, one is likely to find two explanations. The simplest version is a morality play. For a long time, the evil pirates of the East and South have been freeloading on the original genius of Western inventors and authors. Finally, tired of seeing pirated copies of *Presumed Innocent* or Lotus 1-2-3, and infuriated by the appropriation of Mickey Mouse to sell shoddy Chinese toys, the Western countries—led by the United States—have decided to take a stand.[9] What's more, the stand they take is popularly conceded to have more moral force than that of United Fruit protecting its investments in Central America or Anaconda Copper complaining about nationalization in Salvador Allende's Chile. In this case, the United States is standing up for more than just filthy lucre. It is standing up for the rights of creators, a cause that has attracted passionate advocates as diverse as Charles Dickens and Steven Spielberg, Edison and Jefferson, Balzac and Victor Hugo.[10] Thus the normal complaints of carping liberals within the United States have been distinctly muted. Using U.S. power in the service of property is one thing, using it in the service of the rights of creative genius is another.

The second story adds a utilitarian hook to the moral imperative of the first story. In a way that should be familiar from the discussion of information economics, it argues that intellectual property is necessary to avoid public goods problems.[11] Unless the creators of public goods are protected in some way—whether through tax and transfer or through the creation and enforcement of private property rights—there will be inadequate incentives and underproduction. In this scenario, although the current attention to intellectual property rights may look like the rich nations trying to solidify their advantages over the poor nations, there are actually perfectly good *nonideological reasons* to protect intellectual property. Analysts of this persuasion patiently explain to poor countries that the Western position is backed by both self-interest and sound economics, and hope thus to convince them that their instrumentalist approaches to foreign intellectual property rights will be fatal in the long run.

A sense of this type of argument may be gained from the introductory remarks to an analysis of international intellectual property as a classic public goods problem: "The less developed countries

(LDCs) which largely oppose the TRIPs [Trade Related Aspects of Intellectual Property] initiative, must be presented with a set of arguments that rests independent of the ideological content of American policy goals. *While the end is approximately the same,* it is hoped that the road traveled here is more palatable and that the framework adopted in this paper—a form of efficiency analysis grounded in the neoclassical trade paradigm and supplemented by recent developments in cooperation theory—provides a more appropriate perspective."[12]

Politicians and diplomats also play this card, alternating their moral and utilitarian claims to show that respect for intellectual property rights is actually a prerequisite for international development. The following quote from the former USTR, Carla Hills, is a fine example of the genre: "My preferences, as I earlier said, would be for complete protection of intellectual property. And so the higher the protection, the more I think it benefits developing countries, who thereby then attract the transfer technology, investment, and creative endeavor. And, of course, the more you protect intellectual property, those established firms are willing to pour more into research and development to try to address mankind's problems, whether they be disease or constructive building of agricultural crops or what have you, all for the betterment of peoples wherever they may be located."[13]

What is the response to the current dramatic expansion of intellectual property? Most of the current critiques focus on the distributional *unfairness* of strong intellectual property protection. Implicitly accepting Carla Hills's argument that stronger intellectual property rights encourage innovation and the circulation of ideas, they argue on egalitarian grounds for some modification of the system. For example, such a critic might argue that some of those who do poorly in the current intellectual property system, such as the developing nations, should receive benefits in the form of mandatory technology transfers, royalty reductions, and so forth. I agree with some of these criticisms, but I think they concede too much. As my analysis of information economics has shown, there is *no* reason to assume that the current level of intellectual property strikes the right balance between incentives to future production, the free flow of information, and the preservation of the public domain in the interest of potential future creators. Quite the contrary. There are strong reasons to believe that the system of incentives set up under the current author-centered vision of intellectual property will actually *impede* innovation and scientific progress, diminish the availability of our cultural heritage, inhibit artistic innovation, and restrict public debate and free speech.

The Intellectual Land Grab

First let us begin with the conventional distributional criticism. Why should we assume that expansion and strengthening of the international intellectual property regime benefits the developed world at the expense of the developing world? The conventional response assumes that the advantage of the developed world comes entirely from its technological lead. The analogy is the resources of the deep-sea bed. During the 1970s it became apparent that there were significant mineral resources on the deep-sea bed. These resources were owned by no one. If the first nations with the technology to exploit these resources are given sole title to them, the developed world will benefit disproportionately. If all nations can commodify innovation, then those who have the GNP, the scientific base, and the most developed cultural production industries will be able to commodify more. Clearly, this has a huge measure of truth to it. But an overemphasis on the *material* causes of tilt in the international regime, leads us to underestimate the way in which the conceptual structure of the regime is linked to, and is an aggravating part of, underlying disparities. I have tried to show that the basic assumptions of the regime mean that certain kinds of contributions to culture and scientific progress are validated, authorized and thus rewarded, while others are made invisible.

The author concept stands as a gate through which one must pass in order to acquire intellectual property rights. At the moment, this is a gate that tends disproportionately to favor the developed countries' contributions to world science and culture. Curare, batik, myths, and the dance "lambada" flow out of developing countries, unprotected by intellectual property rights, while Prozac, Levis, Grisham, and the movie *Lambada!* flow in—protected by a suite of intellectual property laws, which in turn are backed by the threat of trade sanctions. There are, of course, many reasons for this imbalance. It is not simply the design of an intellectual property system around an author figure that explains such results. Disparities in technology and wealth would mean that, *whatever* the intellectual property system adopted, the developed countries would better be able to exploit, market, and profit from the objects of intellectual property. *But an intellectual property system centered on the ideal of the transformative and original creator compounds these tendencies. It does so because the traditional competitive advantage of the developing countries has been in supplying raw materials and an authorial regime values the raw materials for the production of intellectual property at zero.*

Examples are legion. Centuries of cultivation by Third World farmers produces wheat and rice strains with valuable qualities—in the resistance of disease, say, or in the ability to give good yields at high altitudes. The biologists, agronomists, and genetic engineers of a Western chemical company take samples of these strains and engineer them a little to add a greater resistance to fungus or a thinner husk. It seems to me that, even here, the author analysis adds something to the story. The chemical company's scientists fit the paradigm of authorship. The farmers are everything authors should not be— their contribution comes from a community rather than an individual, from tradition rather than innovation, from evolution rather than transformation. Guess who gets the intellectual property right? Next year, the farmers may need a license to resow the grain from their crops. Calling this practice "the great seed ripoff," Representative John Porter actually introduced a resolution into Congress that would have called for the United States not to proceed with intellectual property negotiations under the GATT until there has been a study on "protecting the rights of those in the Third World." A news article on the resolution immediately follows this observation by offering a view of this issue from the other side, that is to say, from within the author-centered view of intellectual property. "The 'industrial world' view on the issue is that poor countries pirate drug recipes or high-yield seeds, violating the patent laws of industrial countries to avoid paying royalties on the order of $3 billion a year to U.S., Japanese and European firms."[14]

At the moment that I finished this book, international concern about this issue seemed slowly to be awakening. On September 25, 1995, *Time* carried a story called "Seeds of Conflict" describing the controversy surrounding W. R. Grace's patent on a pesticide derived from the seeds of the Indian neem tree. The problem is that the neem tree's seeds have been used by Indian farmers as a pesticide for centuries. Grace's pesticide is a clear improvement over the traditional version; its shelf life is longer. For this and other reasons, *Time* was skeptical about the claims that the use of the seeds constituted "genetic colonialism."

> Labeling Grace's actions a rip-off, though, requires something of a stretch. The company didn't steal away with the seeds and market them; it built a plant in Tumkur, near Bangalore, to process them, providing jobs for 60 Indians and contributing to the local economy. Some critics charge that demand from Grace's plant is the cause of a recent jump in neem seed prices that has driven some small farmers out of business, but that is difficult to prove. And while India [which currently does not permit the patenting of agricultural products] will eventually have to change its patent laws as a member of the World Trade Organization under the General Agreement on Tariffs and Trade, that still wouldn't keep farmers from using neem seeds in traditional ways.[15]

The article concluded, however, with an approving quote by an attorney who spoke of the need to "share benefits" and "to create some kind of compensation . . . to promote development of biological resources in a sustainable way." This article and others like it are not the only sign that the problem has been recognized. Darrell Posey and Graham Dutfield's handbook, *Beyond Intellectual Property Rights: Towards Traditional Resource Rights for Indigenous and Local Communities,* provided indigenous communities with the first accessible summary of the existing intellectual property, human rights, indigenous rights, biodiversity, and environmental rules that bear on the issue.[16] But if things are changing, they are changing all too slowly. And even countries, such as India, which have taken a stand against the patenting of life forms, will soon be forced by the GATT to change their position and their intellectual property laws—all in the name of "free" trade.

So much for the linkage between distribution and conceptual structure. Whether I am right or wrong about the distributional effects, I think it can be convincingly demonstrated that an exclusively author-centered regime will have negative effects on efficiency. In many ways, this may be the more important point to make. To condemn a system as unfair is one thing; to argue that it does not work, that it may sometimes actually *impede* innovation, is another. Again, the key to the analysis is the blindness to "sources" produced by a system that has as its paradigmatic case an individual artist making something *ex nihilo.*

Shamanic Sources and Periwinkle Effects

Shamans from the Amazon basin have generations of lore about the properties of herbs and flowers. Some of the these plants are placebos; others are extremely valuable. Drug companies have found that if they test the plants from the shamans' "black bag," they yield a high percentage of valuable drugs. As the *New York Times* reported, "While skeptics may argue that the lore of the native healers is mere superstition, the ethnobotanists see shamanic knowledge as the result of a trial and error process refined over thousands of years. Ethnobotanists hope to take a scientific short cut to discovering new uses for the tens of thousands of plants with which native peoples are intimately familiar." One of the most fascinating experiments reported by the *Times* involved the AIDS virus. In test tube trials, "of the twenty plants collected on the shaman's advice, five killed the AIDS virus but spared the T cells. But of eighteen plant species gathered randomly, just one did so."[17]

A more widely publicized example concerns vinca alkaloids from the rosy periwinkle, a native of Madagascar. The plant was used indigenously to treat diabetes, was investigated by the Lilly company, and forms the basis of a compound now used in chemotherapy treatment.[18] According to the British newspaper *The Independent,* the plant "has yielded a drug to cure Hodgkin's disease and a trade in the drug worth $100m a year."[19] The article goes on to quote the World Wide Fund for Nature to the effect that "if Madagascar had received a significant part of this income, it would have been one of the country's largest (if not the single largest) source of income." In the days of recombinant DNA techniques, genetic information may be one of the largest resources of the developing countries. "Madagascar is the unique home of perhaps 5 per cent of the world's species. It is the biological equivalent of an Arab oil sheikdom. Yet, without an income from its huge biological wealth, it has chopped down most of its forests to feed its people." Now *there's* a public goods problem. Precisely because they can find no place in a legal regime constructed around a vision of individual, transformative, original genius, the indigenous peoples are driven to deforestation or slash and burn farming. Who knows what other unique and potentially valuable plants disappear with the forest, what generations of pharmacological experience disappear as the indigenous culture is destroyed? In both cases, a large part of the problem is the fact that the indigenous peoples share in none of the profits of development. It is always possible, of course, that huge profits could destroy the culture just as effectively as penury. But the decision to impose the author vision without acknowledging, or even understanding, its implications is also the decision not even to try to solve these problems.

These facts have not gone *completely* unnoticed. Environmental groups and groups devoted to the preservation of indigenous peoples have criticized the way that tribal lore and biological largesse find no place in the language of intellectual property. Dr. Jason Clay, director of the group Cultural Survival, put the position simply: "It's a question of intellectual property rights. People whose medical lore leads to a useful product should have a stake in the profits. Unless we return some of the profits to them, it's a kind of theft. We have to figure out ways to make the rain forests pay for themselves, so that these peoples can continue to exist."[20]

The "colonial" form of intellectual property has been around for hundreds of years. In 1800 the Makushi Indians showed explorers the plant from which they extracted curare for their arrowheads. Western chemists found that curare was an excellent muscle relaxant. It is still being used to this day. According to Dr. Mark Plotkin of Conservation International, "the Makushis never received any compensation for the discovery of a product worth millions."[21] Even plans to set up data banks on the genetic resources of tropical resources raise concerns that companies will no longer have any incentive either to preserve the forest or to reward its inhabitants for the use of their lore. Precisely because of our increasing ability to record genetic information *as information,* its connection to its natural habitat will become less necessary. Conrad Gorinsky, a Guyanan biologist working in Britain, "calls the plans 'bunker biology,' because they ignore the traditional tribal knowledge that is the fount of our wisdom. He fears that the [proposed treaty on genetic sovereignty] could act as an incentive to loot the biological riches of the rain forests over a few years, secreting the results in [Western] their laboratories and gene banks. A gene in the lab, [Western scientists] will argue, is worth two in the bush. But once the riches are taken, who will save the forest then?"[22]

A patent lawyer or an economist could argue that we cannot criticize intellectual property regimes for failing to maintain the genetic diversity of the biomass (or whatever.) Perhaps that is true, although it seems highly problematic to me. But even if we close our eyes to distributional, environmental, and all other "subsidiary" effects of our intellectual property regimes, and analyze those regimes solely on their ability to maintain and increase the production of information, we find that, for the reasons developed in this book, they are unlikely to achieve that very restricted goal. An author-focused regime that makes the contributions of sources "invisible" is unlikely to reward those contributions—even when an economic analysis might show this to be desirable. Sources may become a "commons" whose exploitation is justified or obscured by an author theory, leading to predictably tragic results—cutting down the genetic miracle of a rain forest to grow subsistence crops, for example. The result *may* be a reduced flow of genetic material to laboratories and a consequent reduction in research and innovation.

I would not want the reader to get the impression that this analysis is relevant only to developing countries, to shamans, or to romanticized accounts of the collective genius of indigenous peoples. In developed nations too, the blindness of an author-centered regime to the importance of the public domain can also lead to overly expansive intellectual property rights that deny future creators—novelists, scientists, programmers—the raw material they need to make new products. The tendency to undervalue the public domain is a worldwide phenomenon.

Classroom Copies

Again it is hard to know just which examples to pick. In the realm of the printed word, it is easy to find unduly restrictive decisions about the fair use exception in copyright. Cases such as the *Kinko's* case end up by restricting the accessibility of information and ideas even within the areas specifically marked out by the copyright statutes as examples of "fair use."[23] The *Kinko's* decision concerned the creation of anthologies of photocopied material for classroom use. Kinko's Graphics assembled the packets for the professors concerned and then sold them for a profit. Kinko's claimed that this constituted fair use. Here are the words of the copyright statute, section 107: "Notwithstanding the provisions of section 106, the fair use of a copyrighted work, including such use by reproduction in copies . . . for purposes such as criticism, comment, newsreporting, teaching, (including multiple copies for classroom use), scholarship, or research is not an infringement of copyright."[24]

In the *Kinko's* case, Judge Constance Baker Motley listed a number of factors as determinative of fair use—including the "transformative value" of the secondary work as compared to the original. Let us set aside the question of whether this makes a nonsense of the language of the statute; except by dipping further into postmodernism than Judge Motley seems willing to go, how can "multiple copies for classroom use" ever be "transformative"? Beyond the language of the statute, the use of the transformative test reintroduces an authorial paradigm into all portions of fair use doctrine. This may seem reasonable until one remembers that fair use was supposed to be the *limitation* of the monopoly granted to authors who got their rights by being transformative. Does the exception make sense if it merely parallels the rule? Authors may only be trumped by *other* authors? I would argue that it is a better interpretation of the fair use exception to assume that it allows for socially beneficial uses in general, but also maintains the availability of a public domain for future creators. This availability should be both specific and general. Future creators need to be able explicitly to make use of past objects of intellectual property—for example, the parody of a prior work—a use in which the transformativeness criteria *might* make some sense.[25] But there also needs to be a general availability to the culture as a whole, and that is exactly the goal served by the multiple copying provisions of section 107. Future creators need to be educated—and we might even assume that they will be better educated if they are exposed to the widest possible range of ideas and opinions. Thus, if we care about future creation we might want specifically to *guarantee* the availability of multiple copies for classroom use; indeed section 107 seems to do just that. For most of the opinion, however, Judge Motley seems to assume that the only way in which future creation can be guaranteed is by giving more intellectual property rights: "An important additional factor is the fact that defendant has effectively created a new nationwide business allied to the publishing industry by usurping plaintiff's copyrights and profits. This cannot be sustained by this court as its result is complete frustration of the intent of the copyright law which has been *the protection of intellectual property* and, *more importantly, the encouragement of creative expression.*"[26]

This quotation exhibits exactly the same pattern that I have described elsewhere in this book. It starts with a circular argument: "the intent of copyright law has been the protection of intellectual property." Then it proceeds to the blank assertion of a goal. "The intent of copyright ... is the encouragement of creative expression." But even this, of course, has no bite on the case without a specific set of background assumptions, basically (1) that products of intellectual property are produced either *ex nihilo* or, at least, with the minimum of cultural debts and therefore (2) that the best way to encourage the production of more creative expression is to give more and stronger intellectual property rights to authors. This view ignores the importance of the public domain to future producers precisely *because* it starts with the view of authors and authorial production I have described.

The Electronic Frontier

The tendency of an author-centered regime to undervalue the public domain is not confined to books or even to cultural production in general. In computer programming, where innovation is particularly prized, we find the same pattern. First, intellectual property rights are dramatically expanded. Second, this expansion is internationalized through multilateral treaties backed by the threat of trade sanctions.

Until the late 1980s, software developers relied mainly on copyright and trade secret law to protect their programs. A change in the policy of the Patent Office allowed the patenting of software. Some computer scientists and software engineers felt that patents were being granted on quite basic computer programming tricks worked out long ago by hackers. Although done in the name of encouraging programming innovation, this set of actions has aroused considerable protest from some of the most innovative programmers.[27] Richard Stallman—an MIT computer scientist, winner of the Grace Murray Hopper Award and recipient of a MacArthur Foundation "genius grant"—has founded a group called the League for Programming Freedom. The League's goal is to challenge what Stallman sees as the inhibiting effects of commodification on both the development of new technology and the *dispersal* of market power *over* information technology. Stallman's own efforts have been in the direction of setting up a "Copyleft" system to counter the excesses of patent and copyright. Some reactions have been more extreme. An underground group called Nu Prometheus dedicated itself to stealing and revealing the "source codes" for single supplier CPUs such as the MacIntosh so as to encourage other suppliers to compete with Apple. The idea of theft in the service of competition is a perfect example of the conflicts I describe in this book. (Apple eventually did decide to permit others to manufacture its CPU.)

Stallman's objection is not merely an academic one. Reports of recent hearings held by the Patent and Trademark Office on how to improve software patents indicated that there was substantial disagreement on whether software should be patented at all.

> On one side is the camp that claims that the use of patents will stifle technical innovation and jack up overhead legal costs—costs eventually passed on to consumers—to levels barring everyone but the heavyweights from entering the market. Though this line of reasoning is mostly expounded by developers from small companies and the 600 members of the League for Programming Freedom, some major industry players such as Oracle Corp., Adobe Systems Inc., and Autodesk Inc. also lined up on this side . . . The opposite camp argues that patents are no more harmful to innovation in software than in any other industry and counters with an equally disturbing suggestion that, without patents, American software inventions will be primed for the picking, particularly by foreign developers.[28]

Interestingly, the latter position is greeted with skepticism by some of the most pro-business, "free market" conservatives. "Business author George Gilder argues that the prevailing attitude toward intellectual property leaves American companies extremely vulnerable to the Japanese, who hold many U.S. patents and understand how to litigate in our courts as well as any domestic corporation."[29]

The expansion of intellectual property is not limited to the formal reach of the rules. On the domestic scene, U.S. computer companies have begun a practice of aggressively litigating both software and hardware patents. Patent litigation increased by nearly 50 percent during the 1980s. For some firms it has become a staple source of revenue. Texas Instruments, for example, is reported to make *more money from litigating patents than it does from operations*.[30]

Part of the explanation for this surge in litigation can be found in the business cycle. The collective wisdom in the industry is that during times of declining competitiveness firms seek to mine alternative sources of revenue. Intellectual property rights have come to be seen as one such source. Such litigation explosions are most likely to occur *after* the first dynamic growth phase of a new technology, as imitation drives the factor-price frontier to the right and diminishes capital accumulation. Many of the same trends can be seen in the international economy. U.S. and Western European companies have long since lost the edge in labor costs. As they now lose their technological edge to the high-tech, comprador economies of the Pacific rim, we should expect to see them look for a *legal* edge instead. And so they do, using their governments as an enforcement device in a way that would have been entirely familiar to the eighteenth-century traders of the East India Company.

Apart from explanations rooted in the cycle of technology and capital accumulation, there are also legal reasons for the expansion in both the ambit and the enforcement of intellectual property in the patent law. The first is the fact that, during Ronald Reagan's presidency, the Justice Department stopped antitrust actions against companies that refused to license patented technology.[31] Second, the Congress formed the Court of Appeals for the Federal Circuit to handle all patent appellate litigation.[32] Between 1921 and 1973 the circuit courts had found nearly two-thirds of adjudicated patents invalid.[33] The Federal Circuit was rather different. "Between 1982 and 1985, the court invalidated only forty-four percent of the patents it adjudicated on appeal from trial courts, a marked contrast to the old invalidation rate of approximately sixty-six percent. Perhaps more importantly, patent lawyers believe the court favors patentees—and presumably advise their clients accordingly."[34] More recent reports claim that the court is now upholding patents *80 percent* of the time.[35]

If we put all of these tendencies together we have a truly disturbing trend. Some things never patented before—for example, software and genetically engineered life forms—are now being patented. Partly because the Patent Office has no expertise in software matters, it is widely thought to grant too many patents and to cover processes that had previously been considered to be part of the public domain. Companies are litigating their patents more aggressively, so that those patents which are granted have a much higher chance of being enforced. The new court structure is much more receptive to claims of patent infringement in general. Finally, until recently, the Justice Department had given up enforcing the last hope of those who decry the anticompetitive tendencies of patents, namely, the antitrust laws. Even now, their enforcement is pallid and half-hearted.[36] Each of these changes has removed an important protection of the public domain, some of them legal, some of them cultural, some of them institutional, some based on simple inaction. The assumption of the early days of the industry that all benefitted from the contributions of all has been replaced by the aggressive insistence on private property rights—even when the result may be to slow down innovation as a result. The courts are looking favorably on these claims, and the government has, for some time, apparently given up caring about the effect this has in concentrating market power in the hands of a few firms. Put all these together and you see how the idea of the original, transformative genius, can be used to produce its antithesis—in terms of competition, innovation, and the concentration of market power.[37]

The Author in Cyberspace?

One real accomplishment of the Clinton presidency has been to focus attention on the information infrastructure of the economy. Admittedly, the definition of infrastructure has sometimes been a little narrow—as if information only flowed between computers—but the idea is a very important one and Vice President Gore's oft-repeated commitment to "universal access for all Americans" is to be lauded unconditionally. Unfortunately, when it comes to *implementing* that idea of universal access, the familiar blindnesses of intellectual property reappear. On September 5, 1995, the Administration released its "White Paper" on intellectual property rights on the National Information Infrastructure—a report on intellectual property in cyberspace and a proposed piece of legislation implementing the findings of the report.[38] How does the author fare in cyberspace? Very, very well.

If the White Paper is implemented, the information superhighway will become an information toll road. The privatization of the public domain is unparalleled. Fair use rights will be cut back, individuals will be denied the right to give away their copies of digital works to their friends, even if they delete their own copies of those works. In fact, according to the White Paper, even *reading* a document on the screen of your World Wide Web browser—without saving it to your floppy drive or hard disk—becomes a copyright violation![39] How did all of this happen? In this case we have a report, not simply a piece of legislation. Thus it is possible to track not only the results of decision making about intellectual property in a digital environment, but the reasoning and rhetoric that produced those results.

One of the most striking things about the White Paper is its apparently disingenuous character. Like its predecessor, the Green Paper, the White Paper relies on a three-stage rhetorical strategy. First, it purports to summarize the current state of intellectual property law; then it modestly suggests that the provisions of the current law should be extended to the new technologies of the electronic frontier. Finally, it discusses the objections that have been made to such a plan.

In the abstract, this could hardly sound more reasonable. Indeed, the general tone of the report is a convincing one: that of the learned expert who explains the arcane details of copyright to the laity and offers a few uncontentious technical suggestions to cap the deal. Unfortunately, nothing could be further from the truth. The "summary" of the current state of intellectual property law is in fact a brief for publishing interests; it makes a point of concentrating on any court case or statutory provision that *extends* the reach of intellectual property rights, while minimizing or—more troublingly still—omitting altogether—the countervailing decisions, policies, and doctrines. (The Working Group's discussion of fair use law is a good example, as Pamela Samuelson pointed out when the Green Paper came out.[40] In the White Paper, the one-sided story continues.) The result is reminiscent of a "summary" of contemporary attitudes to birth control that quoted only from sources approved by the Catholic church. Taking this inflated view of intellectual property as its starting point, the White Paper asks itself rhetorically whether there are justifications for offering digital publishers a lower level of protection than this (figmentary) status quo? Unsurprisingly, its answer is in the negative. Finally, the White Paper does mention the fact that there are objections to its method. Unfortunately, the list of objections seems to have been drafted by *Saturday Night Live*'s Emily Latella—the lady who asked why there were all those bumper stickers urging us to "Save Soviet Jewelry." Unlike Emily, the White Paper doesn't say "Never Mind" when its manglings are pointed out; though exactly the same faults were criticized in the Green Paper draft, the White Paper prefers silence to rebuttal.

The really depressing thing about the report is that it fails to accomplish its stated goal: to examine what level of intellectual property rights would be necessary in cyberspace. The problem isn't simply the tendency to give a pro-author account of the existing law. Even if the White Paper's summary of intellectual property law were accurate, there might well be reasons why a different level of protection might be appropriate in the digital environment. For example, the global reach and ease of access that the Net offers clearly facilitate illegitimate copying. But they also cut down enormously on advertising and on the costs of distribution, potentially yielding a higher percentage return for a lower level of investment. Thus, with some products more intellectual property protection might be required, while with others a lower level of protection would still produce a return adequate to encourage future production. Some "digital products" require enormous investments of time and energy, are of lasting value, require no "tied" subsidiary services to make them work, and can be copied for pennies. Others require little investment precisely because of their digital nature, do not require extensive research and development, or can be protected by denial of access (databases and search engines), by preemptive release of "demo" or partially disabled shareware versions (Doom), by being first to market, by "tying arrangements," such as help lines, technical assistance, or paid advertising (Netscape), and so on. The point is that the digital environment is *complicated;* the same technical factors that make copying easier also yield other ways for producers to recover their investments, or otherwise encourage further innovation. Rather than take these complexities seriously, the White Paper simply assumes that, on the Net, a right-holder needs all the rights available outside the Net plus some new ones as well. To the point that there are multiple ways for producers to secure an adequate return on their investment of time and ingenuity, the White Paper opines weakly that not everyone will choose to enforce to the full the rights the report proposes to give them. This is rather like responding to the argument that a capital gains tax cut is not necessary to stimulate investment with the rejoinder that some investors may decide to give the extra money to charity. Yes, it may happen, but that doesn't go to the question of whether the change was necessary in the first place.

More relevant to this book, though, are the logical fallacies and baseline errors with which the White Paper is loaded. As I have shown here, intellectual property rights are limited monopolies conferred in order to gain present and future public benefit; for the purposes of achieving those goals, the "limitations" on the right are just as important as the grant of the right itself. To put it more accurately, since there is no "natural" absolute intellectual property right, the doctrines which favor consumers and other users, such as fair use, are just as much a part of the basic right as the entitlement of the author to prevent certain kinds of copying. Even the source of the Congress's authority in intellectual property matters—Article 1, Section 8, clause 8 of the Constitution—mentions two limitations on intellectual property rights. One is functional: "To promote the Progress of Science and useful Arts"; and the other is temporal: "by securing for limited times to authors and inventors." Thus intellectual property is a particularly inappropriate area to talk about property rights as if they were both natural and absolute. Yet this the White Paper does with a dogged consistency and an unlikely passion. Observe in the following quotation how the White Paper first sets up its own inflated idea of intellectual property as the baseline, then implies that right-holders actually have an absolute property right in the continuation of that level of protection. Amazingly, the "limitations" that define intellectual property rights instead become a "tax" on right-holders. "Some participants have suggested that the United States is being divided into a nation of information haves and have nots and that this could be ameliorated by ensuring that the fair use defense is broadly generous in the NII [National Information Infrastructure] context. The Working Group rejects the notion that copyright owners should be taxed—apart from all others—to facilitate the legitimate goal of 'universal access.' "[41]

Of course, given the goals of copyright law, it would have made just as much sense if the argument had been reversed, taking the fair use rights of users and consumers as the baseline. The White Paper wants to give expansive intellectual property rights because it believes, wrongly in my view, that this is the best way to encourage private companies to fund the construction of the information superhighway. In response, a more skeptical Working Group might have said: "Some reports have suggested that the difficulties of encouraging companies to develop the National Information Infrastructure could be ameliorated by ensuring that intellectual property rights are broadly generous and fair use rights curtailed in the NII context. The Working Group rejects the notion that consumers, future creators and other holders of fair use rights should be taxed—apart from all others—to facilitate the legitimate goal of encouraging investment in the information superhighway."

But not only does the White Paper illustrate the pervasive power of baseline fallacies in information economics, it also shows how the author-vision downplays the importance of fair use and thus encourages an absolutist rather than a functional idea of intellectual property. In a footnote to the passage quoted above, the Working Group explains further. "The laws of economics and physics protect producers of equipment and tangible supplies to a greater extent than copyright owners. A university, for example, has little choice but to pay to acquire photocopy equipment, computer, paper and diskettes ... It may, however, seek subsidization from copyright owners by arguing that its copying and distribution of their works should, as a fair use, not be compensated."[42]

This completes the picture given above. Fair use rights are a "subsidy" sought by universities. But wait a minute. Even if the *only* goal of intellectual property law were to encourage future innovation and information production, this argument would be fallacious. Future creators need some raw material to work *with,* after all. Fair use is one important method of providing that raw material. It can also be seen as part of the implicit quid pro quo of intellectual property; we will give you this extremely valuable legal monopoly, backed with state power and enforced through the courts (and by the FBI). In return, we will design the contours of your right so as to encourage a variety of socially valuable uses. The White Paper wants to give copyright holders the "quid" while claiming that the "quo" is a tax, or a forced subsidy. Only the unfamiliarity of intellectual property conceals the ludicrousness of the argument. It's as if a developer had negotiated a fat package of cash grants and tax breaks as the price of building a new stadium in Washington, D.C., but then wanted to claim an absolute property right in the benefits of the deal while insisting that to make him fulfill his side of the bargain would be to confer a "subsidy" on the city.

Defending the Current System

The response to the kinds of criticisms I have offered here is generally to offer counter-examples, some of which I would happily accept. Is it not true that the current system has provided the large sums of capital necessary to produce and test new drugs? Are there not inventors or software engineers who have been able to stand against the large companies because they are armed with an intellectual property right to protect their innovations? Don't academics sometimes shamelessly photocopy entire books and hand them out to their classes? Won't we need new intellectual property rights in cyberspace? Is it not true that if a drug company in Chile or a software company in Argentina develops a patentable product, the international regime will protect them as well as it protects DuPont or Microsoft? To some of these I would respond, "Absolutely"; to others, "Maybe" or "Sometimes."

Take the drug example, for instance. The current system does provide a return that encourages investors to put money into companies that do pharmaceutical research. This is clearly a good thing, and anyone who tells you we do not need *some* system for ensuring such a return is a fool. However, the current system rests on assumptions and not evidence. (The fact that the drug companies put more into advertising than research and development is about as close as popular debate has come to this point.)[43] In the different areas in which intellectual property is available, we fail to consider the extent to which innovators can recover their investment by methods other than intellectual property—packaging, reputation, being first to market, trading on knowledge of the likely economic effects of the innovation, and so on. What's more, the current system values at zero the contributions of the public domain, and in some areas that practice may actually slow down the production of new products. At the very least, the system should balance the incentives and the efficiency aspects of information production better than it does at present.

My response to the other examples is similar. Yes, it is true that there are cases in which the current system actually fulfills a socially and morally attractive function. It would be strange if there were not. We do need to encourage innovation, and the idea of the transformative iconoclast is a profoundly appealing one. But this is not the question. The real set of questions might go something like this. Does this system rest on evidence or on faith? Do we want to consider a system that would have more protection for information production and less protection for the production of innovation? Do all the types of innovation that get protection actually need it? If not, is it necessary, for reasons of administration and formal realizability, to cast our net so wide? In its overall effects, does this system disproportionately help or hurt developing countries and the individual author or creator? Does this system undervalue the public domain and, if so, will it actually end up diminishing future innovation and impeding future innovators?

In different areas, in different industries, the answers to these questions will be different; indeed, that is my point. A system built on a single Procrustean concept of information production and ownership will miss the mark, and, as I have tried to show, that is the system which our embedded ideas about information have driven us toward. We cannot examine our current system by a trial of anecdotes in which individual examples do the work of analysis. Just as my stories of shamanic sources and periwinkle effects mean nothing without the accompanying analysis of information economics, so individual stories of rapacious intellectual pirates or noble inventors cannot—by themselves—provide an adequate grounding for the system.

. . . .

The process I have been describing is of intellectual property rights expanding worldwide. In biotechnology, computer software, conventional publishing, and a number of other areas, the tendency has been to extend and enforce intellectual property rights and to ignore or minimize the importance of the public domain—the claims of sources and audience, the interests of future producers. The process is truly an international one. On the institutional level, the GATT has been used both to expound and to enforce the developed world's view of intellectual property. The threat of trade sanctions, of the Special 301 "watch lists," of the removal of most favored nation status have all been added to the arsenal of the producers of intellectual property. But more than this, a particular conceptual apparatus of intellectual property has been established more firmly, both on the domestic and the international level. This way of thinking about intellectual property has a specific conception of "original" creation by a transformative individual at its heart. In many parts of the international information economy, this conception—though formally neutral—functions as a one-way valve for property claims. It favors the developed countries, not entirely, but disproportionately. Cultural forms, dances, patterns, traditional medical knowledge, genetic information from the plants of the rain forest, or from peasant-cultivated seed varieties, all flow out of the developing world unprotected by property rights. In return the developed countries send their cultural forms—Mickey Mouse, the X-Men, Pearl Jam, Benetton, Marlboro, and Levis. The developed world also sends its wonderful medicines—Prozac and Tagamet—its computer programs—WordPerfect and Lotus 1-2-3—its novels and its industrial designs. Almost all of *these* things, of course, are well protected by intellectual property rights.

The traditional move at this stage of the argument is to make all of the developed world's products seem tawdry and shallow, while those of the developing world are noble and fine. I think there is *some* merit to this point, but not a lot. Cultural shallowness is not an exclusive possession of the rich, and the antibiotic Augmentin works better than the bread or potato mold from which its antecedents come.

My point is a different one. First, I think this system is colossally unfair. If one has the slightest concern for distributional justice in one's criteria for property regimes, this regime must surely fail. Second, I think the system undermines the very goal it claims to promote. The distributional inequities are purchased at the cost of *inefficiency*, rather than efficiency. The rosy periwinkle story is one that precisely exemplifies the utilitarian failures of the current regime.

Equally important to the politics of the situation is the fact, as I have said repeatedly, that the process is not just one which a First World "we" are doing to a Third World "them." It is a process that is being carried on inside the legal systems of the developed world, expanding intellectual property rights and privatizing the public domain. Often the people who carry out this privatization are well-meaning; the author is a sympathetic character, after all. One has only to look at the *Kinko's* decision or software patenting to see the appeal of intellectual property rights on both utilitarian and aesthetic grounds. Yet with the idea of romantic authorship at its core, the tendency of an intellectual property system is to run one way—with sources, audiences, and future creators on the losing end. (The table in Chapter 13 offers a schematic layout of the process.)

. . . .

At the beginning of this book I said that intellectual property might have the same relationship to the information society that the wage-labor nexus had to the industrial manufacturing society of the 1900s. I also said that this relationship remains underanalyzed, if it is analyzed at all. The legal and institutional forms for the international political economy of information are under construction and, so far as I can see, they have an author-shaped hole at their center. Yet there has been remarkably little concern about these issues. Intellectual property just does not occupy the same position in the imagination as human rights or environmentalism. The liberal left has been slow to grasp the distributional impact of the intellectual property regime I describe, let alone the regime's failure to accomplish its own stated goals or its potentially negative effects on the environment or on cultural heritage. Recently, however, that blindness to the effects of intellectual property has begun to lift. Near the end of this book, I have included as an appendix the text of the Bellagio Declaration, the statement of the Bellagio Conference on Cultural Agency/Cultural Authority. The conference was organized by two colleagues who share a fascination with "author effects"—Peter Jaszi and Martha Woodmansee—and it brought together computer scientists, environmentalists, anthropologists, literary critics, authors, publishers, and legal scholars from all over the world to discuss the effects of intellectual property on their communities and their fields. I had the honor of being one of the drafters of the declaration designed to capture the sense of the meeting. My point of view is admittedly a partial one—in both senses of that word. Still, one of the remarkable things about the conference was the extent to which the participants, from so many different countries and areas of interest, found the author analysis useful in linking up and helping to explain problems that, until then, had appeared entirely distinct. I offer it to the reader as a small piece of evidence that there might be something to what I say.

CHAPTER 12

Private Censors, Transgenic Slavery, and Electronic Indenture

Less obvious, but no less important, than the distributional and efficiency consequences of an author-centered regime are the effects that this regime can have on politics, morality, and the marketplace of ideas. As I have pointed out, information issues are often settled by a process of "typing." Admittedly, the process of typing goes far beyond the contours of this book. In its more general sense it is one of the fundamental methods we have for making—and avoiding—moral judgments. It is a fundamental way of *making* moral judgments because much of our moral discourse has the misleading form of a syllogism: I know that torture is wrong; the question is, "Is this torture?" I know that free speech is to be protected; the question is, "Is this speech?" The moment of typing, classifying, and defining becomes the moment of moral decision. It is a fundamental way of *avoiding* moral judgment for the same reason. The thing-like or "reified" nature of categories can operate to obscure a moral issue, to resolve by pretheoretical definition an issue that would be troubling and painful if faced directly. "The Declaration of Independence's promise of equality for 'all men' does not apply to blacks or women because they are not within the relevant category of 'men.' " I will not enter here into the larger question of whether or not this process of "moral lexicography" should be the canonical method for working out the right thing to do.[1] Suffice it to say that we often act as though it was, and thus, right or wrong, the contours of the definitional process are *important*.

When dealing with information issues, this process of typing is not merely *important* to analysis and debate; as the previous chapters show, it's often all there is. Questions of information regulation, commodification, and access are shaped by two neglected processes of interpretive construction. First, such issues are often decided by pigeonholing them into implicitly contradictory stereotypes of "public" or "private" information. These conflicting stereotypes have their roots in basic assumptions about politics, the market, and privacy in a liberal state. Second, the tension *between* these stereotypes is often apparently resolved by the use of a seductive image: the romantic author whose original, transformative genius justifies private property and fuels public debate. I pointed out that this leads to bad results in terms of economic efficiency, scientific innovation, and wealth distribution. Now I turn to the political and moral impact of "typing," and specifically author-centered typing.

Private Censorship

Policing the Language

In the early 1980s, a nonprofit California corporation called San Francisco Arts and Athletics, Inc., tried to organize a "Gay Olympic Games" with the avowed aim of fighting prejudice against gays.[2] The United States Olympic Committee brought suit against it, claiming—in effect—that the USOC "owned" the word "Olympic" and that it could decide who could use the word and who could not. Under the ironically named Amateur Sports Act of 1978 Congress had authorized the USOC to prohibit some kinds of "commercial and promotional" uses of the word. I say that the name of the act was ironic because its key provisions were designed to ensure adequate *commercial* exploitation by the USOC of the word "Olympic" and the symbols associated with the games. It was, in other words, a state grant of a monopoly rent on a piece of the linguistic landscape. The statute treated "Olympic" as if it were equal to "Kleenex" or "Hoover." In some ways the rule was actually more sweeping, since it lacked even the normal defenses to trademark infringement. The U.S. Olympic committee had let other groups use the name—"the Special

Olympics," "Youth Olympics," and so on. Nevertheless, the USOC refused to let the SFAA use the word "Olympic" next to the word "gay" (perhaps on the theory that nothing could be more foreign to the traditions of ancient Greece than homosexuality). Rejecting both First Amendment and equal protection claims by the SFAA, the Supreme Court agreed that the USOC had the right to prohibit the use of the word—even where there was no danger of confusion with the "real" Olympics.

"Congress reasonably could conclude that the commercial and promotional value of the word 'Olympic' was the product of the USOC's 'own talents and energy, the end result of much time, energy and expense.' "[3] Just as with the publicity rights cases I analyzed earlier, this "homestead law on the English language" is justified by appeal to a notion of a talented and industrious author.[4] Just as with the copyright cases, the public formation of the Olympic ideal over the last two millennia becomes merely a "source," subsumed within the transformative powers of the USOC's "talents and energy."

What of the free speech issue? The USOC appears explicitly to discriminate in deciding who can use the word "Olympic" (youth, some disabled groups) and who cannot (gays, the aged). But despite the fact that the state first gives the USOC this sovereignty over an important word and then enforces the USOC's decisions, there is no issue of censorship here. The USOC—as author of the word that makes up its own title—is a *private* actor, and we are dealing here with *commercial* usage. There is no state action because we are in the private sphere—authors are not governments. There is no free speech issue because we are in the marketplace and not the polity. This is moral geography with a vengeance.

The uninitiated are likely to be puzzled by this dazzling chain of definitions. Where does it stop? Could the Congress reserve the use of the word "democratic" to the Democratic Party, prohibiting any other group—profit or nonprofit—from using the word either as a fund-raising slogan or as a title of a rival organization? What does it matter that the word "democrat" has a rich tradition going back at least two thousand years? So does the word "Olympic." Far from ruling out such a dystopian world of private censorship, the Supreme Court went out of its way to concede that it remained a possibility. "There is no need in this case to decide whether Congress ever could grant a private entity exclusive use of a generic word."[5] The rationale could be the same, surely. We need only change the language of the court's opinion slightly. "Congress reasonably could conclude that the commercial and promotional value of the word 'democratic' was the product of the Democratic Party's own talents and energy, the end result of much time, energy and expense." How unfair then for *Social* Democrats, the Students for a Democratic Society, the Californians for Economic Democracy, or Democracy Radio to promote themselves using this word. Could a local group challenging a PTA practice—Durham Parents for School Democracy—be enjoined from using the word? What if the Democrats decided that they would only let heterosexual groups use the word? Or white groups? How about an author selling a book that used the word in the title? At some point along this slippery slope, I am sure the Court would want to get off, but I am unsure how or where.

I will let Chief Justice Rehnquist have the last word in this issue. Two years after the Gay Olympics case, the Supreme Court had to decide whether or not the First Amendment prohibited the conviction of a Gregory Lee Johnson for burning an American flag in front of the Dallas City Hall. (And chanting, in dubious meter, "America, the red, white, and blue, we spit on you.") The Court held that the First Amendment did protect such behavior. This decision prompted a rash of editorials, proposed constitutional amendments, and heady declarations—some of patriotism, some of respect for the First Amendment. (Or, as in Justice Brennan's opinion, patriotism *as* respect for the First Amendment.) For liberals, this decision was proof that the First Amendment still held its power. For conservatives, it was proof that the country was, as they had said all along, going to hell in a handbasket. In the midst of all of this hoopla, the question of private censorship was understandably absent from the popular consciousness. Thus even keen readers of Supreme Court opinions— if such animals exist—could be forgiven for missing the following paragraph in Justice Rehnquist's dissent.

> Only two terms ago in *San Francisco Arts and Athletics, Inc. v. United States Olympic Committee*, the Court held that Congress could grant exclusive use of the word "Olympic" to the United States Olympic Committee . . . As the Court stated, "when a word [or symbol] acquires value 'as the result of organization and the expenditure of labor, skill, and money' by an entity, that entity constitutionally may obtain a limited

property right in the word [or symbol]." Surely Congress or the States may recognize a similar interest in the flag.[6]

Justice Rehnquist has a point. Under the Gay Olympics decision, Congress *should* be able to "privatize" the flag—to take it out of the public domain, by "author-izing" the United States to treat it as a protected mark. This point however, does not lead me to believe that the flag case was wrongly decided; rather I believe that the Olympic case was. *A free speech discourse that imagines that the only threat to vigorous public discourse is direct censorship by the state is blind to the multiple ways that state-granted property rights fence off the public domain, even directly restrain certain kinds of "speech."* In America, you are not *allowed* to call your games the Gay Olympics. We think of ourselves as defenders of free speech—ever vigilant against the risk that the police will be sent in to close down the presses. Meanwhile, behind our backs, the public domain can be privatized and sold off. Never fear. Authors, even state author-ized authors, aren't censors. It's a matter of definition.

A World Outside the Public World

In September 1993 a reviewer in the *Washington Post* noticed that David Leavitt's new novel, *While England Sleeps,* seemed to be strongly reminiscent of the life of Sir Stephen Spender. This aroused the interest of David Streitfeld, a journalist for the *Post* who has a professional interest in controversies over literary and scientific plagiarism. He called David Leavitt, who at first acknowledged quite freely that he had used Spender's autobiography as one of his sources. "It's an incident that is on the public record. When someone publishes an autobiography that in some ways is more history than literature, to use an historical event as a springboard for a novel didn't seem particularly problematic."[7] Streitfeld also asked Spender's reaction, sending him a copy of the book to illustrate the parallels. Spender was horrified. He called the use of his life story "plagiarism." After some legal wrangling, Leavitt's British publishers decided to withdraw the novel from publication and have all existing copies pulped. In June of 1995 it was announced that a "revised" edition was to be published by Houghton Mifflin. The Spender family again expressed outrage. Sir Stephen Spender died one month later.[8]

Leavitt is one of the new generation of gay writers. While sexual identity is central to his work, his novels don't seem as agonized about it as those produced by the Stonewall generation of gay activists. For him, Spender's life during the 1930s suggested a rich array of material—the Spanish Civil War, conflict over sexual identity, and so on. Spender's autobiography seems to have been particularly fascinating to Leavitt, because it is less explicit than today's books in discussing these issues. "There were things suggested but not articulated that I found fascinating. For instance, choosing between a heterosexual and a homosexual relationship, as well as what happens when a private relationship becomes in some way public because it is involved in a war." To the stew of moral issues involving plagiarism, moral rights, free speech, the public domain, and so on, perhaps one can add another issue—a generational difference of sensibility over sexual identity, perhaps even a trace of "outing."

What are we to make of all this? Spender wishes to prevent David Leavitt from writing about his life. His concerns are mainly *personal* and *aesthetic*—he does not want his privacy invaded and he believes that Leavitt has done a bad job. "Suppose the novel was by Tolstoy? He'd be welcome to my material."[9] On both grounds I am inclined to sympathize with Spender—what's more, Leavitt seems to have been badly advised over, and unbecomingly grudging in, his acknowledgments. At a couple of places, he comes very close to old-fashioned plagiarism. But forget Leavitt's qualities for a moment and focus on the larger issue.

If he had never written an autobiography, Spender would presumably have felt exactly the same way when he saw the—comparatively well-known—story of his life used as a source of fictional material. He would actually have had *more* justification as far as the privacy claim is concerned. But he would have been without recourse.[10] As an author, a person who has *sold the story of his life to the world*, Spender can get Leavitt's publishers to withdraw and pulp the book. His legal claim was based on the 1988 Copyright Act, which—paralleling European "moral rights" provisions—bans "distortion or mutilation" of an author's work in a way that prejudices his or her "honesty or reputation." One might imagine that the sight of a book being withdrawn and destroyed—particularly a book on a controversial topic—would prompt concern from civil libertarians of all camps. Can we withdraw the lives of famous and controversial people from the public domain? What about those who have not shunned publicity themselves, and whose own biographies—both personal and textual—exemplify the moral and political issues of their time? In fact, there was little or no civil libertarian response to the pulping of the novel. The British Society of Authors hailed the decision ringingly (if somewhat ambiguously) as "important for the integrity of writers."[11] Authors aren't censors. It's a matter of definition.

Transgenic Slavery

Transgenic organisms are those that combine genetic material from two species—part-horse, part-dog, say. The hippogriff becomes reality. The transgenic species is not surgically modified. It is changed at the genetic level. Thus the organism is created by design and is potentially capable of "naturally" reproducing itself. For many people, this sounds like science fiction.[12] It is not. Biotechnology *already* offers the possibility of mixing and matching genetically determined attributes of different species to produce new ones. And intellectual property law allows us to own them. U.S. Patent 4,736,866 was granted to Harvard University and Dr. Philip Leder on a transgenic mouse—the so-called oncomouse—containing human genetic material and engineered to be prone to cancers not normally occurring in mice. What happens when the patent application comes for a human-chimp hybrid—unusually strong and agile, with an IQ of 70, a limited vocabulary, and a biddable nature? Then we would really have a new *subject* of intellectual property laws.

> Chimpy™—Able to work in dangerous conditions without the need for pesky safety regulations, guaranteed not to form unions, or indeed to require any wages at all. Deluxe Chimpy™ reproduces to make new little workers. Pre-owned Chimpy's™ available. For underwater work, consider Flipper™, or Moby™. (Chimpy™, Flipper™, and Moby™ are genetically copy-protected. Breeding license required. *FBI notice:* Unauthorized reproduction is a violation of federal intellectual property laws and may be punished by destruction of illicitly bred copies, a $10,000 fine and up to five years imprisonment.)

The Patent Office has said that it will not grant patents on human beings because the Thirteenth Amendment prohibits the ownership of one human being by another. ("Neither slavery nor involuntary servitude, except as a punishment for crime whereof the party shall have been duly convicted, shall exist within the United States, or any place subject to their jurisdiction.") The question then becomes, what is a human being? To most people, the inclusion of human genetic material in a mouse does not make it human—no freedom from the badges or marks of slavery for the oncomouse. What if a chimp is given hands based on human genetic material, or a voice box? Is it only when we get to the brain that we begin to say "human, all too human"? Or what if we could make creatures that *looked* like human beings externally, but that were not sapient—for sex toys, say? Take a biological shell with the body of Marky-Mark or Vanna White and the brain of a hamster. (I refrain from the obvious repartee with conspicuous restraint.) Is it making things in our own image that triggers the protection of the Thirteenth Amendment? To put it another way, is the Thirteenth Amendment to be understood as a subset of the First Commandment?

All this does not lead me to conclude that "Chimpy" will be accepted any time soon. Distaste for the idea may come to us via Kant, Ecclesiastes, or Mary Shelley, but, whatever its source, there is more revulsion against making humanoids in the lab than against the other possible developments I discuss in this book. The patent claim for the sapient chimp-human hybrid may well be rejected because of a kind of naturalistic abhorrence—one with which I have some sympathy. Indeed, it seems fairly likely that there would be a greater reaction against ownership of biological creations that were nonsapient—the genetically engineered, fashion-model "meat-puppet"— than against the creation of arguably sapient entities that look nothing like human beings (artificial intelligences, transgenic dolphins, and so on). Those who write about artificial intelligence (AI) and transgenic species often start from the assumption that the immorality of slavery is the immorality of dominating other intelligences, a violation of the Enlightenment ideal of recognizing common reasoning powers, even when they are hidden under unfamiliar exteriors. In practice however, the *social understanding* of the Thirteenth Amendment might turn out to be, as I suggested earlier, a subset of the prohibition of idolatry and graven images—a prohibition of making beings in our own image. Looks may turn out to be more important than consciousness, just as Madison Avenue has always told us.

Samuel Butler has fallen out of favor as a creator of dystopias, but a few of the writers on artificial intelligence have discovered the passage in which he speculated on machine consciousness. In the persona of an Erewhonian philosopher, Butler points out that machine consciousness could not be judged by our current conceptions of intelligence—and does so in a way that would make Marvin Minsky proud:

> Consciousness, in anything like the present acceptation of the term, having been once a new thing . . . why may not there arise some new phase of mind which shall be as different from all present known forms of consciousness as the consciousness of animals from that of vegetables? It would be absurd to define such a mental state (or whatever it may be called) inasmuch it must be something so foreign to man that his experience can give him no help towards conceiving of its nature; but surely when we reflect upon the manifold phases of life and consciousness which have been evolved already, it would be a rash thing to say that no others can be developed and that animal life is the end of all things . . . There is no security against the ultimate development of a mechanical consciousness in the fact of machines possessing little consciousness now. A mollusc has not much consciousness . . . Assume for the sake of argument that conscious beings have existed for some twenty million years: see what strides machines have made in the last thousand! May not the world last twenty million years longer? If so, what will they not in the end become? Is it not safer to nip the mischief in the bud and to forbid them further progress?[13]

Artificial intelligence may be a little further away than sapient transgenic species—but not much. The phrase is generally used to refer to the possibility of electromagnetic devices that would possess consciousness. (This usage is in itself interesting. Why should the attempt to achieve *electromagnetic* artificial intelligence be the main locus of the philosophical and moral debate about the nature of consciousness? Many of the same issues are raised with transgenic species, biomechanical "wetware," or nonhuman animals, for that matter. Yet on the gut level, it is mechanical artifacts, rather than biological artifacts, that make people wonder about the meaning of awareness, intelligence, and personhood. Naturalistic assumptions strike again?) The debate over AI is a fascinating one, full of Turing tests and Chinese rooms, but I cannot enter into it here. Instead I want to bring up the following question: Suppose at some time in the near future there are rapid developments in expert systems, fuzzy logic, learning feedback loops, or whatever. Suppose we get a situation where there is actual social disagreement about whether artificial intelligence has been achieved. What happens when Microsoft's experimental machine appeals for sanctuary or when the demonstrators outside IBM claim that the Thirteenth Amendment is being violated by their current research programs? What happens in the case of reasonable dispute?

The point I mean to make is that—with both AI and the transgenic species example—the authorial paradigm offers us a way to reinvent slavery and to hide the reinvention from ourselves. The idea of physical ownership of a "naturally born" human being is anathema to us. We cannot imagine a situation in which one person comes to own another legitimately; neither cash nor conquest can provide an adequate basis for such a property right.[14] But what about an *intellectual* property claim? *If,* and it is a big *if,* the basis for social feelings about the evil of slavery is a natural rights formulation about the inherent equality of natural persons, then transgenic species and AI both offer a number of soothing and profitable ways to distinguish intellectual property from slavery. These are not "natural" persons but artificial ones. We recognize that corporations—as "artificial" legal persons—do not have the full range of rights possessed by natural persons. It would be "consistent" to say the same thing about these newly created sapient entities.

Above all, the distinctive feature of the cases I have discussed here is that the claim being asserted is that of the inventor/author/creator, rather than that of the slaver/master/conqueror. Without the slave-master, the slave still exists—and is better off in terms of liberty. Without the "author," the human-chimp hybrid or the artificial intelligence has no existence at all. Under a number of libertarian property theories, this would negate any finding of "harm."[15] Suppose, as I suggested earlier, that the strongest popular revulsion will be not against the ownership of another's consciousness, but rather against the ownership of something that *looks* human. The language of authorship, with its tendency to see the created object as arising *ex nihilo,* free from the claims of culture and morality, could well provide a dangerous way of concealing the moral issues involved in the ownership of intelligences that do not look human. Creation of nonhuman intelligences could be understood as the ultimate act of authorship. The language of the Declaration of Independence is instructive: "that all men are created equal, that they are endowed *by their Creator* with certain inalienable rights." In the most simplistic sense, we can imagine the "author" of the transgenic species or the artificial intelligence saying, "If it weren't for me, they wouldn't be here. I *am* their creator, and *I* gave them no such rights."

CHAPTER 13

Proposals and Objections

In the last two chapters, I tried to show that the author-vision can obscure disturbing political, economic, and moral consequences, and that it is presently doing just that on an international scale. For one thing, if one conclusively presumes a romantic vision of originality, one is more likely to neglect the importance of the public domain. This neglect means that property rights for "authors" can actually *restrict* debate and slow down innovation—by limiting the availability of the public domain to future users and speakers. The Gay Olympics case, the patenting of software, the *Kinko's* case, and the story of the rosy periwinkle show that this is not merely a possibility but a fact. Our current definitional denial of these consequences merely makes them all the more likely. The table on page 156 provides a summary of my analysis.

In this chapter I deal with some of the more likely objections to my analysis, and then offer some proposals for change, both political and legal. In most legal scholarship, the detailed proposals for reform are the capstone of the piece, but there are three reasons why I shy away from that position here. First, I am attempting to construct a social theory of the information society. To concentrate only on the specific policy proposals is to lose sight of the larger project. Even if that project is a failure, it is a *large* failure rather than a small one. Durkheim wasn't writing a book about the best height for bridge parapets.

I have arranged these tensions in two vertical sets. Each set is not a list of corollaries; indeed, they are sometimes internally contradictory. Thinking of the subject of intellectual property as "information" rather than "invention" does not commit one to Northrop Frye's view that artistic works can only be created from other artistic works. In fact, any particular portion of an information regime is likely to "mix and match," like a restaurant patron picking four dishes from column B and one from column A. *Nevertheless*, the entries in each column are most likely to be found in popular and scholarly discourse when linked to their vertical neighbors. Under the guise of resolving these problems, the effect of the author-vision is to make the items in the middle column either disappear or recede in importance.

Subject Matter	Information	Innovation
Economic Perspective	Efficiency	Incentives
Paradigmatic Conception of Problems	Transaction Cost Problems: barriers to the free flow of information lead to the inhibition of innovation / inadequate circulation of information	Public Goods Problems: inadequate incentives for future production lead to the inhibition of innovation / inadequate circulation of information
Reward (If Any) for . . .	Effort / Investment / Risk	Originality / Transformation
View of the Public Domain	Finite Resources for Future Creators	Infinite Resources for Future Creators
Vision of the Productive Process	Development Based on Existing Material: "Poetry can only be made out of other poems; novels out of other novels. All of this was much clearer before the assimilation of literature to private enterprise."[a]	Creation *ex Nihilo*: "Copyright is about sustaining the conditions of creativity that enable an individual to craft *out of thin air* an *Appalachian Spring*, a *Sun Also Rises*, a *Citizen Kane*."[b]
Normative Starting Point	Free Speech / Free Circulation of Ideas and Information	Property Rights: the creator's "natural" right, the reward for past creation, the incentive to produce again

a. Northrop Frye, *Anatomy of Criticism*, 96–97 (1957).

b. Paul Goldstein, "Copyright," 38 *Journal of the Copyright Society of the U.S.A.* 109, 110 (1991) (emphasis added).

Second, there is the danger that I would replicate the very deterministic and technocratic errors I criticize. The structure of thought I have described here is wildly overdeterministic in the way it equates the abstract need for some set of incentives with the actual current arrangement of intellectual property rights. My analysis pointed out that undervaluation of the public domain is reflexively produced when one builds an intellectual property system around an expanded idea of originality. Thus mine is at least a two-sided, rather than a one-sided, account. Still, to claim that my analysis could—without further empirical evidence—set the correct level of incentives, or dictate the appropriate duration of copyright, would be ridiculous. (Though not quite as ridiculous as the claims of the proponents of the current system, who say they can do exactly that from an even weaker theoretical basis.) Third, if we are truly living in an information economy, it is particularly vital that the intellectual property system be opened up to democratic oversight and control. Like most property systems, intellectual property is a system designed by elites. But to a greater extent than with other property systems spurious claims to the "technical" and "scientific" status of the subject matter have curtailed the possibility of democratic dialogue. Thus the more detailed suggestions I make here are *examples* of the direction in which the intellectual property system should move, rather than the imperious dictates of "correct" analysis. My goal is to diminish the number of spuriously scientific and determinist prognostications about the intellectual property system, rather than to add to it.

Objections

Apart from the arguments already dealt with, the most common objections I have encountered deal with my focus on ideology and the social construction of knowledge. Rather than taking my points piecemeal, these responses seek to dismiss the importance of the author vision *tout court.* I have encountered three basic versions: "It's just words." "It has to be this way." "And anyway it's good."

"It's Just Words": The Rhetorician

It is true that the regulation of information entails a lot of "author talk," but you are mistaken in thinking anyone believes it. The idea of

an "original" author or inventor is just a conventional figure of
speech, a convenient rhetoric to justify an intellectual land grab.

If it were true that the authorial vision was only used as a rhetorical
device, used hypocritically *by* disbelievers *to* disbelievers, I should
still think it worthy of study. "Hypocrisy is the homage that vice pays
to virtue."[1] By studying a society's sanctimonious rhetoric we can
understand its normative orthodoxy. I would certainly be willing to
admit that the image of the romantic author is *sometimes* used consciously as rhetoric; when Time Warner enlists Byron, Proust, or even
D. W. Griffiths as the champion for their flow of royalties, we may
be a little suspicious of the message. But, attractively cynical though
it is, I simply do not accept the assertion that the author vision I
describe is *only* rhetoric.

First, authorship is not merely a handy argument; it is a premise,
the major premise, of our intellectual property system. We could have
an intellectual property system that merely tried to provide adequate
returns on investment in information production—one that is just as
happy ensuring payment to the person who invests time and labor
in collecting names and numbers for a telephone directory as the
person who, after much work, invents something new. Instead, originality is our touchstone—not just our rhetoric. Second, those who
speak so cynically of mere "rhetoric" portray themselves as being
entirely above the society that consumes this rhetoric, free from its
cultural assumptions and untouched by its deepest beliefs. I find myself unconvinced by both the specific assertion and the general attitude. The idea of the original, transformative creator is coded deep
into our speechways and our patterns of thought. Not only is it a
legitimately attractive idea, an iconic vision of human potential, but
it forms the baseline against which we judge other accounts of art,
science, and information production in general.

"It Has to Be This Way," Response 1:   The Resigned Cynic

> You may be right in saying that the language of authorship is a cen-
> tral one, but that is just because it serves the interests of the most eco-
> nomically powerful actors. Microsoft, Pfizer, and Time Warner want a
> certain kind of intellectual property regime and that is the one they
> get. The system expresses the interests of the most powerful, always
> has and always will. Consequently, while your project may be very

nice as an academic exercise, it is of no conceivable importance to anyone.

This argument takes the position that ideology is of no importance and that legal regimes are based merely on economic self-interest. In most versions, it adds a relatively crude determinism—that "the big companies" have a single set of interests that they consciously pursue and get enacted into law. (Interestingly, the determinist argument is often coupled with the rhetorical argument, to produce the surprising assertion that authorial language is mere rhetoric, just froth and show, while a regime built around the author figure is historically inevitable. In this rather puzzling picture, the authorial paradigm is both irrelevant *and* inexorable.) I have heard the determinist objection from a wide range of people—a Marxist patent law scholar, a science fiction cyberpunk author, a liberal legal historian, an iconoclast computer programmer. Some Chicago School economic analysts of law express similar conclusions, but without the sigh of regret. Entitlements in a legal system go to those who are able and willing to pay the most for them—and a damn good thing too.

Obviously there is some truth to this picture, but as the *sole* explanation of the current situation, I think it substitutes cynicism for analysis. First, it is hard to identify a group of corporations with consistent interests in the intellectual property field, broadly or narrowly conceived. Take computer software as an example, and Microsoft as the hardest case for my argument. Surely at least Microsoft has a simple set of interests in intellectual property? (Namely, "More, More, More.") Yet even here, in the very worst case for my thesis of a complexity of interests, the reality turns out to be a little more complicated. Microsoft wants broad protection of operating systems—but not always too broad, because otherwise Microsoft Windows would be held to have infringed on the "look and feel" of the Apple operating system.

If we look beyond Microsoft, a company that is in the economically enviable position of having copyrighted the alphabet, we find that the complexity increases. When it comes to issues such as decompilation, the large software companies have interests both in the protection of software (their own) and in a *limitation* on the protection of software (their competitors'). More generally, in the absence of a strong ideology of authorship, we might expect attitudes toward intellectual property to move in cycles as bulges of new companies enter the market. Even within this generational analysis, we would expect further variation across industries depending on the ease with which investment in research and development can be recouped without intellectual property protection. Some new market entrants may want an expansive conception of the public domain so that they can utilize the accumulated expertise of their predecessors, while others may believe that investment in a new area can only be justified by the possibility of a monopoly rent on the likely results. Differences in risk preference would presumably also play a role. Even with the long-term players, views should shift more over time as market posture shifts. As a participant in a project to break into the operating system market, IBM has a rather different attitude toward intellectual property than it did when its mainframes defined the universe of computers.

If we actually find that corporate lobbying centers on the expansion of intellectual property regimes, both domestically and internationally, does this refute my analysis of the author paradigm, or reinforce it? Given the actual diversity of interest that a more detailed economic analysis reveals, it seems possible that corporations' perception of self-interest is just as often a *result* of the author paradigm as it is a *reason* for it.[2]

Second, and more important, the author-vision produces economically irrational results. The "periwinkle effects" detailed in Chapter 11 are a prime example. Precisely because the system is built around the idea of originality, it tends to undervalue the importance of sources, of the public domain. At present it may be in the *individual* interest of the individual drug company to secure biological material and ethnobiological knowledge for free. But it is in the collective interest of the companies in the drug industry to ensure the continued existence of their raw materials. Thus we have the classic argument for state intervention to avoid free rider problems; so long as one company could "free-ride" on the preservation efforts of others, each will hold back, hoping the others will do the work. It would not be rational for any one drug company to change the way it operates, but it would actually be in the interest of all to shift to a regime in which it was mandatory to devote some proportion of profits to the maintenance of biological diversity and perhaps cultural survival. *Failure to do so may signal the uncritical acceptance of a particular ideology of information production rather than a cool-headed pragmatism about self-interest.* Again, I would argue that the corporate perception of self-interest is just as often a *result* of the author paradigm as it is a *reason* for it. Finally, even if there were *no* truth in the argument I put forward here—even if all corporations had somehow rationally converged on a monolithic position on intellectual property—we would still want to work out whether the corporate position was in the long-term interest of anyone else. Even the most fatalist of the cynics wants to know something about the reality on which his cynicism is based, if only so he can be assured that his sigh of resignation is perfectly pitched.

"It Has to Be This Way," Response 2:
The Historical Determinist

> The author paradigm you describe was an inevitable *functional* by-product of the development of widespread print technology at the end of the sixteenth century. To talk as if we had any choice among paradigms is profoundly misleading. If, indeed, the author vision is doomed it will be because it does not fit the material realities of contemporary information technology and not because we "decide" it is a bad idea. For example, within the copyright arena narrowly conceived, greater ease of copying will make the authorial paradigm obsolete, if the possibility of levying individual fees for each electronically metered "use" does not make it moot first. Consequently, the attempt to explain the negative effects of this kind of thinking to some imaginary audience is an entirely futile one. Economic and technical changes called the author figure forth and only those forces can lay it to rest.

This is a deeper, but no less enervating, determinism than that of the person who believes that "the big corporations" are the moving hand of history. On a crude level, it has become our orthodoxy that social meaning in general, and law and ideology in particular, are mere adjuncts to technological and economic change. My reaction to this argument is a complicated one. Obviously such change is important, but I fail to see the simple definite correlations between technological change and legal innovation that are so often assumed.[3]

At first sight, it seems reasonable to believe that the second thing off the Gutenberg press was the romantic author, but both history and analysis tend to clutter the artful simplicity of this thesis. Yes, it is plausible that the greater the ease of copying, the more the need for *some* kind of "copy"-right.[4] The possibility of large-scale profit *from* books and the possibility of large-scale copying *of* books arise at the same moment. It is the ease of "copying" that makes information a potential public goods problem in the first place. But what kind of regime do we have to solve this, built around what kind of assumptions? The Stationers Company in Elizabethan England had an apparently functional system of allocating and registering the privilege to publish certain books, protected by a quasi-legal system of dispute resolution by the guild. At least within a pervasively regulated industry such as Elizabethan printing, guild allocation could have fulfilled some of the functions of copyright in guaranteeing that no one would try to horn in on anyone else's literary turf.[5] (Think of the protections against competition on allocated routes within the regulated airline system.) At the other extreme, one could imagine a comprehensive system that simply tracked the public goods problem case for case, giving monopoly property rights to all those who produce goods, one unit of which can satisfy an infinite number of users at close to zero marginal cost. This would cover many of the problems of a copyright regime, but it would also cover the "unoriginal" telephone directory produced in the *Feist* case. We have neither of those systems. Why?[6] It is unconvincing to say that the printing press *requires* the authorial–original creator model I describe here—as if technology and economic organization existed in some Tupperware container that seals out ideology, aesthetics, and the social construction of reality. We should uncouple the factitious determinacy of the *actual* legal regime and ideology we end up with from the technologically driven need to have *some* legal regime or ideology.

The determinist makes a category mistake—identifying the concrete social forms produced by the last four hundred years of our history with the abstract *idea* of functional needs. When we turn from history to prognosis, the same thing happens. Yes, developments in information technology will certainly have a huge effect on both the utility and the unintended consequences of our intellectual property regime (though the arrow of influence runs both ways—from technology to ideology *and* back again.) That is one of the premises of this book, after all. But the specific consequences of those technological developments are harder to figure out. Perhaps greater ease of copying will undermine an author-centered regime, or make it seem even more important. The latter is where I would put my money. Perhaps electronic metering of use will make copyright superfluous, or perhaps it will simply be used to enforce a copyright-based regime. Perhaps the appropriative, cut and paste technology of the Internet will make us question the very idea of originality, or perhaps the Net will remain an electronic ghetto, cut off from the "respectable" world of literary production (no modems in Proust's cork-lined room). *Perhaps* the psychic and ideological attractions of authorship will continue to manifest themselves long after aesthetic theory and information technology have supposedly left them far behind. I have explained why I think so. Whether I am right or wrong, the simple argument from technology fails to move me. The determinist imagines self-interpreting technologies "announcing" their needs to a world of rationally adaptive social institutions. That is an interesting picture, but one that belongs in 1950s science fiction rather than social theory.

"And Anyway It's Good":   The Defender of Authorship

> How can you deny that there is something noble in authorship and in the larger idea of basing intellectual property rights on originality? There is a difference between originality and mere grunt work, and the former is worthier than the latter—in both Kantian and utilitarian terms. Shakespeare deserves better intellectual property protection than Grisham, let alone a telephone directory; Einstein deserves more recompense than Nintendo. What's more, if *anyone* ought to believe in property rights based on originality, it is someone who believes—as you seem to—that iconoclasm is to be valued and that the human capacity to wreak great changes in our life plans, our cultures, and our societies is one of the proudest attributes of the species.

Strange as it may seem, I *do* think that there is something noble in originality in general and authorship in particular. I don't know if anyone takes the caricatured position that it is impossible to distinguish between the cultural contributions of Shakespeare and Grisham. I certainly do not and I would be quite happy rewarding the former more than the latter, based precisely on the degree of original material they added to the public domain (although our current system doesn't, and Shakespeare didn't have any copyright protection at all). Finally, if one is going to be romantic about something, our ability radically to transform culture, self, and society is a pretty good candidate.

The first problem is that this argument proves too much. In order to have any practical utility, the definition of originality has to be broadened so much it loses much of its romantic appeal. Earlier I quoted Holmes swooping down from the Olympian heights of art to the reality of a circus poster: "The work is the personal creation of an individual upon nature. Personality always contains something unique. *It expresses its singularity even in handwriting,* and a very modest grade of art has in it something irreducible which is one man's alone. That something he may copyright."[7]

Intellectual property covers the tax-preparation book as well as *Othello,* the manual for WordPerfect as well as the poetry of Elizabeth Bishop. There is nothing wrong with this; quite the contrary. In fact, it is because the definition of originality has been stretched so far that the regime is not already paralyzed by its inability to cover the kinds of "information–public goods" problems I described earlier. In those cases where the gatherer of information can be smuggled under the mantle of romantic authorship, the artifact will still be covered, though the overall pattern of coverage will be extremely unsatisfactory on any *utilitarian* ground. (For example, the person who puts together a book of "lucky lottery numbers" will get copyright protection, whereas the person who compiles a telephone directory will not. Useful alphabetical listings are not "original," unlike wholly spurious arrangements of numbers and silly text.) But whatever the accidental virtues of the system, one cannot defend it as if its definition of originality was anything but "thin."

Second, if we *really* cared about originality, we would cover a lot of things that we do not presently cover. Albert Einstein and Stephen Hawking get *no* intellectual property rights for their discoveries of "natural laws," while the inventors of the Slinky and the paper clip can really rake it in (unless their inventions were "obvious"). Suppose for a moment that our intellectual property system really *was* designed to produce an adequate amount of invention and original discovery. One would think that the paradigmatic case for protection would be the foundational discovery which produces no immediately useful product. That is the one that is least likely to be compensated in other ways, after all. Yet that is exactly the discovery we do *not* protect. Strike two against the strong defense of originality.

Third, if one truly worships Great Artists or Inventors, one is under an obligation to concede that the current system can make their lives a lot more difficult. The tendency of the current system to undervalue the importance of the public domain can deprive the truly creative among us of the raw material necessary to create their next transformative artifacts. Examples of this process abound, but the most recent to catch my eye was a letter written to the official publication of the Association for Computing Machinery, *Communications of the ACM*.[8] The letter was a protest against Clause 1.5 of the ACM's new Code of Ethics, a clause that announced a "moral imperative" for members to "honor property rights, including copyrights and patents." The letter was signed by seven prior recipients of the ACM's highest awards, including Marvin Minsky and Richard Stallman, founder of the League for Programming Freedom, which opposes software patents on the grounds that they inhibit innovation, slow down research, and convey few useful benefits for society. The fascinating thing here is that opposition to extensive intellectual property regimes is coming from precisely the people that those regimes purportedly honor and defend: the innovative geniuses and inventors. This demonstrates the fallacy in assuming that creators' interest is only in increasing intellectual property protection. It also should give one pause before concluding that all opposition to intellectual property is based on "author envy."

Proposals

A large portion—the most important portion—of this book is devoted to understanding the various ways we now think about information. It deals with the tensions within our current patterns of thought and the unintended consequences that might occur as we rely—consciously or not—on those patterns to create the legal and institutional frameworks of an information society. But my goal is prescriptive as well as descriptive. The general issues and concrete suggestions that follow are rooted in my analysis of information discourse in the market, the polity, property, and the family. They are not, of course, *entailed* by that analysis. A more detailed set of suggestions is provided by the Bellagio Declaration (see Appendix B).

General Issues

There is, in both classical liberalism and market economics, an ironic tendency toward an egalitarian idea of information. Both the market and liberal democracy deal with hard value judgments by aggregating individual acts of choice. Should vanilla ice cream cost more than chocolate, should teachers be paid less than missile engineers? Should human growth hormone go to the rich basketball player or the poor dwarf? How do we decide the government's policies or pick society's leaders? Both systems answer that question by addition. In the market, everyone makes their rational consumer choices, "votes" with her dollars, and the self-regulating system produces prices— societal valuations—as the result. In the realm of democracy, everyone just votes. In the political or economic terrain thus constructed, each person pursues her own life plan. The system's legitimacy comes from the fact that it treats each participant's choice equally— with formal neutrality. If you have a dollar to spend, the market doesn't care how you spend it. If you have a vote and a political "voice," you may deploy them as you choose.

Criticism from the left has always focused on the "if's" in the preceding sentence. Freedom to spend one's dollar as one wishes is of little use to the person without the dollar in the first place. The promise of egalitarian democracy is somewhat undercut by the fact that both in voting and in other forms of political behavior wealth is such a significant predictor of success. The general criticism focuses on the aridity of a system that postulates as a formal matter that all are equally free to make the same choices—whatever the distribution of resources. The classic example is that both rich and poor will be punished equally for making the "choice" to sleep under the bridges in Paris. The question of disparate actual resources is not relevant.

There is an irony in these criticisms when we turn to the subject of information—a simple point of great potential significance for the information society. *Both the market and liberal democracy use the idea of rational choice as their nostrum for every normative issue, often ignoring the questions of resource distribution that would make that choice a reality. But even the most formally arid system based on rational choice requires that its participants have one actual resource—information—if the choice is to function as a normatively appealing bedrock.* On this one issue, about this one resource, both the market and democracy move from the realm of formal, negative liberty toward that of substantive positive liberty. The journey is not always completed, as my discussion of insider trading illustrated. But as that discussion also showed, the impulse is there.

The second idea of information is in some ways the opposite of the first. Issues ranging from the Bork hearings to the debate over credit records or the analysis of blackmail offered here all testify to the strength of our notion of informational privacy: the idea that there is some kind of natural right to control information about ourselves, to restrict access, (intermittently) to prohibit commodification, and to control dissemination.

One should be careful not to make too much of this. No social results flow automatically from such a picture of the world. Information too can be recharacterized as something all are presumed to have or as a resource about which the system is conclusively indifferent—"Caveat emptor" or "Ignorance of the law is no excuse," for example. When claims of privacy butt heads with the market need for accurate consumer information, privacy often loses. But even at our most carefully qualified and hedged, we would be silly not to realize that when dealing with this resource our society's languages of entitlement are less grammatically hostile to the claims of the dispossessed and the marginalized. This is not just a description of a useful rhetorical ploy; the way we think about the world sets up limits for us. It prepackages certain normative claims as potentially valid, others as marginal, and it prevents still others from even being understood as valid speech acts.

This part of my discussion does not provide a neat set of programmatic proposals. Instead, it is intended as a sort of guidebook for those who are engaging in scholarship, activism, or decision making on a specific information issue. But the moral geography of information issues I described here is important for another reason. It maps out the landscape of "public" and "private" information, the territories that abut the information property issues on which I have spent so much time.

THE PUBLIC DOMAIN

We need to show much greater concern for the public domain, both as a resource for future creators and as the raw material for the marketplace of ideas. Despite all the ballyhoo about the information highway, there has been little or no coalition politics on this issue. The reporters who were outraged by the restrictive meaning given to journalistic fair use in *The Nation* case need to form common cause with the programmers in the League for Programming Freedom. Rap musicians who wish to "sample" other recordings in their songs should see their interests tied not only to parodists and appropriationist artists but to the software companies that want the antitrust law enforced against Microsoft and to environmental activists trying to save the biologically diverse public domain of seed "land races." These groups in turn should realize that they have interests in common with developing nations that object to the patenting of life forms, and so on, and so on. At the moment, the doctrinal divisions between different areas of intellectual property are mirrored in the isolation of the individual groups who are seeking to restrict the privatization of the public domain. My analysis here suggests a philosophical, moral, and even an economic agreement, concealed by the absence of an overall picture of the struggle. In just the same way as PEN, Amnesty International, the ACLU, journalists, and teachers' unions understand apparently discrete "free speech issues" as being linked together, the coalitions that have been drawn into the fight over the public domain need to understand the connections between their diverse battles.

Preserving the public domain does not always mean getting rid of property rights. Sometimes the problem is that a property system constructed around the idea of authorship recognizes only certain kinds of contributions, and does so in such a way as to reduce the likelihood that the public domain itself will survive. The discussion of shamanic sources and periwinkle effects in Chapter 11 offers pertinent examples. In these cases, the answer will be not to have fewer intellectual property rights, but rather to have different ones. At this point, a critic might say that my analysis is contradictory. Having spent all this time saying we had too little concern for the public domain and too much intellectual property, I am now arguing for the creation of new forms of intellectual property. I have nothing against contradictions, some of my best friends are contradictions, but in this case I think I am not guilty of one. My point is not that we always need *fewer* intellectual property rights, or that we always need *more* intellectual property rights. Rather, my point is that an author-centered system has multiple blindnesses and that we should strive to rectify some of them. In general, these blindnesses result in the creation of too many intellectual property rights, because a strong author-centered system minimizes the importance of the public domain, and conceives of information issues predominantly from the incentives point of view. But these blindnesses also result in the undervaluation of nonauthorial contributions to the production process, often in a way that would curtail the possibility of future production, or in the suppression of the interests of the audience or market for the product. In an essay accompanying the Bellagio Declaration (see Appendix B), my fellow drafters and I put it this way:

> Our analysis indicates three overlapping areas of neglect in an overly author-centered vision of intellectual property: neglect of unacknowledged sources and non-authorial modes of scientific and cultural production, neglect of the interests of the "audience," and neglect of the importance of conserving the public domain for the benefit of innovators and consumers alike. Measures designed to counteract these tendencies do not fall neatly into a simple choice to have "more" or "fewer" intellectual property rights. Indeed, one of our criticisms of contemporary discourse about intellectual property is its simplistic binary format. We favor a move away from the author vision in two directions; first towards recognition of a limited number of new protections for cultural heritage, folkloric productions, and biological "know-how." Second, and in general, we favor an increased recognition and protection of the public domain by means of expansive "fair use protections," compulsory licensing, and narrower initial coverage of property rights in the first place.

DATABASES

A reconfigured intellectual property regime would be attentive to the times when the current system provided too little protection as well as too much. For example, the focus on "invention" may well provide too little incentive for the compilation of databases, or may cause socially unproductive labor to be expended in trying to arrange those databases in an "original" way just to bring them under the mantle of intellectual property. However, there are many ways to finance such information production. The technology itself may provide a method for controlling access; the tax system might offer incentives; and so on.

The creation of expensive and useful databases may also impose indirect costs on and generate benefits for public discourse. These too should to be taken into account. At present Mead Data Central's NEXIS service allows journalists electronically to search fifteen years' worth of the big newspapers in the United States in just a few seconds. Say a state senator gives a speech attacking homosexuals. I check to see if his name was ever mentioned in any newspaper, only to find that he was himself picked up, before he entered public life, for soliciting in a public bathroom. (In this case, we might think that the privacy objection has been "waived," though it is worth noting that one of the greatest protections of privacy is the anonymity purchased through bad recordkeeping. To the extent that information technology makes information instantaneously retrievable, it has obvious costs for privacy.) But what about the more tangible costs of this excellent service, namely, the expense of paying for it? What happens if only the big news media can afford it? Do we need some form of publicly subsidized service? Or does this form of research push journalists even further toward the recitation of disconnected prurient facts, an uneasy hybrid of railway timetable and a peep show? The point is that these questions need to be addressed directly, not defined out of existence, as is often done under our current system.

SUI GENERIS SYSTEMS

In discussing information economics, I argued that there was no such thing as a generic public goods problem. Instead, there were a host of problems: underproduction, overproduction, diminution of the public domain, and so on. In addition, the different *loci* for intellectual property rights present strikingly different characteristics, yet we tend to cram them all into the same categories in a way that would have made Procrustes proud. The table at the beginning of this chapter could be used as a kind of checklist for each area. In some industries or areas of life, information production might seem as worthy of protection as innovation. Some innovations might offer high returns even in the absence of intellectual property protection, because of the ability of the innovator to trade on the knowledge of the likely effect the innovation will have on the market. Others might have such a short half-life that the ability to be first to market offers ample rewards. Still others might present us with a dilemma in which every reward for innovation has the direct effect of stifling future innovation.

Obviously, no intellectual property system could be perfectly sensitive to all these market differences, even if we could identify them in advance, or associate them with particular classes of products with a high degree of confidence. That is not the question. Any legal rule ends up covering both too much and too little. The question is not whether the system could solve all these problems, but whether—as seems likely—we could do better than the two-sizes-fit-all scheme we have at the moment. A reasonable place to start would be to study sui generis systems for particular types of information products—software is the most salient example.

INTERNATIONAL EQUITY

One central theme of this book is that many of the "human rights" and even more of the "international development" issues of the twenty-first century will be intellectual property issues. Earlier I described the regressive and inefficient operation of the current international intellectual property system. I am not under the illusion that this expression of sentiments provides an algorithm with which to resolve the world's intellectual property problems. In fact, it raises as many questions as it answers. My hope, however, is that they are better questions. What we have right now is an exponentially expanding intellectual land grab, a land grab that is not only bad but dumb, about which the progressive community is largely silent, the center overly sanguine, and the right wing short-sighted.

. . . .

It is certainly possible to maintain our faith in the premises of the current system while we fiddle with its effects. Patent systems could have more general transfer of technology requirements built into them; copyright regimes could have compulsory low-cost licensing for educational use in developing nations; "neighboring rights" regimes could make up for some of the current shortcomings in the treatment of sources; and so on. As the prior paragraphs suggest, I have nothing against incremental progress. I am quite happy to make moderate, reformist suggestions about the protection of databases and the appropriate interpretation of the fair use provisions of the copyright act. Here are some examples of reforms based on the analysis I have put forward.

- Copyright should subsist only for twenty years, with a broadly defined fair use protection for journalistic, teaching, and parodic uses—provided that those uses were not judged to be in bad faith by a jury applying the "beyond a reasonable doubt" standard.

- Software should be covered not by patent law or by copyright, but by a sui generis system that would take more account of the costs of creation, the possible returns in the absence of intellectual property protection, and the extent to which an intellectual property right would concentrate market power and erect roadblocks to further development.

- Drugs derived from the ethnobotanists' pharmacopeia should be subject to a 10 percent tax and the proceeds split equally between the indigenes and a fund to promote biological diversity.

- Patents should be voidable at the instance of any party who can prove that an adequate return would have been provided merely by being first to market, with the state paying the legal fees for successful suits.

- All intellectual property right systems should be subject to periodic auditing by the General Accounting Office, an auditing to test whether—with each type of product—the intellectual property right was providing too high or too low an incentive to future production and research, and to attempt to balance that incentive against the monopolistic and anticompetitive results of intellectual property protection.

Although I give these only as examples of the kinds of reforms that should be considered, I think they are well worth pursuing. I am particularly interested in opposing the worldwide expansion of intellectual property rights, backed with trade sanctions. But my real concern lies with the general *ideology* of the intellectual property system.

The author-vision that I have described here is not merely a set of mistakes in thinking about the balance between incentives and efficiency, public domain and private right. It is the focal point of a language of entitlement, an ideology every bit as rich and important as that of wage labor and the will theory of contract. Those who are negatively affected by this language of entitlement—be they programmers, satirists, citizens of the developing world, or environmental activists—see only the impact within their narrow bailiwicks. Focusing on effects, they fail to see the structure underlying those effects. Thus they lose the possibility of both theoretical analysis and the practical recognition of common interests. This truth may not set us free, but it is a start.

Conclusion

nformation is different. If the shift to an information society means anything, it means thinking about information as one of the most important resources in the society. We do not do this in a vacuum, in some sterile cultural "clean room." We are always already inside, or between, a set of histories, ideologies, institutions, and practices. And in those practices, in the languages of market, family, property, and politics, information is different from other resources. Classical liberalism is not a doctrine hospitable either to egalitarian controls *over* resources or to positive rights *to* resources. When the resource concerned is information, however, the answer is much more equivocal. The discussion of insider trading showed just *how* equivocal. To oversimplify, information is the only resource of civil society that is "supposed"[1] to be distributed in an egalitarian manner; it is the only resource where both microeconomics and the First Amendment seem to push in the direction of free availability and transmission. Courts show a singular willingness to void bargains because of information disparities between parties, even when they are reluctant to strike down bargains directly for other kinds of power disparities. On the other end of the spectrum, the idea of privacy is remarkable both in the way it puts control over information—as opposed to any other resource—at the heart of personhood and in its degree of support for state intervention to give citizens actual control over this resource even when they cannot purchase such control through the marketplace.

We see the strength of these embedded—and potentially contradictory—ideas of information in each new area of regulation. What we lack is a sense of the connections *between* the different ideas. The romanticists of the Internet repeat the mantra "information wants to be free" at the same moment that the cypherpunks condemn the Clipper chip for violating electronic privacy and the National Telecommunications Information Agency (NTIA) claims that the information highway will be based on the principle of universal access. Do these positions complement or contradict each other? Each group can give you, as it were, a set of directions that will bring you to its own position. But as yet they have no *maps*.

In between the egalitarian, public ideal of information and the personal, private one lies the realm of property and that is where I focused in much of this book. I have given a slew of examples, ranging from environmental concerns in the rain forest to dark electronic dystopias. My point, however, is a simple one. Much of the current case law, scholarly literature, and international debate gives the impression that if we wished to consider issues of distributive justice, or of international development, or of citizens' interest in a thriving public domain, we would have to give up a rigorous analytical system that carefully balances incentives to production against the needs of current use. From my perspective, nothing could be further from the truth. The analysis is massively indeterminate at every stage. It is based on claims for which there is inadequate empirical evidence. It relies on an aporetic set of economic ideas in which most issues could convincingly be portrayed as *either* a public goods problem requiring commodification or a monopoly–transaction cost problem requiring competition and the free flow of ideas. As a system it is held together by definitional fiat, despite that fact that the definitions of "idea," "expression," "parody," "originality," "fact work," "fair use," "nonobviousness," and "natural law" merely reproduce the very tensions they were designed to resolve. Finally, the system is both grounded on and imbued with an ahistorical and romanticized vision of authorial creation: it takes as a universal premise that which should be its occasional conclusion.

Admittedly, there are a number of things the authorship vision does well. It conceals the indeterminacy of much of the utilitarian analysis. More positively, the concerns it stresses are real. Authors and inventors often *do* need to be encouraged, protected, lauded, and rewarded. The romantic vision of authorship offers an attractive idea of creative labor—transcending market norms, incorporating both work and play, and entailing a world in which workers have a real connection to and control over the fruits of their labors. This is a vision that we might want to expand far beyond the limited realm of property in information. As currently constructed however, intellectual property law in particular and information issues in general seem to be in the thrall of an idea that is taken as truth where it should be questioned as dogma.

In my analysis I have assumed that we are moving toward a society more centrally concerned with the production, manipulation, and use of information. As assumptions go, this seems to be a reasonable one. Obviously, any judgment about the best way to analyze information issues will depend in part on the fears (and hopes) we have about this process. Classical liberalism lays great stress on the dangers posed by a runaway state, and so liberalism as a political doctrine has much to say about the best means for the restraint of state power. *What fears do we have about information and the much heralded information age?* From here it is hard to tell what the future holds, or what kind of ideas and cultural traditions will be of use. Inevitably, we rely on historical analogies to grasp the situation, and just as inevitably, the analogies mislead as well as enlighten. But this seems no reason to give up the attempt. In an information world, what would be the equivalent of Hegel and Weber's analyses of the public-private split, Marx's labor theory of value, Pigou's analysis of externalities? Here are three possibilities that draw on the ideas developed here.

Information Class

I am concerned with ideas and lines of thought that tend to be suppressed by the current way of thinking about information and society. This is a familiar intellectual exercise. Writing about the industrial revolution and the transformation of capitalism, Marx turned the rhetoric of private property and entrepreneurialism on its head, arguing that wealth was socially produced but privately appropriated. According to Marx, law, ideology, religion, and philosophy all operated so as to obscure this "skimming off" of surplus value. In place of a market theory of value, and the confused positivist–natural right theory of property of his time, he offered a labor theory of value, transforming workers from "another factor of production" into "the *real* producers of value."[2] Forget for a moment that I used the bugbear name of Marx. Forget even the incoherent theory of labor value that he produced to answer his own question. Concentrate on the idea behind his theoretical project. How should we understand "value" in the information society? Whose contributions will our system recognize and reward, whose will it ignore, or genuinely fail to see?

One danger dimly prefigured here is that we are moving toward a new, highly stratified class system—a world broadly divided between manipulators of information and "sources." In a society where one group compiles, modifies, redesigns, and commodifies information gleaned in part from the genes, consumption patterns, and culture of the rest of the population, the rhetoric of justification and entitlement bids fair to be based on author talk. Just as the market–natural right vision of property could be used to claim that workers were receiving exactly the proportion of social wealth to which they were entitled, so the authorship vision can be used—both rhetorically and theoretically—to obscure, undervalue, or simply ignore the contributions of "sources." Precisely because author talk is genuinely attractive, because it does express desirable moral and utilitarian ideas, its power is likely to be all the greater. How does one break the grip of a rhetoric of entitlement that systematically obscures and undervalues the contributions of one part of the population and magnifies those of another part of the population? One method is to propose an alternative rhetoric of entitlement. For Marx, the labor theory of value was the *true* theory, rather than a way of thinking that helped to expose the partiality and contentious quality of the settled arrangements of his society. By contrast, I merely aspire to show the suppressed side of information and intellectual property, not to dethrone the author and crown the source instead.

The examples that I gave ranged from the *Moore* case to insider trading, from copyright doctrine to indigenous medical lore in the Amazon, and the tragedy of the commons in the forests of Madagascar. Using them, I argued that for complex reasons relating to the ideology of public and private spheres in a liberal society, the regime of intellectual property is built around a particular romanticized conception of authorship. I argued that this regime often has the effect of devaluing sources and that, even within the conventional language of policy analysis, such a devaluation seems sometimes to have very bad consequences. (And sometimes to have very good ones—but more by accident than by design.) This, surely, is something we want to know. Apart from this pragmatic concern, I have a more intangible one—*Ideologiekritik* rather than policy analysis. Marx's errors notwithstanding, it *is* important to see the lacunae and contentious assumptions involved in a particular society's discourse of entitlement—the language in which entitlement to that particular society's primary resources is both described and justified.[3] To have a critical understanding of the rhetoric of entitlement in an information society, one would need an analysis of conventional discourse about information, as well as of the more complicated, more sophisticated, and more highly formalized version of that discourse provided by the language of microeconomics. I have tried to provide both here. Idea does not produce reality. Our vision of the world does not entail our social structure, but neither can our social structure exist without relying on, without *being*, a complex way of understanding the world.

If there is a class structure that comes with the author-vision I described, it will not be one in which authors, programmers, artists, and engineers inherit the earth. In fact, one of the truly remarkable things about the author vision of entitlement is how indifferent it is to the needs or interests of actual authors or creators. Imagine the young software engineer, trying to start a new software company in the approved iconoclastic, entrepreneurial manner. He finds that many of the programming tools he wants to use have already been patented by large companies, some of which now make *more money from litigating patent claims than they do from actually producing something new* (a result that could make only a lawyer happy). What would Shakespeare do if the Stationers' Company owned the alphabet? In the end, our software engineer ends up working for Microsoft, and the tendency toward oligopoly continues. This tendency is enhanced precisely by the fact that we think of authors or creators as "original"—that is what defines them. If originality is the warrant for property rights creation *ex nihilo* will be our unconscious model of the productive process, and our undervaluation of the public domain will follow as the night follows the day. Intellectual property rights (in fact, all property rights) produce monopolies as well as incentives; they produce incentives because they are monopolies. If we undervalue the public domain, we will tend to give too many intellectual property rights, thus delivering a powerful anticompetitive, oligopolistic chunk of state-backed market power into the hands of the established players. Result? Authors and creators lose. We all lose.

Information Overload

My second alternative future is a strongly counter-intuitive one, one that violates not only the basic assumption of post-Enlightenment thought that more information is always a good,[4] but also the assumption that the rate of progress of science and society will vary directly with the rate of accumulation of information. I offer the scenario anyway, not because I believe it will necessarily become reality, but because the very possibility of this set of events tends to be suppressed by the uncritical acceptance of an Enlightenment view of information.

It could be that we are headed for an information overload—a brownout caused by overproduction and consumption of information. This is an idea that ought to be familiar to the legal profession. During the 1980s, bright young lawyers worked hundred of thousands of hours on contested leveraged buyouts. They pored through corporate documents, built up electronic databases to keep track of their research, searched for any case, treatise or law review article that could give their side an edge, and checked every possible line of authority on computerized legal research services. They even rechecked the final product an hour before filing just to make sure that no more recent decision had been added. On the other side, opposing attorneys did exactly the same thing. Even if one believes that all those leveraged buyouts actually led to a more efficient allocation of resources, it is hard to believe that the legal process would not have been just as efficient and just as equitable if both sides had commanded a slightly lower level of effort.

This legal equivalent of the nuclear arms race could be described in terms of market failure, or inefficient discovery rules, or prisoners' dilemmas, or hyperlexis. But any thorough analysis would have to concede that one of the problems was not just hyperlexis, but Hyper-LEXIS—an explosion of the availability of information that, under a particular a set of societal assumptions and background rules, sometimes leads to a socially irrational investment of resources. There is no a priori reason that the scenario of information overload must be confined to the adversary system. We might imagine a world in which inventors were overwhelmed by the difficulty of searching patent banks, where specialists found it impossible to keep up in their fields, where researchers worked in increasing isolation—an isolation produced by the sheer quantity of available information. Increasing specialization, balkanization of the disciplines, an irrational fixation on "authority" and cross reference, and a scholarly habit of conspicuous citation,[5] even an erosion of public debate by information overload—these signs are not so very alien from the world we live in that we could afford to dismiss them completely. Nor are they so different from the results one would expect in a world that romanticized authorship and focused overwhelmingly on incentives to the immediate producer. That might be food for thought.

In the 1930s, welfare economists used the example of the factory that spews pollution onto the landscape, but pays nothing for it. In that case, they declared, overproduction is caused by a failure to internalize all externalities. If the full social costs of production were taken into account, the factory's products would be uneconomical. Who knows, maybe a future Pigou will write an analysis of the blindness of information economics at the close of the twentieth century[6] and will point out that we were oblivious to the "information pollution" we were creating, that our economics did not force us to internalize the consequences of our overproduction, leaving us free to continue to "pollute."[7] Like the welfare economics of the thirties, the economics of information welfare might well lay part of the blame on an ideological insistence on the image of the isolated economic actor. For us, that actor is the author, and our romance is almost as great as the romance with which the classical economists endowed the self-reliant economic atoms of the laissez-faire Lochner era.

Information Politics

What of the realms in which the author figure apparently does not play so great a role? What of public debate, privacy, or requirements for the disclosure of information advantages in market transactions?[8] It is here that I find myself being most optimistic. My own views are loosely egalitarian and favor an expanded and decentralized view of democracy.[9] But egalitarianism and democracy are norms that liberalism confines to a comparatively narrow sphere and a restricted ambit—as evidenced by everything from the state action requirement (unequal treatment by private actors is not a violation of the Constitution) to the notion of formal equality in the public sphere. One way to express my conclusions is that, on information issues, liberal political theory is less restrictive, and consequently, from my perspective, many of the criticisms aimed at liberalism are less powerful. Precisely because information is conceived of as being different from other forms of wealth and power, precisely because it seems like an "infinite" resource, it does not get exiled to the world of civil society, and information disparities are not simply taken as "given," as a postulate that must be accepted before we begin. Thus to me it seems that judges are more willing to strike down bargains on the basis of information disparities than other forms of (nonphysical) power disparities, that legislatures are willing to criminalize insider trading but not other forms of market advantage, that people who see nothing wrong in the state's refusal to *fund* abortion clinics find *Rust v. Sullivan* troubling.[10] (*Rust* was the case that upheld the "gag rule" on doctors in federally funded Title X programs; the "gag rule" forbade the mention of abortion as a medical option, even if the doctors thought it medically desirable.) When we are analyzing SEC mandated disclosure statements or the extent of a tort law duty to warn of the dangerous tendencies in a product, there is more of a willingness to look at outcomes and results rather than formally equal access—to take into account the actual education level, social class, and native language of those who are the targets of the warnings, rather than conclusively assuming a formal equality.

Whatever the practical limits of the "exceptions" to my comments here—and I would accept them to be significant—it seems at least that we often do not confine egalitarian norms as narrowly when we are dealing with information rather with some other form of wealth or power. If we are, indeed, moving toward a more information-based society—whatever that means—then we are doing so with an available reservoir of egalitarian cultural understandings and political ideals. This fact, in and of itself, guarantees nothing at all. But it is not unimportant and, from my perspective, it is a very good thing.

What about privacy? Egalitarian and redistributive political solutions can be supported by arguments keyed to the requirements of the individual ("to flourish, every human being needs . . .") or supposedly deduced from abstract distributional principles. The interesting thing about privacy is that it offers up a view of human personality that has normative implications about the control of resources. To be fully a person, one must have control over . . . The resource named is information. Again, a society that often has a hard time imagining that persons need control over food, shelter, medical care, and so on, can find room for the idea that the most intimate sphere of personhood must be defined in part by a right to control information—the right of privacy.

In 1890 when Samuel Warren and Louis Brandeis wrote their famous article, "The Right to Privacy," the idea that personhood entails control over information may not have seemed like much of a challenge to the distribution of power in society. In a society based on the transmission, accumulation, and manipulation of information, it might seem rather more of one. Of course, it *could* turn out that the ideal of privacy was precisely the basis needed for a discourse of entitlement in an information society. It could be manipulated to allow an electronic society to justify the appropriation of intimate details, just as the labor theory of property was used by Locke to "boot himself up" into market society. Again, one must resist the temptation to reason from rhetoric to reality. Nevertheless, it seems to me that the gradient of argument runs the other way. Using the concept of privacy, one is arguing downhill when challenging the imperial tendencies of a data-based society and arguing uphill when supporting them.

The question that remains to be answered is whether the social harm we should be most concerned about is underproduction, overproduction, the tragedy of the commons, the commercialization of an electronic public sphere, the corrosive effect of information technology on privacy, or merely straightforward distributional inequity. This book cannot answer that question. Indeed, I have tried to show that there are conceptual reasons why the question is unanswerable *in the abstract*. But it does show that the ways that we think about information at the moment may actually blind us to important aspects of each one of those problems, making us that little bit more helpless in the face of them. But some of our current ideas about information also offer reservoirs of strategy, tactics, and social belief which—when viewed in the abstract—seem egalitarian in the extreme. To someone like me, who believes a lot of our social ills come from the restriction of egalitarian norms, that fact has an optimistic ring.

....

I have offered a theory of information, but the theory is more like a road map or a tool kit than a blueprint or an algorithm. One cannot *deduce* social consequences from the existence of an authorship theory of intellectual property or an information-centered vision of privacy. This book has pointed out tendencies and gradients of argument. It has described in detail the reasons that the romantic vision of authorship spreads far beyond copyright. It has shown the aporias at the heart of information economics. It has prognosticated about the way that the rhetoric and ideology of the past will interact with the social arrangements of the future. It suggests that the information age may be constructed in part around the conflicting valences of a romantic individualistic notion of information production, an egalitarian notion of public information, and a positive liberty theory of privacy. It points out the dangers of an author-centered ideology of entitlement, and argues for a large-scale restriction of intellectual property rights, an expansion of the public domain, and a greater sensitivity to the needs of both sources and audiences. These are important things to understand, surely. But where do they leave us as a practical matter?

Information is different. This book has tried to point out some of the potential, some of the freedom to reimagine and remake our society, that this difference might offer. If this freedom is real, it exists partly in the precarious balance *between* the gravitational pulls exercised by each of the information stereotypes described here. But analysis gets one only so far. This is, at best, a potential freedom. No theory can grant it to us. It must be taken through collective action and imagination, through the postulation of a fictive "we" that becomes real only in the context of a practice which presupposes the very community it calls into being. The intellectual land grab I have described here can be halted, and even pushed into reverse. We do not *need* to turn the information society into a world of private censors and a sterile, narrow public domain, a world of slow technical progress in which the divide between the rich and poor countries is widened farther, where intellectual property rights become the vehicle for oligopolistic concentrations of corporate power worse than those of a cyberpunk dystopia. In fact, in cold hard economic terms, leaving aside most of the moral and political commitments that actually make me care about these issues, we would be better off if we change the path we are currently on. There are even powerful communities out there, ranging from software developers and drug companies to civil libertarians and environmentalists, that have much to gain from changing our path—if they can see and act on this precarious moment of common interest. The opportunity may be missed, we may take it and mess it up, or it may ultimately seem never to have existed. And what else is new? But it would be sad to look back in fifty years time and say, "if only . . ." Almost anything is better than that.[11]

. . . .

An Afterword on Method

Many academic books nowadays begin with an elaborate treatise on method, a preemptive strike against likely misunderstanding, a denial of various disfavored types of conceptual imperialism. The theorists' list of methodological disclaimers has taken the place of the seventeenth-century scholar's anticipatory propitiation of popes and princes. Each has similar protestations of fidelity to orthodoxy and hopeful invocations of the names of possible protectors. Although today's academics seldom write as well as their seventeenth-century predecessors, they have the same nervous tone, utter the same reassuring denials of heresy, even appeal to the protective authority of the great. I have some doubt about the utility of these methodological apologias. But given my prior work, I probably seem in dire need of one. It is hardly fashionable to write a book about an ideology exhumed from legal materials and credited with social importance. It also seems strange coming from someone whose previous academic work has been on the virtues of "local" theory. Accordingly, here is a note on what I thought I was doing.

Societies justify themselves; they have to. A society is not merely a particular configuration of people and productive resources within a geographical boundary; it is also a set of stories—moral, political, religious, and economic—about why the existing order is desirable, or inevitable, or natural, or neutral (or, more confusingly, all of the above). This is the first great insight of the study of social theory. The second insight is that a host of qualifications is needed before one can talk about the first insight in a way that reveals more than it obscures. Here is mine.

For a start, these justificatory stories are not monolithic, or monolithically apologetic. Sometimes an apparently reactionary body of cultural material is turned to ends subversive of an existing order. In seventeenth-century England, naturalistic arguments were routinely invoked to describe and thus justify the status quo. From the evidence we are left, it seems clear that large numbers of people saw the world through a mental framework in which inequality, social hierarchy, and the power of the landed gentry were both "natural" and biblically sanctioned. (Here, as in many other cases, the construction of reality is more important than the arguments that are deployed within an assumed reality, though the latter are certainly evidence of the former.) Nothing could be more protective of the status quo than this set of naturalistic assumptions, or so one might think. Yet the radical democratic movements of the seventeenth century were able to turn this naturalistic pattern of beliefs on its head. "When Adam delv'd and Eve span / who then was the gentleman?" If there had been no social inequality in the Garden of Eden (the theological equivalent of the perfect market), then one could deduce that any social inequality in contemporary society was the result of the Fall— a human artifact or accident with no command on our loyalties. These are hardly the ideas one would expect from a society numbed by a monolithic set of naturalistic assumptions.

Still more qualifications are needed. There is the identity-politics qualification; often one group in a community has attitudes very different from those suggested by the pieties of the dominant culture. Yet there is also the hegemony qualification; sometimes sets of beliefs that seem to an outsider very clearly to support one particular group are embraced by the dominated together with the dominator. "False consciousness" theories are normally associated with the left, but they actually cross ideological lines. Even those who decry the idea of "false consciousness" when it is used by others tend to deploy it themselves. Cold Warriors who condemned the smug certainty of Leninism and emphasized indigenous resistance to Communism also had to deal with the idealistic embrace of corrupt and oppressive nomenklatura-run state socialism by some of the very people who suffered under it. Admittedly, very few examples of this process will be accepted by all concerned. For some, Phyllis Schlafly's embrace of the chains that bind her would represent proof of the possibility of false consciousness. Others would see proof of false consciousness in the supposed ability of elite feminists to "brainwash" working-class women into renouncing the sex roles that protected them, when they were offered in return an abstract ideal from which only the fortunate few could benefit. Neither the feminist nor the antifeminist, however, can object to the *notion* of hegemony, and that is my point.

After the hegemony qualification comes the visibility qualification; these story lines or sets of assumptions vary in the ability of the participants in the culture to *see* them, let alone criticize them. For example, in the contemporary United States, it is possible to challenge the assumption that the "free market" will always produce the right answer. It is harder to challenge the language of freedom and choice in which such discussions are often couched and hardest of all to question the epistemology of autonomous subjects on which it depends. Some criticisms are seen as legitimate attempts to explore the internal problems of a system of beliefs, some are seen as challenges to the system itself, and some cannot even be understood as meaningful speech acts.

For those who are repelled by any analysis containing the word "ideology" or "legitimation" or "critical," it is vital to stress the "wavicle" qualification. Just as light must be conceived of as both a particle and a wave, so we should be able to conceive of an ideology—a structure of beliefs, a set of justificatory stories, a way of constructing reality—as having the potential to be *simultaneously* apologetic and critical, a legitimating veil and an incisive theory of justice. The notion of formal equality enunciated in the language of classical liberalism is a theory of justice with extraordinary power and utopian vision. We all use it, like it or not, when we attempt to understand some new situation and decide whether it is just. What's more, I would say we are the better for it. Yet the normative ideal of formal equality—the law is just if it treats all citizens in a way that is formally equal—obscures as well as reveals. Both rich and poor will be prosecuted for sleeping under the bridges in Paris. Do we therefore have justice?

In the same way, the language of entitlement to information I describe in this book is both apologetic and critical. It is far from being a monolithic aid to the powerful, an immutable system of oppression, a functionally determined expression of the interests of a particular class, or the dynamics of a particular stage in economic development. In fact, one of the more interesting things revealed by this study (and by the study of history in general) is the polysemic and open quality of languages of entitlement. This indeterminate and multivocal quality of our moral traditions seems to me to be a good, rather than a bad, thing. In fact, it may have a positive but theoretically neglected role to play in cultural criticism. If there is indeed a symbiotic relationship between social practices and the systems of thought that describe them and prescribe for them, how can we ever criticize? Why doesn't norm simply follow the contours of fact, like a chair cover following the outline of a chair? Part of the answer, I think, is that there is not just one set of cultural practices, one set of norms, and one set of interpretations. To put it another way, the indeterminacy *within* justificatory systems and the simultaneous existence of *conflicting* justificatory systems are two important reasons that we can make normative criticisms in the first place. Freedom is often to be found in the tension *between* traditions. This could be called the postmodern qualification.

For my purposes here, the most important qualification is that these stories, these languages of power, are not stable. They change through time, evolving internally and in reciprocal relation to social pressure, technological change, and a host of other, less easily enumerated factors. Because of the powerful and unfortunate legacy of determinist social thought, this (rather obvious) point has to be followed by yet another qualifier. History does not have stages, like stations on a railway line. ("Leaving Feudalism, next stop Capitalism. This train does not stop in Mercantilism or The Comprador Economies. Mind the doors, please.") Historians such as Fernand Braudel have shown that there was capitalism in the thirteenth century and that there is feudalism in the twentieth. Nor does history have a drive wheel, a single determining factor or relationship that powers all other change through an intricate system of societal gears. Nevertheless, we would be impoverished by our own sophistication if we could not point out that the rhetoric, beliefs, and networks of assumptions that described, explained, and supported a thirteenth-century agricultural society are not the same as those of a nineteenth-century industrial one. More daringly still, we should still be able to mention that one of the reasons for the difference is that the society's central method of production and main form of wealth had changed.

My focus here is on just such a process of rhetorical and interpretive change, the tectonic shift to a society in which information is, and is recognized to be, one of the principal forms of wealth. The justificatory stories of classical liberalism, market, household, and property right all have things to say about entitlements to information. As I pointed out at the beginning of the book, if the future is made from fragments of the past, then the discourse of entitlement in an information society will have to draw on images of information that were produced in a society where information bore a very different relationship to technology, to power, to wealth, a different relationship even to our own bodies. What will happen? What unintended consequences, what perverse systems of rewards, will be generated? What historical relics will suddenly become extraordinarily important? What well-established ways of thinking will be discarded as ludicrous and outmoded? What groups will get an initial advantage from the normative terrain and what groups will find themselves struggling to enunciate claims delegitimated by the very structure of thought and perception in which they are developed? The response to all these questions, of course, is that no one knows, but this book is a first stab at imagining some of the more likely answers.

The Bellagio Declaration

The following declaration comes from the Bellagio Conference on Cultural Agency/Cultural Authority. The conference was organized by two of my colleagues in the authorship project, Martha Woodmansee and Peter Jaszi, and funded through the generosity of the Rockefeller Foundation and the Washington College of Law, American University. The conference brought together computer scientists, environmentalists, anthropologists, literary critics, authors, publishers, and legal scholars to discuss the effects of intellectual property on their disciplines. I had the honor of being one of the drafters of a declaration designed to capture the sense of the meeting.

The Declaration

WE, the participants at the Bellagio Conference on intellectual property, come from many nations, professions, and disciplines. We are lawyers and literary critics, computer scientists and publishers, teachers and writers, environmentalists and scholars of cultural heritage.

SHARING A COMMON CONCERN with the effects of the international regime of intellectual property law on our communities, on scientific progress and international development, on our environment, on the culture of indigenous peoples; in particular,

APPLAUDING the increasing attention by the world community to such previously ignored issues as the preservation of the environment, of cultural heritage, and biodiversity; but

CONVINCED that the role of intellectual property in these areas has been neglected for too long, we therefore convened a conference of academics, activists, and practitioners diverse in geographical and cultural background as well as professional area of interest.

DISCOVERING that many of the different concerns faced in each of these diverse areas could be traced back to the same oversights and injustices in the current international intellectual property system, we hereby

DECLARE the following:

FIRST: Intellectual property laws have profound effects on issues as disparate as scientific and artistic progress, biodiversity, access to information, and the cultures of indigenous and tribal peoples. Yet all too often those laws are constructed without taking such effects into account, constructed around a paradigm that is selectively blind to the scientific and artistic contributions of many of the world's cultures and constructed in fora where those who will be most directly affected have no representation.

SECOND: Many of these problems are built into the basic structure and assumptions of intellectual property. Contemporary intellectual property law is constructed around the notion of the author, the individual, solitary and original creator, and it is for this figure that its protections are reserved. Those who do not fit this model—custodians of tribal culture and medical knowledge, collectives practicing traditional artistic and musical forms, or peasant cultivators of valuable seed varieties, for example—are denied intellectual property protection.

THIRD: Such a system has strongly negative consequences. Increasingly, traditional knowledge, folklore, genetic material and native medical knowledge flow *out* of their countries of origin unprotected by intellectual property, while works from developed countries flow *in*, well protected by international intellectual property agreements, backed by the threat of trade sanctions.

FOURTH: In general, systems built around the author paradigm tend to obscure or undervalue the importance of "the public domain," the intellectual and cultural commons from which future works will be constructed. Each intellectual property right, in effect, fences off some portion of the public domain, making it unavailable to future creators. In striking respects, the current situation raises the same concerns raised twenty years ago by the impending privatization of the deep-sea bed. The aggressive expansion of intellectual property rights has the potential to inhibit development and future creation by fencing off "the commons," and yet—in striking contrast to the reaction over the deep sea bed—the international community seems unaware of the fact.

FIFTH: We deplore these tendencies, deplore them as not merely unjust but unwise, and entreat the international community to reconsider the assumptions on which and the procedures by which the international intellectual property regime is shaped.

IN GENERAL, we favor an increased recognition and protection of the public domain. We call on the international community to expand the public domain through expansive application of concepts of "fair use," compulsory licensing, and narrower initial coverage of property rights in the first place. But since existing author-focused regimes are blind both to the importance of the commons and to the interests of non-authorial producers, the main exception to this expansion of the public domain should be in favor of those who have been excluded by the authorial biases of current law.

SPECIFICALLY, we advocate consideration of special regimes, possibly in the form of "neighboring" or "related" rights regimes, for the following areas:
—The protection of folkloric works.
—The protection of works of cultural heritage.
—The protection of the biological and ecological "know-how" of traditional peoples.

IN ADDITION, we support systematic reconsideration of the basis on which new kinds of works related to digital technology, such as computer programs and electronic data bases, are protected under national and international intellectual property regimes. We recognize the economic importance of works falling into these categories, and the significant investments made in their production. Nevertheless, given the importance of the various concerns raised by such a regime—concerns about public access, international development, and technological innovation—we believe that choices about how and how much to protect databases should be made with a view to the specific policy objectives such protection is designed to achieve, rather than as a reflexive response to their categorization as "works of authorship."

ON A SYSTEMIC LEVEL, we call upon states and nongovernmental organizations to move toward the democratization of the fora in which the international intellectual property regime is debated and decided.

IN CONCLUSION, we declare that in an era where information is among the most precious of all resources, intellectual property rights cannot be framed by the few to be applied to the many. They cannot be framed on assumptions that disproportionately exclude the contributions of much of the world community. They can no longer be constructed without reference to their ecological, cultural and scientific effects. We must reimagine the international regime of intellectual property. It is to that task this Declaration calls its readers.

Discussion

Contemporary intellectual property law is constructed around the notion of the author, the individual, solitary and original creator, and it is for this figure that its protections are reserved.[1] The "author" in the modern sense is the sole creator of unique works of art, the originality of which warrants their protection under laws of intellectual property—particularly those of "copyright" and "authors' rights." The notion, however, is neither natural nor inevitable. Rather, it arose at a specific time and place—eighteenth-century Europe—in connection with a particular information technology—print. Nevertheless, it remains the dominant paradigm in our global, multicultural, post-colonial electronic age, a paradigm that stretches beyond copyright to influence all types of intellectual property rights. We must recognize that there is a politics to "authorship"; as presently understood, it is a gate through which one must pass in order to be given property rights, a gate that shuts out a disproportionate number of non-Western, traditional, collaborative, or folkloric modes of production.

Although intellectual property rules are defended as economically necessary, kneejerk reliance on "authorship" may in fact destructively undervalue important contributions to art, science, and culture. Examples are legion. Drugs drawn from the rainforest or from indigenous pharmacopeias do not economically support the protection of either. Traditional patterns and dances can be taken without permission or recompense, perhaps diminishing the chance that the culture that originated them will survive. Exclusively authorship-focused systems also run the risk of cherishing the ownership of ideas over their circulation, the purses of the potential audience over their minds.[2] There is no guarantee that the current system of intellectual property maximizes free speech and informed democratic debate, and much evidence that it does not.

In general, systems built around the author paradigm tend to obscure the importance of "the public domain," the intellectual and cultural commons from which future works will be constructed. The assumption of these systems is that one must reward creators in order to ensure new production. Yet the "reward" has its costs. Each intellectual property right, in effect, fences off some portion of the public domain, making it unavailable to future creators. If one is concerned about promoting future production of books, ideas, inventions, and works of art, then one must be just as careful in one's protection of a vigorous and diverse public domain, a "commons" of scientific, literary, and artistic raw material, as one is in one's protection of the author's rights and incentives. Recently, there has been a dangerous international tendency to suppress the former concern and to concentrate only on the latter.

The process has taken place with remarkably little recognition or outcry. In striking contrast, during the late sixties and early seventies, the members of the General Assembly of the United Nations showed great prescience in enunciating the concept of the "common heritage of mankind." They declared that the resources of outer space and the deep seabed must be available to all, that they should not be entirely consumed by the first nations to have the technological capacity to do so. In striking respects, the current situation with respect to intellectual property rights is similar. Certainly the same distributional and developmental issues are raised. For example, under the current regime, corporations from nations with the most advanced technology may manage to secure patents on the majority of rainforest–derived drugs before an indigenous drug industry develops. The aggressive expansion of intellectual property rights also has the potential to inhibit future creation by fencing off "the commons." Despite these similarities, the international community has been comparatively silent on the issue. One reason for this silence may be the perception that intellectual property rights are not a "zero-sum game," that, unlike rights to manganese nodules or oil, they are potentially of infinite extent and thus that future producers are always left enough raw material out of which to create their own works. But this perception is more a by-product of faith in the author vision, than a careful analysis of literary, artistic, and scientific production. Patents given on commonly used lines of computer code may impede the production of future programs. Extensive copyright and publicity rights may allow public figures to control access to vital information about themselves. Patents on seed landraces based on indigenous varieties may actually inhibit the maintenance of genetic diversity and local cross-breeding. The blandishments of the international information industries notwithstanding, more intellectual property rights may actually mean *less* innovation, less heterogeneity in culture and environment and a less informed world of public debate.

The international community must move towards a just world order of intellectual property rights, and in what follows we appeal to national governments and international organizations to consider specific measures toward that objective. At the same time, we acknowledge our local responsibilities, and those of the constituencies we represent: to resist, where necessary, unjust extensions of intellectual property regimes.

Our analysis indicates three overlapping areas of neglect in an overly author-centered vision of intellectual property: neglect of unacknowledged sources and non-authorial modes of scientific and cultural production, neglect of the interests of the "audience," and neglect of the importance of conserving the public domain for the benefit of innovators and consumers alike. Measures designed to counteract these tendencies do not fall neatly into a simple choice to have "more" or "fewer" intellectual property rights. Indeed, one of our criticisms of contemporary discourse about intellectual property is its simplistic binary format. We favor a move away from the author vision in two directions; first towards recognition of a limited number of new protections for cultural heritage, folkloric productions, and biological "know-how." Second, and in general, we favor an increased recognition and protection of the public domain by means of expansive "fair use" protections, compulsory licensing, and narrower initial coverage of property rights in the first place.

Where the first point is concerned, we recognize the importance of incentives for cultural conservation, in the form of grants of exclusive rights. Indeed, such grants may be essential to provide recognition to the contributions of those groups and individuals who the present system tends to exclude. But we do not propose to address this problem of exclusion merely by expanding the "authorship" construct, with all its legal and ideological associations. We advocate consideration of alternative regimes—perhaps based on expansion of the system of "neighboring" or "related" rights. By this terminology we refer to legal regimes like those which, in some countries, protect the interests of performers, of broadcasters, and sound-recording producers. These laws, although they participate in some of the assumptions and contain some of the features of traditional copyright or "authors' rights" laws, are not justified on the grounds that they extend protection to "works of authorship." Rather, they exist to recognize the special economic and/or cultural contributions of groups whose activities fall outside the traditional definition of "authorship."

Specifically, we advocate consideration of new regimes, possibly in the form of "neighboring" or "related" rights, in the following areas:

—The protection of folkloric works.
—The protection of works of cultural heritage.
—The protection of the biological and ecological "know-how" of traditional peoples.

In each case, this consideration should entail inquiry into the appropriate individual, group, or state entity in whom intellectual property rights should be vested, into the duration and intensity of those rights, and into the means by which reasonable public access to the categories of works in question would be assured, including such devices as "fair use" privileges and systems of compulsory licensing.

The same considerations should be borne in mind as the international community enters into a systematic reconsideration of the basis on which new kinds of works related to digital technology, such as computer programs and electronic databases, are protected under national and international intellectual property regimes. We recognize the economic importance of works falling into these categories, and the significant investments made in their production. Nevertheless, given the importance of the various concerns raised by such a regime—concerns about public access, international development and technological innovation—we believe that choices about how and how much to protect databases should be made with a view to the specific policy objectives such protection is designed to achieve, rather than as a reflexive response to their categorization as "works of authorship."

Moreover, whether intellectual property protection takes the form of traditional copyright or authors' rights regimes, or of new ones in the nature of "neighboring rights," it is critical that its elaboration be undertaken with a commitment to the preservation of the "public domain" as a cultural and intellectual commons from which all people, from all nations, are free to draw. In an effort to redress unfairness in the existing global scheme of intellectual property, it is important that we do not err in the direction of uncritically and unqualifiedly increasing the level of protection available for all forms of cultural production.

We are acutely aware of the importance of access to information for cultural, economic and educational development, and we support new measures on the part of international organizations to promote access to new information technologies in developing countries. At the same time, we recognize that it is critical to support more traditional forms of information distribution, such as book publishing, in those countries, through initiatives to make capital available and to encourage the licensing of copyrights on reasonable terms.

Likewise, the international intellectual property community can and should do more to recognize the special situation of the countries of Eastern Europe and the former Soviet Union, by extending to them for a limited term (under multilateral and bilateral agreements) a special regime identical or similar to that applicable to developing countries under the Appendix provisions of the 1971 Act of the Berne Convention.

In conclusion, we would suggest that—at least historically—laws of intellectual property, as well as laws of neighboring and related rights, have been designed by a few individuals and applied to many. The goal of a just world order of intellectual property may be best advanced by addressing the process by which intellectual property laws are made and revised, to provide more representation for interests other than those of governments and information industries— through the inclusion of more non-governmental organizations and community groups in the dialogue. For a long time, intellectual property has escaped attention in international discussions of justice, self-determination, economic development and human rights. If that assessment was ever true, it has ceased to be so now. The advent of the information society, the collaborative networks typical of production on the electronic frontier, the increasing importance of intellectual property rights to corporate balance-sheets and national balances of payment, the global circulation and commodification of culture—all of these events conspire to thrust upon us the need to imagine and simultaneously to *build* a world intellectual property system that is both just and wise.

. . . .

This document was framed by lawyers, anthropologists, environmentalists, computer experts, literary critics, publishers and activists. Inevitably, each of us would change some word or phrase, or shift some emphasis. Its signatories agree however, to the central themes and spirit of this Declaration and to the urgent sense of concern that motivated it. Institutional affiliations are provided for identification purposes only.

....

Notes

Preface

1. When I use the word "problems," I do not mean to imply a simple issue of means-end fit, with all else assumed away. (The tap drips; how can we fix the drip?) The issue is a deeper one, in which both ends and means are contested and contestable. (Lower the water pressure? Get rid of indoor plumbing?)
2. Simon L. Garfinkel, Richard M. Stallman, and Mitchell Kapor, "Why Patents Are Bad for Software," 8 *Issues in Science and Technology,* 50 (Fall 1991).
3. See Appendix 1.
4. Alvin Toffler, *Future Shock* (1970); see also John Naisbitt, *Megatrends: Ten New Directions Transforming Our Lives* (1982); Taichi Sakaiya, *The Knowledge-Value Revolution: A History of the Future* (1991). It is notable that one of the most thoughtful commentators on the information revolution is not an academic—but rather a cattle-ranching, Grateful Dead lyricist. John Perry Barlow, "The Economy of Ideas: A Framework for Rethinking Patents and Copyrights in the Digital Age (Everything You Know about Intellectual Property Is Wrong)," *Wired,* 84 (March 1994); "Decrypting the Puzzle Palace," 35 *Communications of the ACM* 25 (1992); "Stopping the Information Railroad," available on the World Wide Web at URL http://www.ora.com/gnn/bus/ora/features/barlow/index.html.
5. Anne W. Branscomb, *Who Owns Information?* From Privacy to Public Access (1994).
6. Bruce Sterling, *The Hacker Crackdown: Law and Disorder on the Electronic Frontier* (1992).

7. M. Ethan Katsh's well-crafted book is a fine example. See *The Electronic Media and the Transformation of Law* (1989). Katsh believes that greater access to information may undermine the "abstractions of the law" "such as rights." Id. at 262, 265. He seems to believe that this process will make the law more "humane," a word that appears here—as it does in some early critical legal theory—to be an antonym of "abstract." See James Boyle, "The Politics of Reason: Critical Legal Theory and Local Social Thought," 133 *University of Pennsylvania Law Review* 685 (1985). Yet his other positions in the book are marked by a mainstream liberalism that prod me into wondering whether Katsh would really *want* "abstractions" such as the "rights of free speech" to be undermined. When he says that the information age will make law more like a conversation, I find myself wondering who will get to talk and who will have to listen. Finally, when he says that privacy will "change," I find myself beset by dystopian images entirely unlike the ones that appear, from his tone, to be evoked for him by that phrase. Id. at 168–197. All of Katsh's assessments may be right—a transformation devoutly to be wished, no doubt—but it is hard to escape the conclusion that he is able to be so vague and yet so optimistic precisely because he is talking about *information*—the life blood of the Enlightenment.

8. There are exceptions of course. Michel Foucault and Peter Jaszi started me thinking about many of these issues. See Michel Foucault, "What Is An Author?" in *Textual Strategies: Perspectives in Post-Structuralist Criticism*, 141 (J. Harari ed., 1979), Peter Jaszi, "Toward a Theory of Copyright: The Metamorphoses of 'Authorship,'" 41 *Duke Law Journal* 455 (1991). Mark Poster, David Bolter, and Jane Gaines have all written fascinating books about the intersection between the information society and cultural studies: Mark Poster, *The Mode of Information: Poststructuralism and Social Context* (1990); David Bolter, *Writing Space: The Computer, Hypertext, and the History of Writing* (1991); Jane Gaines, *Contested Culture: The Image, the Voice, and the Law* (1991). Thomas Streeter has written interestingly about communication studies, information theory, and critical legal thought in "The Cable Myth Revisited: Discourse, Policy, and the Making of Cable Television," 4 *Critical Studies in Mass Communication* 174–200 (1987). Doubtless, there are others I should mention.

1. The Information Society

1. Dickens's lectures and broadsides are only the most famous example of the many complaints leveled by foreign writers against American literary piracy. See Sidney Moss, *Charles Dickens' Quarrel with America* (1984).

2. "Nimbus Announces Breakthrough Holographic Labelling Technology for Compact Discs" *PR Newswire* (September 11, 1995).
3. Actually, when it comes to this issue, I am something of a heretic. On the one hand, I agree with the ACLU's Privacy Project that the technology poses a profound threat to both privacy and liberty. On the other hand, I have greater faith than the ACLU in the enduring inefficiency of both the market and the state. In the Conclusion I suggest that a general study of information offers two modest reasons for optimism. First, in our current society, information issues are about the most advantageous ground on which to fight issues of unequal control and power. The very idea of privacy is centered on control over information. To put it crudely, we are willing to speak expansively of the need for the state to step in to ensure an individual's privacy, something we do with few other valuable resources. Second, the pervasive Enlightenment discourse of information makes it seem as though more information is always a good. In fact, as any librarian will tell you, the opposite is just as likely to be true. In the section on information brownout, I discuss the way in which failure to consider information externalities could lead to an information explosion in which the capacity for processing would be overwhelmed by the capacity for production. Big Brother may be watching, not you, but a computer screen with an hourglass icon and the legend "Please Wait."
4. "DNA is a long, unbranched polymer composed of . . . four types of subunits [nucleotides]." The subunits contain the bases adenine (A), cytosine (C), guanine (G), and thymine (T). DNA carries genetic information in its long chain of nucleotides. See *Molecular Biology of the Cell*, 95 (Bruce Alberts et al. eds., 2nd ed. 1989).
5. Diamond v. Chakrabarty, 447 U.S. 303 (1980).
6. Lawrence M. Fisher, "Mining the Genome: Big Science as Big Business—A Special Report; Profits And Ethics Clash in Research on Genetic Coding," *New York Times*, sec. 1, p. 1, col. 3 (January 30, 1994).
7. Larry Thompson, "Genes, Politics, and Money: Biology's Most Ambitious Project Will Cost a Fortune, But Its Value Could Be beyond Measure," *Washington Post*, Z12 (February 24, 1987).
8. Michael Schrage, "What Happens When Marketers Learn How We Wear Our Genes?" *Washington Post*, G3 (November 12, 1993).
9. In personal terms, this project had a very different point of origin than is suggested by the preceding discussion. It began when I noticed a few similarities between an insider trading issue and an issue in copyright. I began to wonder what would happen if instead of treating these as separate legal issues I looked at the way our legal culture deals with information in general. This led me to group together several apparently disparate legal categories—the regulation of blackmail, genetic information,

intellectual property, privacy, and so on. I discovered that there are few systematic studies of the rhetorical, ideological, political, and, ultimately, legal structures through which we deal with information. Among legal scholars, only economic analysts of law have seemed interested in dealing holistically with information, rather than with the doctrinal boxes into which law has traditionally divided it. The two most striking examples are Frank H. Easterbrook, "Insider Trading, Secret Agents, Evidentiary Privileges, and the Production of Information," 1981 *Supreme Court Review* 309, and Edmund W. Kitch, "The Law and Economics of Rights in Valuable Information," 9 *Journal of Legal Studies* 683 (1983). Yet even the economic analysis seemed often to repeat the pattern of assumptions I was interested in, rather than to study it. I should note here that, though I disagreed with them at many points, the economists' studies proved extraordinarily useful (indeed, Easterbrook's "Insider Trading" made me feel considerably more confident about my own strange list of information issues). In a manner familiar from legal realist scholarship, these studies suggest that doctrinal divisions may obscure the need for enlightened policymaking. Easterbrook, for example, was concerned that "if the Court puts information cases in securities law or evidence law pigeonholes, it may overlook the need to consider the way in which the incentive to produce information and the demands of current use conflict." While I agree with the impulse to treat information holistically, my goals are rather different. Later in this book, I argue that the law and economics literature is beset by a number of conceptual "baseline" and Hohfeldian errors and that it presents an ideology of "authorial" incentive as if it were not ideology but empirical fact.

Nonlawyers have come close to my concerns here. Kim Scheppele's book *Legal Secrets* gives a thoughtful contractarian analysis of secrets in cases related mainly to fraud, privacy, and professional requirements of confidentiality. In the process Scheppele offers a critique of Chicago-style law and economics and an interesting defense of egalitarian informational ethics. Kim Scheppele, *Legal Secrets: Equality and Efficiency in the Common Law* (1988). Literary critics have also contributed to the issue. In a recent book, Susan Stewart offers a fascinating analysis of the intersection of law and a range of "crimes of writing"—forgery, literary imposture, pornography, and graffiti—and the relevance of this intersection to notions of subjectivity and authenticity. Susan Stewart, *Crimes of Writing: Problems in the Containment of Representation* (1991). Bernard Edelman's *Le droit saisi par la photographie* (published in English as *Ownership of the Image*, 1979) goes in the other direction, giving an Althusserian analysis of law through an examination of intellectual property law relating to photographs. In the process Edelman raises some of the problems of objectification, originality, and commodification that I deal with here. Finally, Mark Rose's *Authors and Owners: The Invention of Copyright* (1993) offers an excellent analysis of the historical connections between "authorship" and copyright in England. Rose's work has both parallels to and differences from Martha Woodmansee's pioneering article on the same issues in Germany, "The Genius and the Copyright: Economic and Legal Conditions of the Emergence of the 'Author,'" 17 *Eighteenth-Century Studies* 425, 443–444 (1984), and from my discussion of the valences of an ideology of authorship for interpretation and entitlement. James Boyle, "The Search for an Author: Shakespeare and the Framers," 37 *American University Law Review* 625 (1988). For a critical comparison of our approaches see David Saunders and Ian Hunter, "Lessons from the 'Literatory': How to Historicise Authorship," 17 *Critical Inquiry* 479, 491–500 (1991). See also David Saunders, *Authorship and Copyright* (1992).

10. Nevertheless, I will argue later that it is far from clear that the developed world's *actual* current positions on intellectual property are in anyone's long term interests at all.

11. Interestingly, despite the fact that many legal scholars talk as though the arrow of influence runs only from economy and technology *to* law, they also continue to cling to the orthodox set of ideas about the incentive structure of intellectual property—namely, that the existence of a particular legal regime is necessary to produce adequate innovation. In fact, to *prove* conclusively that legal forms have shaped technological development is fairly difficult since the demonstration must be—to a significant extent—counterfactual. It seems reasonable to say that a world without any intellectual property protection for software might see more effort put into programming that is embedded in the hardware. Yet to insist on a particular set of causal nexi is to fall into the overdeterministic rhetoric of the functionalist legal theories one is trying to criticize. See Robert W. Gordon, "Critical Legal Histories," 36 *Stanford Law Review* 57 (1984). Lower-level effects are a little easier to demonstrate. One can certainly find examples of legally influenced changes in the *organization of technological development*. For example, court decisions have given wide protection to computer programs that have been studied—and "decompiled"—by rival firms in the development of their own products. In the wake of the decision many software companies introduced so-called clean-room programming, in which the actual programmers have no direct contact with rival products. Legal influence on *engineering* can also be seen—subtly in terms of responses to product liability standards and rather more obviously in legislative enactments such as the digital audio tape legislation, which explicitly *dictates* the form of the recording equipment. Audio Home Recording Act, 17 U.S.C. §1001 (Supp. IV 1992). For

an example of the effects of intellectual property rules on art forms see David Sanjek, " 'Don't Have to DJ No More': Sampling and the 'Autonomous' Creator," 10 *Cardozo Arts and Entertainment Law Journal* 607 (1992) (detailing the difficulties that rap and house music have with the current legal regime because of their practice of "sampling" other musical works).

12. I use a case only for simplicity of exposition. In fact, I would argue that one can draw the same lessons from many different types of legal materials, ranging from legislative debates to abstract law review arguments. Although the conventions of each form differ widely, there is a common need to offer a plausible language of entitlement and incentive, coupling working assumptions about the political and institutional topography of our society (judicial and legislative, public and private) with the mundane facts of the issue. Thus both a harrumphing legislative debate over a proposal to ban commercial telephone autodialers and a tedious case-crunching law review article arguing for a particular interpretation of constitutional Fourth Amendment doctrine, will offer valuable information to someone who wants to understand the social construction of "privacy."

13. Patent law offers just as rich a field for analysis. I excluded it partly because of a tentative judgment that it depends on basically the same conceptual structure as copyright law. Both areas apply a notion of "originality" that suppresses the importance of the culture, the language, and the scientific community. Both exhibit the same structural pattern of internal binary division, although the content of the divisions is not identical. (Consider the copyright protection of expression, not idea, and the patentability of function, not form.) In each case, it is the *manifestation* of the appropriate kind of genius that receives protection, while the remainder is given to the public realm. My own background leads me to use the idea of romantic authorship as the organizing concept. I leave open the question of whether one could perform a similar analysis using the idea of the "inventor."

14. Joseph A. Schumpeter, *The Theory of Economic Development* (1949); William Wordsworth, *Essay, Supplementary to the Preface*, in *Literary Criticism of William Wordsworth*, 158 (Paul M. Zall ed., 1966).

15. Paul David, in his book *Technical Choice, Innovation, and Economic Growth: Essays on American and British Experience in the Nineteenth Century*, 2 (1975), explains that he has found it much more useful to conceive of innovation in terms of modification of particular existing processes rather than in terms of sweeping industry-wide transformation. "The economist's now conventional conceptualization of technological innovation as a change of a neoclassical production function—an alteration

of relationships between inputs and output across the entire array of known techniques—has turned out to be less helpful than one might wish. On more than one occasion, regrettably, it has led historical discussions of invention and diffusion into paradox and confusion." Id. at 2. David's conclusion is that "a deeper understanding of the conditions affecting the speed and ultimate extent of an innovation's diffusion is to be obtained only by explicitly analyzing the specific choice of technique problem which its advent would have presented to objectively dissimilar members of the relevant (historical) population of potential adopters . . . Doing so, however, calls sharply into question the penchant historians of technology have displayed for separating their task into two distinct undertakings: writing 'the history of common practices' and the 'history of inventions,' and supposing that it will prove useful to continue to pursue each enterprise rather independently of the other." Id. at 5.

In this book, I stress that the fixation on authors, inventors, and entrepreneurs tends to obscure the importance of continuity, indebtedness, and evolution and to overemphasize that of transformation, originality, and revolution. Having claimed that this vision of creation undervalues genre, tradition, and source, I point out that it also ignores the contradictory roles that information is expected to play—even within the world of microeconomics. Consequently, I argue that one cannot draw the kind of general conclusions that most economists and historians have drawn about the relationship of any particular kind of information, *or* innovation, to some abstract legal form. For obvious reasons, my use of the larger conceptual category facilitates this argument considerably. David's account, with its stress on dissimilar circumstances, particular empirical evidence, and the intimate relationship between the "innovation" and the practices it modifies, seems to me to support at least part of this effort.

2. Four Puzzles

1. "Nobody has been able to fix the boundary, and nobody ever can." Nichols v. Universal Pictures, 45 F.2d 119, 121 (2d Cir. 1930) (opinion of Hand, J.), and Peter Pan Fabrics, Inc. v. Martin Weiner Corp., 274 F.2d 487, 489 (2d Cir. 1960). The more fundamental question, however, is not *how* to draw the distinction between idea and expression, but *why* to draw it. "Why is it that copyright does not protect ideas? Some writers have echoed the justification for failing to protect facts by suggesting that ideas have their origin in the public domain. Others have implied that 'mere ideas' may not be worthy of the status of private property. Some authors have suggested that ideas are not protected because of the strictures imposed on copyright by the first amendment. The task of distinguishing

ideas from expression in order to explain why private ownership is inappropriate for one but desirable for the other, however, remains elusive." Jessica Litman, "The Public Domain," 39 *Emory Law Journal* 965, 999 (1990) (footnotes omitted). At a later point, I will argue that the contradictory ideological structure described here is the most plausible explanation for copyright's reliance on the idea/expression dichotomy.

2. L. Ray Patterson and Craig Joyce, "Monopolizing the Law: The Scope of Copyright Protection for Law Reports and Statutory Compilations," 36 *University of California at Los Angeles Law Review* 719 (1989) (recounting the district court's willingness to grant, and the circuit court's willingness to affirm, a preliminary injunction against use of West page numbers by Mead Data Central's *Lexis* "star pagination" service). These decisions led Mead to settle for "tens of millions of dollars" in order to obtain a settlement. But see Feist Publications, Inc. v. Rural Telephone Service Co., 111 S. Ct. 1282 (1991), where the Supreme Court held that the telephone white pages are not entitled to copyright and thus that use of them does not constitute infringement.

3. Justin Hughes, "The Philosophy of Intellectual Property," 77 *Georgetown Law Journal* 287 (1988); Alfred Yen, "Restoring the Natural Law: Copyright as Labor and Possession," 51 *Ohio State Law Journal* 517 (1990).

4. Wendy J. Gordon, "Toward a Jurisprudence of Benefits: The Norms of Copyright and the Problem of Private Censorship," 57 *University of Chicago Law Review* 1009 (1990).

5. "The most notable features of present-day copyright doctrine relating to 'fact works' are its incoherence and instability." Peter Jaszi, "Fact Works and All That—A (Slightly) Structuralist Overview," in *Fundamentals of Intellectual Property Law Practice before Agencies, Courts, and in Corporations,* 348 (1987).

6. Apple Computer, Inc. v. Microsoft Corp., 821 F. Supp. 616 (N.D. Cal. 1993). See also David L. Hayes, "Apple v. Microsoft under a Microscope," 11 *The Computer Lawyer* 1 (February 1994).

7. For example, the Supreme Court refused to allow *The Nation* to copy excerpts of President Gerald Ford's autobiography despite the fact that news reporting is mentioned as one of the statutory exemplars of the fair use exception. "The promise of copyright would be an empty one if it could be avoided by merely dubbing the infringement a fair use 'news report' of the book." Harper and Row, Publishers, Inc. v. Nation Enterprises et. al., 471 U.S. 539, 556 (1985). If the printing of excerpts from an ex-President's memoirs by a news magazine is seen merely as an *assertion* of "news reporting," then what counts as actual news reporting, sufficient to meet the fair use test? For a magisterial study of fair use law, which actually discusses both the utilitarian and the utopian goals that copyright law ought to promote, see William W. Fisher III, "Reconstructing

the Fair Use Doctrine," 101 *Harvard Law Review* 1659 (1988). Fisher is more sanguine about the *Nation* case. Later in this book, I argue that even the defenders of an expansive fair use doctrine have paid insufficient attention to the role of the fair use doctrine in constructing the public domain—that is, in providing or disseminating the raw material out of which future intellectual creations may be built. See also Litman, "The Public Domain." William M. Landes and Richard A. Posner ("An Economic Analysis of Copyright Law," 18 *Journal of Legal Studies* 325 [1989]) are, by contrast, very careful to mention this aspect of copyright doctrine and seem to agree that its importance is underrated—a phenomenon for which they offer no particular explanation.

8. David Lange, "Recognizing the Public Domain," 44 *Law and Contemporary Problems* 147 (1981); see Litman in "The Public Domain," where she argues that "the justifications for the public domain become least satisfactory at the most fundamental level" (id. at 999) and proposes that the public domain should be understood "not as the realm of material that is undeserving of protection, but as a device that permits the rest of the system to work by leaving the raw material of authorship available for authors to use" (id. at 968). Occasionally, judges seem willing to recognize this side of the public domain, although they generally "balance" their commentary by a tip of the hat to the idea of the idea of original genius; "In truth, in literature, in science and in art, there are, and can be, few, if any, things, which, in an abstract sense, are strictly new and original throughout. Every book in literature, science and art, borrows, and must necessarily borrow, and use much which was well known and used before ... No man writes exclusively from his own thoughts, unaided and uninstructed by the thoughts of others. The thoughts of every man are, more or less, a combination of what other men have thought and expressed, although they may be modified, exalted, or improved by his own genius or reflection." Emerson v. Davies, 8 F. Cas. 615, 619 (C.C.D. Mass. 1845).

9. Litman, "The Public Domain," 998.

10. Actually, a privilege—in Hohfeldian terms.

11. William M. Landes and Richard A. Posner, "The Private Enforcement of Law," 4 *Journal of Legal Studies* 1, 42 (1975); Arthur L. Goodhart, *Essays in Jurisprudence and the Common Law,* 175–189 (1937); Ronald Coase, "The 1987 McCorkle Lecture: Blackmail," 74 *Virginia Law Review* 655 (1988); Robert Nozick, *Anarchy, State, and Utopia,* 84–86 (1974); Richard Epstein, "Blackmail, Inc.," 50 *University of Chicago Law Review* 553 (1983).

12. James Lindgren, "Unraveling the Paradox of Blackmail," 84 *Columbia Law Review* 670, 671 (1984). Lindgren's own explanation concerns third-party rights and I will discuss it later.

13. James D. Cox, "Insider Trading and Contracting: A Critical Response to the 'Chicago School,'" 1986 *Duke Law Journal* 628 (emphasis added). For even more critical assessments see also J. A. C. Hetherington, "Insider Trading and the Logic of the Law," 1967 *Wisconsin Law Review* 720; Harold Demsetz, "Perfect Competition, Regulation, and the Stock Market," in *Economic Policy and the Regulation of Corporate Securities*, 11–16 (Henry Manne ed., 1968); Michael Moran, "Insider Trading in the Stock Market: An Empirical Test of Damages to Outsiders" (Center for the Study of American Business, Washington University, Working Paper no. 89, July 1984.)

14. Henry Manne, *Insider Trading and the Stock Market*, 1, 5, 10 (1966).

15. Moore v. The Regents of the University of California, 793 P.2d 479 (Cal. 1990), *cert. denied*, 111 S. Ct. 1388 (1991).

16. And I am not the only one to think so. See, for example, John J. Howard, "Biotechnology, Patients' Rights, and the *Moore* Case," 44 *Food, Drug, and Cosmetics Law Journal* 331 (1989); Patricia A. Martin and Martin L. Lagod, "Biotechnology and the Commercial Use of Human Cells: Toward an Organic View of Life and Technology," 5 *Santa Clara Computer and High Technology Law Journal* 211 (1989); Stephen A. Mortinger, Comment, "Spleen for Sale: Moore v. Regents of the University of California and the Right to Sell Parts of Your Body," 51 *Ohio State Law Review* 499 (1990); Thomas P. Dillon, Note, "Source Compensation for Tissues and Cells Used in Biotechnological Research: Why a Source Shouldn't Share in the Profits," 64 *Notre Dame Law Review* 628 (1989); Bernard Edelman, "L'homme aux cellules d'or," 34 *Recueil Dalloz Sirey* 225 (1989); "Le recherche biomedicale dans l'economie de marche," 30 *Recueil Dalloz Sirey* 203 (1991). For the most brilliantly macabre title in the related literature, see Erik S. Jaffe, Note, " 'She's Got Bette Davis['s] Eyes': Assessing the Nonconsensual Removal of Cadaver Organs under the Takings and Due Process Clauses," 90 *Columbia Law Review* 528 (1990).

17. "Biotechnology; Spleen-Rights" *The Economist*, 30 (August 11, 1990); see also Beverly Merz "Whose Cells Are They, Anyway? Commercial Worth of Human Cell Lines Provokes Ownership Disputes," 33 *American Medical News* (March 23, 1990).

18. It also ignores the possibility that one can give up one stick from the bundle of property rights, but still retain the rest. This is an idea which is fundamental to all modern concepts of property, but particularly to intellectual property.

19. Moore v. Regents, 492.

20. Owners of cars (think of speed limits, HOV regulations, emission, safety, and insurance requirements) should also be disturbed by this kind of comment.

21. Carson v. Here's Johnny Portable Toilets, Inc., 698 F.2d 831 (6th Cir. 1983). A disagreeable picture of Johnny Carson emerges from the suit, and one is left wishing that the defendant, who described himself as "the World's Foremost Commodian," could have taken his place on television. Judge Kennedy, in dissent, attacked the decision because (among other reasons) "[the phrase 'Here's Johnny'] can hardly be said to be a symbol, or synthesis, i.e., a tangible 'expression' of the 'idea' of Johnny Carson the comedian and talk-show host." Id. at 844 (Kennedy, J., dissenting). This formulation—one that might have made even Hegel blanch— shows the power of the idea/expression distinction, even outside its normal ambit. Kennedy also mused that Ed McMahon might have a better claim to the phrase, since he was the one who actually used it. Id. at 839. Nevertheless, Judge Kennedy was willing to admit that a distinctive racing car could be an "expression" of the "idea" of the driver normally associated with it. Id. at 844 (citing Motsenbacher v. R. J. Reynolds Tobacco Co., 498 F.2d 821 [9th Cir. 1974]). At a later point, I will discuss the reasons for making such a distinction.

22. Moore v. Regents, 490. The court claims that "by definition, a gene responsible for producing a protein found in more that one individual will be the same in each." Id. at 490 n.30. One's first reaction is to wonder whether the reasoning here is disingenuous or merely accidentally fallacious. Later on I will compare the court's concern with "originality" and "uniqueness" to the concerns stressed by the romantic notion of authorship. My claim is that such a comparison helps us to understand the court's almost obsessional desire to prove that Moore's spleen was not unique, whereas the doctor's research products were.

23. Id. at 495 (footnotes omitted).

3. The Public and Private Realms

1. Karl Marx, "On the Jewish Question," in *The Marx-Engels Reader*, 31 (Robert Tucker ed., 1972).

2. One of Marx's more intriguing suggestions is that the public sphere owes its attraction to the fact that it is a diminished and distorted form of a truly just, egalitarian society. While the Eastern European state socialist societies never provided anything except a dystopian model of drearily brutal oppression, the concern with the limits of egalitarian justice is an issue that bids fair to obsess liberal societies for the foreseeable future.

3. Marx, "On the Jewish Question," 34.

4. These paragraphs can be no more than a summary of the basic ideas. It would take an entire book to discuss the full ramifications of the public-private distinction. In fact, particularly good studies have already been

written on several aspects of the subject. On the influence of classical legal thought and economics, see Duncan Kennedy, "The Role of Law in Economic Thought: Essays on the Fetishism of Commodities," 34 *American University Law Review* 939 (1985). On the effects of legal realism on the current perception of the public-private split, see Duncan Kennedy, "The Stages of the Decline of the Public/Private Distinction," 130 *University of Pennsylvania Law Review* 1349 (1982), and Morton J. Horwitz, "The History of the Public/Private Distinction," 130 *University of Pennsylvania Law Review* 1423 (1982). On the paradoxes produced by the fact that the market can seem public from the perspective of the family, but private from the perspective of the state, see Frances E. Olsen, "The Family and the Market: A Study of Ideology and Legal Reform," 96 *Harvard Law Review* 1497 (1983). For a general discussion see James Boyle, "The Anatomy of a Torts Class," 34 *American University Law Review* 1003, 1023–1034 (1985).

5. Marx also thought that law played a vital role in this process. "Man emancipates himself *politically* from religion by expelling it from the sphere of public law to that of private law. Religion is no longer the spirit of the *state*, in which man behaves, albeit in a specific and limited way and in a particular sphere, as a species being, in community with other men. It is no longer the essence of *community*, but the essence of *differentiation*. It is now only the abstract avowal of an individual folly, a private whim or caprice." Marx, "On the Jewish Question," 35. In this sense, the defining feature of the liberal theory of politics is that it moves religion, wealth, and social class from the realm of public law to that of private law. We can no longer condition public office on a particular religion or social class, nor can we allow citizens to buy shorter jail time or purchase exemptions from military service. We can, however, allow private associations to exclude members on the basis of religion, or private individuals to purchase better health care or education.

6. Gideon v. Wainwright, 372 U.S. 335 (1963); Anthony Lewis, *Gideon's Trumpet* (1964).

7. The question is more complicated than this. The tension is reproduced at each level of the inquiry. Gideon v. Wainwright is a perfect example of the playing out of this issue in constitutional law. First, we have to decide whether the norm of equality applies. Our notion of equal justice fairly obviously does include access to legal services and does not include access to medical services. But even if we say that the norm of equality should apply, we have to decide what equality *means*, with the choice normally being presented in terms of formal equality, or substantive equality. In Gideon v. Wainwright equality means substantive equality—the accused has a right to an actual lawyer, not merely to a hypothetical lawyer if he can pay for one. In First Amendment issues, however, we

have only a formally equal right to speak—the state is not understood to be constitutionally bound to pay the cost of getting my advertisement into the newspaper.

8. For an excellent discussion of the tensions between these ideas, see Frank Michelman, "Law's Republic," 97 *Yale Law Journal* 1493 (1988).

9. Admittedly, conventional privacy doctrine covers a great deal more. Nevertheless, it seems fair to say that other areas of privacy doctrine are explained partly in informational terms (cf. Rust v. Sullivan, 111 S. Ct. 1759 [1991]) and that control over private *information* is a vital part of the contemporary conception of privacy—whether legal or lay.

10. Frank H. Easterbrook, "Insider Trading, Secret Agents, Evidentiary Privileges, and the Production of Information," 1981 *Supreme Court Review* 309.

11. Letter from James Madison to W. T. Barry, August 4, 1822, reprinted in *The Complete Madison*, 337 (Saul K. Padover ed., 1953).

12. See, for example, Harper and Row Publishers, Inc. v. Nation Enterprises et. al., 471 U.S. 539 (1985).

13. Anthony T. Kronman, "Mistake, Disclosure, Information, and the Law of Contracts," 7 *Journal of Legal Studies* 1 (1978); Saul Levmore, "Securities and Secrets: Insider Trading and the Law of Contracts," 68 *Virginia Law Review* 117 (1982).

14. Two hundred years later, Max Horkheimer and Theodor Adorno amazed American college students by suggesting—in considerably less graceful language—that, even in capitalism, there was still mythology and iconography. More surprising still, they argued that these new "mythologies" might be all the more secure precisely because of the effect of disparities of power on the type of abundant but nonrandom "information" provided to the public: "In the enlightened world, mythology has entered into the profane. In its blank purity, the reality which has been cleansed of demons and their conceptual descendants assumes the numinous character which the ancient world attributed to demons. Under the title of brute facts, the social injustice from which they [sic] proceed is now as assuredly sacred a preserve as the medicine man was sacrosanct by reasons of the protection of his gods . . . Through[out] the countless agencies of mass production and its culture the conventionalized modes of behavior are impressed on the individual as the only natural, respectable and rational ones." Max Horkheimer and Theodor W. Adorno, *Dialectic of Enlightenment*, 28 (1972).

15. Olsen, "The Family and the Market."

16. Edmund Andrews, "Telephone Autodialers under Fire," *New York Times*, D24 (October 30, 1991).

17. The same, familiar tensions play themselves out in the public sphere of

debate. Do private citizens have a right of access to privately held communications media in order to participate in public debate? The citizens would portray the television station as a means of public communication, "tinged with a public interest," as in Munn v. Illinois, 94 U.S. 113 (1876), and would demand state intervention to prevent public debate from being ceded to a satrapy of private interests. The television station would portray the same situation as an illegitimate public interference with private property. Does a person who participates in the public world of politics lose her property right in reputation, a property right normally protected by the imposition of a universal tort duty to refrain from defamation?

18. 47 U.S.C. §227 (Supp. IV 1992).

19. Moser v. Frohnmayer, 845 P.2d 1284 (Or. 1993) (holding that an Oregon state statute which prohibited the use of automatic dialing and announcing devices to solicit the purchase of any realty, goods, or services, was invalid); see also Edmund L. Andrews, "Curtailing the Telephone Robots," *New York Times*, D1, D24 (October 30, 1991); Andrew Binstock, "Curbs on Telemarketing Not Working, Study Says; Many Firms Found to Have No Written Policy," *Washington Post*, F1 (July 15, 1994).

20. Although there is relatively little reference in the academic literature to the conflicting requirements that liberal state theory puts on information, most academics would admit, I think, that the language of publicness and privateness is relatively useless for resolving *any* important issue. By this, I do not mean to say that it is meaningless to talk of "public" and "private" issues—quite the contrary. Those terms are central to public discourse. They are also the accepted way in which competing political beliefs are expressed. (Hence the old saw that conservatives think the market is private and the bedroom is public and liberals think the exact opposite.) Robert H. Mnookin, "The Public/Private Dichotomy: Political Disagreement and Academic Repudiation," 130 *University of Pennsylvania Law Review* 1429 (1982). But although they are vital terms with which to express normative conclusions, they are poor guides to analysis or decision making. When lawyers or state theorists attempt to use them as *operative terms,* the "all-things-to-all-people" quality that makes them so useful in political debate simply produces an endless array of mirror-image arguments of the kind described above.

21. Kim L. Scheppele, *Legal Secrets: Equality and Efficiency in the Common Law* (1988), provides an excellent contractarian critique of this tendency. See also *Economic Imperialism: The Economic Approach Applied outside the Field of Economics* (Gerard Radnitzky and Peter Bernholz eds., 1987).

22. William M. Landes and Richard A. Posner, "An Economic Analysis of Copyright Law," 18 *Journal of Legal Studies* 325 (1989); John Shepard

Wiley Jr., "Copyright at the School of Patent," 58 *University of Chicago Law Review* 119 (1991). See also William W. Fisher III, "Reconstructing the Fair Use Doctrine," 101 *Harvard Law Review* 1659 (1988).

23. Edmund W. Kitch, "The Nature and Function of the Patent System," 20 *Journal of Law and Economics* 265 (1977); Edmund W. Kitch, "Property Rights in Inventions, Writings, and Marks," 13 *Harvard Journal of Law and Public Policy* 119 (1990); Louis Kaplow, "The Patent-Antitrust Intersection: A Reappraisal," 97 *Harvard Law Review* 1813 (1984); George Bittlingmayer, "Property Rights, Progress, and the Aircraft Patent Agreement," 31 *Journal of Law and Economics* 227 (1988); Frank H. Easterbrook, "Intellectual Property Is Still Property," 13 *Harvard Journal of Law and Public Policy* 108 (1990).

24. In insider trading scholarship, it would be briefer to cite those articles which do not have recourse to economic analysis. But the following list may give some indication of the breadth of approaches subsumed under the heading. Henry Manne, *Insider Trading and the Stock Market*, 1 (1966); William J. Carney, "Signalling and Causation in Insider Trading," 36 *Catholic University Law Review* 863 (1987); Christopher P. Saari, Note, "The Efficient Capital Market Hypothesis, Economic Theory and the Regulation of the Securities Industry," 29 *Stanford Law Review* 1031 (1977); Dennis W. Carlton and Daniel R. Fischel, "The Regulation of Insider Trading Restrictions," 35 *Stanford Law Review* 857 (1983). See also James D. Cox, "Insider Trading and Contracting: A Critical Response to the 'Chicago School,' " 1986 *Duke Law Journal* 628.

25. Ronald Coase, "The 1987 McCorkle Lecture: Blackmail," 74 *Virginia Law Review* 655 (1988); Richard A. Epstein, "Blackmail, Inc.," 50 *University of Chicago Law Review* 553 (1983); William M. Landes and Richard A. Posner, "The Private Enforcement of Law," 4 *Journal of Legal Studies* 1, 42 (1975).

26. Easterbrook, "Insider Trading"; Edmund Kitch, "The Law and Economics of Rights in Valuable Information," 9 *Journal of Legal Studies* 683 (1980).

4. Information Economics

1. For reasons related to the aporia described here, economists have tried to refine the concept of perfect information so as to limit the breadth of the concept. The accepted formulation seems to be that "individuals are unsure only about the size of their *own* commodity endowments and/or about the returns attainable from their own productive investments. They are subject to technological uncertainty rather than market uncertainty." Jack Hirshleifer, "The Private and Social Value of Information and the Reward to Inventive Activity," 61 *American Economic Review* 561

(1971) (footnote omitted). See also Peter A. Diamond, "The Role of a Stock Market in a General Equilibrium Model with Technological Uncertainty," 57 *American Economic Review* 759 (1967). But see Sanford J. Grossman and Joseph E. Stiglitz, "On the Impossibility of Informationally Efficient Markets," 70 *American Economic Review* 393 (1980).

2. Having always wanted to imitate my ancestor and attach my name to a Law, I would like to call this Boyle's Paradox. Somehow, I doubt that the name will catch on.

3. The analogy underestimates the point, as the theoretical discussion will show in a moment. In any event, like microeconomics, religions are replete with mediating devices between the ideal and the actual. Consider, for example, how the ideal vision of a perfectly merciful God and the actual reality of starving children are mediated through a variety of conceptual devices, including "original sin" and "God moves in mysterious ways." The economic ideas discussed here have more esoteric names, but the basic function is similar.

4. For some qualified exceptions to this statement, see Jacques H. Drèze, "A Paradox in Information Theory," in *Essays on Economic Decisions under Uncertainty,* 105 (1987) (arguing that the value of information can be negative as well as positive); Torben M. Andersen, "Some Implications of the Efficient Capital Market Hypothesis," 6 *Journal of Post Keynesian Economics* 281 (1983–84) (arguing that the concept of information does not have any well-defined meaning in efficient capital market); Grossman and Stiglitz, "Impossibility of Informationally Efficient Markets." The classic article calling for a more rigorous treatment of information is George J. Stigler, "The Economics of Information," 69 *Journal of Political Economy* 213 (1961). According to Stigler, "One should hardly have to tell academicians that information is a valuable resource: knowledge is power. And yet it occupies a slum dwelling in the town of economics. Mostly it is ignored." Id. at 213. Reading the economic literature on information, one is tempted to believe that there was a reason for the marginalization of information noted by Stigler: information plays the same role for neoclassical economics that rent did for classical economics. It is the problem case in which the internal tensions of the discipline come to the surface.

5. In practice, the process of typing is more complicated. Take insider trading, an example I develop in a later chapter. The classic defense of insider trading by Henry Manne, *Insider Trading and the Stock Market* (1966), treats the information issue in the incentive mode—in this case, a privilege to trade on the information acts as a necessary incentive to encourage acts of entrepreneurship by corporate insiders. We have an undercompensated production of a public good. The nonowner entrepreneur engages in large-scale iconoclastic transformation of the economy only to have

others capture most of the profits through imitation. Thus as a society we fail to encourage future acts of entrepreneurship and prevent adequate capital accumulation. Allowing these insider-entrepreneurs to trade will provide an incentive for their future acts of entrepreneurship. The incentives are not merely for the production of *information*, of course, but in other respects the basic form of information-incentive story is there.

The other scholarship on insider trading treats the issue in the perfect-information mode. Taking the model of the efficient capital markets hypothesis as their starting point, some analysts conclude—unsurprisingly—that insider trading is unexceptionable. (In fact, if one takes the hypothesis *seriously* it is definitionally impossible.) The market already reflects all the relevant information. For those to whom this seems too much of an "assume a can-opener conclusion," there is the possibility of linking the two modes of analysis. Legalized insider trading would act as an incentive to produce the information necessary to bring about an efficient capital market. Of course, the greater the "reward," the slower and more costly the delivery of the information, and therefore the less efficient the market. Yet without the reward, no convincing mechanism can be postulated by which the information is produced at all.

As these examples show, there is only a rough correlation between the efficiency mode and the "no commodification" conclusion, on the one hand, and the incentives mode and the "commodification" conclusion, on the other. In other words, although each model has an in-built slant, with each it is possible to reach different conclusions. For example, assume a high time value of information and, even within the incentives picture, no property rights in information are necessary. The inventor and author will gain sufficient reward merely by being first to the market. (This still leaves open the question of the insider trader who wants not a property right but a privilege to trade on the time value of material non-public information.) Assume a very low time value of information—as in a state approaching a perfect market mechanism—in fact, assume that the current market is informationally efficient. From this, one could conclude that insider trading should *not* be illegal since the market already reflects all available information (and the insider wouldn't be able to make a profit anyway). Alternatively, one could conclude that insider trading should remain illegal because the present set of incentives and disincentives for information production has already, by our first hypothesis, produced an informationally efficient market. Or, as we say in technical economic terms, "if it ain't broke don't fix it."

Three points emerge. First, any information issue can always be analyzed as either an efficiency issue or an incentives issue. The policy recommendations produced will tend to diverge depending on which portrayal is chosen. Second, economists have no master principle to tell us whether to analyze any given issue as an incentive point or an efficiency point. Third, to the extent that their practice does reveal a pattern in these choices, the pattern is that in cases where one party can convincingly be portrayed as having the attributes of the romantic author, the incentive aspect is chosen. Fourth, those analysts who do attempt to mediate the two aspects of information cannot banish the fundamental tension between the demands of efficiency and those of incentives. On the level of the perfect market, their analyses of the market mechanism undercut their analyses of the incentives necessary to produce the information, and vice versa. On the level of the actual market, their attempts at reconciliation lack all empirical foundation and must therefore leap headlong from the fact that current systems of intellectual property make *a* balance between incentive and efficiency to the claim that the current balance is the right one.

6. Literally, "in a state of doubt." Philosophers and political theorists have differed both between and among themselves about the appropriateness of using the term "paradox" or "contradiction" to describe the kind of situation I lay out here. My claim is that information can, with formal correctness, be defined both as a commodity, the production and distribution of which can be analyzed within the model, and as a constituent part of the model itself. Aporia seemed the most appropriate word to use because, whether one chooses to see this as a basic theoretical fault line or as a mere quibble which can be solved by changing the level and focus of the analysis, the nature of information is "in a state of doubt," and the outcome of any particular economic analysis will be profoundly different depending on which aspect is chosen. Because "aporia" might be unfamiliar to those who love neither classical rhetoric nor German idealist philosophy, I use the word "paradox" interchangeably. Unless specified otherwise, it is this double, and thus doubtful, quality of information to which I am referring. Other well-known paradoxes have a similar structure—the barber of Seville is both "a man" and "the barber"—if the barber shaves all the men who do not shave themselves . . .?

7. Many economists do not see a paradox here because microeconomics is, after all, the study of trade-offs. As I will show shortly, economic analysts of law tend to start by thinking of information as a commodity and then to introduce the free circulation of information as a countervailing factor that needs to be "balanced" against the need to commodify. See William M. Landes and Richard A. Posner, "An Economic Analysis of Copyright Law," 18 *Journal of Legal Studies* 325, 326 (1989) ("Copyright protection . . . trades off the costs of limiting access to a work against the benefits of providing incentives to create the work in the first place.")

Actually, except for the fact that it ignores the distributional side of things, this is not a bad formulation in that it tends to recast every issue as an ad hoc balancing act, depending on highly contextual and specific local factors. Yet by downplaying the extent to which this "balancing act" diminishes the scientific pretensions of the pure version of the theory, economic analysis attempts to keep its credibility while maintaining the illusion of rigor. Professional economists employ this tone of certainty less often than practitioners of "law and economics." Cf. id. at 333 ("In principle, there is a level of copyright protection that balances these two competing interests optimally ... We shall see ... that various doctrines of copyright law, such as the distinction between idea and expression and the fair use doctrine, can be understood as *attempts* to promote economic efficiency"; emphasis added) with Hirshleifer, "The Private and Social Value of Information," 572 (because of the possibility of speculation on prior knowledge of invention and the uncertainties of "irrelevant" risks, patent protection may or may not be necessary in order to produce an appropriate incentive to invention).

It also makes one a little skeptical to note that, when done by economic analysts of law, this ad hoc balancing of empirically unspecified and unquantified factors tends to track the distinctions made by the existing case law with surprising fidelity—surprising, that is, unless one had already assumed that the common law was working its way toward the economically efficient solution. See George L. Priest, "The Common Law Process and the Selection of Efficient Rules," 6 *Journal of Legal Studies* 65 (1977). In recent years, however, it seems that economists have begun to acknowledge that the problems in reconciling efficiency and incentives in information issues go deeper than this. See Grossman and Stiglitz, "Impossibility of Informationally Efficient Markets," 405. Lawyers, too, have had their moments of skepticism, the most famous being Stephen Breyer, "The Uneasy Case for Copyright: A Study of Copyright in Books, Photocopies, and Computer Programs," 84 *Harvard Law Review* 281 (1970). The most sophisticated recent analyses have been those of Wendy Gordon. See Wendy J. Gordon, "Fair Use as Market Failure: A Structural and Economic Analysis of the Betamax Case and Its Predecessors," 82 *Columbia Law Review* 1600 (1982); Wendy J. Gordon, "An Inquiry into the Merits of Copyright: The Challenges of Consistency, Consent, and Encouragement Theory," 41 *Stanford Law Review* 1343 (1989); Wendy J. Gordon, "Toward a Jurisprudence of Benefits: The Norms of Copyright and the Problem of Private Censorship," 57 *University of Chicago Law Review* 1009 (1990) (book review).

8. Grossman and Stiglitz, "Impossibility of Informationally Efficient Markets," 405.

9. This clash is a general one, not limited to information questions. Frank
H. Easterbrook has recently argued that both judges and economists over-
state the extent to which intellectual property rights (and in particular,
patent rights) confer a monopoly. Intellectual property rights, he argues,
are no different from rights to tangible property: "Problem: Patents are
not monopolies, and the tradeoff is not protection for disclosure. Patents
give a right to exclude, just as the law of trespass does with real property
... A patent *may* create a monopoly—just as an auto manufacturer *may*
own all of the auto production facilities—but property and monopoly
usually differ." Frank H. Easterbrook, "Intellectual Property Is Still Property," 13 *Harvard Journal of Law and Public Policy* 108, 109 (1990). If Easterbrook is merely pointing out that the economic consequences of granting
different patents will be different given the varying possibilities of substitute goods and so forth, the point is a good one. Indeed, it is precisely
such empirical difficulties that undermine economists' more sweeping
statements about the efficiency of the patent system as a whole. See Hirshleifer, "The Private and Social Value of Information." As to his other point,
Easterbrook may be right that judges overestimate the monopolistic qualities of *intellectual* property.

Nevertheless, his article, like many pieces of economic analysis, seems
to commit the opposite error—to underestimate the extent to which *all*
property rights can have monopolistic or quasi-monopolistic effects.
Property rights are frequently trumped *against* market forces; this point
causes considerable problems for economic analysis. Thus an economist
would ask: "If I value your house more than you do (measured by our
relative ability and willingness to pay), why should I not be able to compel you to sell it to me whether you like it or not?" Indeed, the general
tendency in Chicago School economic analysis is to use offering price
rather than asking price as a measure. See Duncan Kennedy, "Cost-Benefit
Analysis of Entitlement Problems: A Critique," 33 *Stanford Law Review* 387
(1981); cf. C. Edwin Baker, "The Ideology of the Economic Analysis of
Law," 5 *Journal of Philosophy and Public Affairs* 3 (1975). Under that measure, a forced sale would be moving resources to their highest use value.

But because we make a pretheoretical classification of the issue as being
about "settled property rights," we use asking price rather than offering
price as the measure of value. You get to keep the house unless your
asking price is equal to or lower than my offering price—in other words,
unless you are willing to sell it to me. Yet if there is a "public interest"
involved, or an existing clash of land uses, we shift doctrinal boxes into
eminent domain or nuisance and change our measure of valuation back
to offering price. We need a general principle or algorithm that would
identify those issues that should be analyzed in terms of the free-flowing

calculus of utility (and offering price) and those issues that should be analyzed in terms of settled property rights (and asking price). Without such a principle, economic analysts seem to be guilty of exactly the kind of mushy ad hoc balancing for which they reproach other legal scholars. See Duncan Kennedy and Frank Michelman, "Are Property and Contract Efficient?" 8 *Hofstra Law Review* 711 (1980).

It is, of course, true that there may be no problem as to any given property right. You may loathe my house, and the patent may be for a device that no one wants to use. This hardly resolves the more general theoretical problem, however, and it also tends to reduce all property (and intellectual property) questions into endlessly particular, empirical inquiries—negating the possibility of exactly the kind of grand statements about the efficiency or inefficiency of entire doctrinal areas for which economic analysis is renowned.

10. Obviously, there are a number of reasons for this—many of them good ones. Later in this book, I will suggest that one of the not-so-good reasons is an unacknowledged and largely unconscious reliance on a particular model of authorship as the norm against which to measure all information issues.

11. 248 U.S. 215 (1918).

12. William W. Fisher III, "Reconstructing the Fair Use Doctrine," 101 *Harvard Law Review* 1659 (1988).

13. Id. at 1766–1779.

14. Landes and Posner, "An Economic Analysis of Copyright Law," 326. In another context, one might expect that Landes and Posner would engage in one of those charming "assume a can opener" flights of fancy, in which we merely assume that authors will contract for the right to use exactly the inspirational sources needed, no less and no more. After all, Judge Posner can imagine that contingency fee lawyers will come flocking to prisons in order to pursue meritorious claims for damages: "Encouraging the use of retained counsel thus provides a market test of the merits of the prisoner's claim. If it is a meritorious claim there will be money in it for a lawyer, if it is not it ought not to be forced on some hapless unpaid lawyer." McKeever v. Israel, 689 F.2d 1315, 1325 (7th Cir. 1982) (Posner, J., dissenting). Why should Posner not imagine T. S. Eliot paying small royalties to everyone from Dante to the inventors of the tarot pack? Interestingly, Landes and Posner seem to assume from the beginning that such a solution is completely impractical. Instead, they maintain that the best way to encourage production is to limit the creator's legally protected interests from the beginning. Perhaps authors are allowed to exist in a world less stringently constricted by the devices of economic fantasy.

15. Recourse to the traditional categories of copyright law—expression may be owned but not ideas or facts—merely begs the question. We *could* choose to analyze expression in our "commodity" mode and facts and ideas in our "free circulation of information" mode. Having thus assumed away the very aporia we need to resolve, we could study the production of texts under the current regime—to find our methodology triumphantly confirmed as we rediscovered the very pattern of choices that we ourselves had made moments before.

16. Grossman and Stiglitz, "Impossibility of Informationally Efficient Markets," 404 (emphasis added). The time lags, or other imperfections in the transmission of information through price, that are necessary for those who create information to trade on it, are crucial to the discussion of insider trading. See Chapter 8. In an article that studies the informational mechanisms of market efficiency, Reinier Kraakman and Ronald Gilson have argued that the "efficiency paradox" can be seen as a phenomenon that occurs only when the market is fully efficient. "While we do argue that an evolutionary bias pushes the market *toward* efficiency, the Efficiency Paradox arises only when *full* efficiency is achieved. Our very emphasis on information costs recognizes that prices need not be perfectly efficient with respect to any particular information." Ronald J. Gilson and Reinier H. Kraakman, "The Mechanisms of Market Efficiency," 70 *Virginia Law Review* 549, 623 (1984). Nevertheless, they acknowledge that this notion of limits does not explain the apparent inconsistency between Grossman and Stiglitz's conclusions and their own analysis of two particular market mechanisms—universally informed and professionally informed trading—an analysis which does "explicitly point to reaching such an efficient equilibrium." To their eyes, however, "the conflict between these perspectives is more apparent than real." Their solution is an interesting variation of an analysis that should be familiar by now. Briefly put, their idea is that the first trader to gain access to, or to develop, some useful information will be able to profit from it—thus receiving an adequate incentive—and that the equilibrium can thereafter be maintained at a very low cost. "The empirical literature does not demonstrate that the originators of [a useful insight] failed to gain a return on their efforts. Rather, it is reasonable to suppose that they did earn an acceptable return on the information, but that the secret was subsequently dissipated through discovery by competitors, (or even academics.) So understood, the question posed by the Efficiency Paradox is not whether incentives exist to induce the *original* innovation. Rather the puzzle is to explain how an efficient equilibrium is *maintained* once the innovation becomes so widely known that profit is no longer possible for those who exploit it . . . Because of joint cost characteristics, mainte-

nance of the equilibrium is effectively costless, and the Efficiency Paradox disappears."

The first part of the argument, which finds its incentive in the originator's temporally limited monopoly in trading on the value of the information, is very similar to Hirshleifer's musings about the patent system (Hirshleifer, "The Private and Social Value of Information"), as well as to Manne's description of insider trading as the necessary compensation for entrepreneurial acts (see Chapter 8). Given only a privilege to trade, the originator needs no more extensive legally protected interest (on the model of copyright or patent, say) in order to encourage future information creation. The second part of the analysis relies on a traditional philosophical method for getting around state/process paradoxes, paradoxes such as Zeno's tale of the arrow that can never reach its target because it must pass though an infinite series of smaller and smaller distances. With the initial process simply postulated, we have no trouble thinking about the arrow quivering in the target, the equilibrium being maintained. Yet, as I think Kraakman and Gilson would agree, if we move from the abstract modeling of *possible* market mechanisms to the actual analysis of a particular market, to postulate this is to assert that which must be proved. In the abstract there is no way of knowing whether the temporal advantage of being first in possession of information and having a privilege to trade is an *inadequate* compensation, requiring greater intellectual property rights or an *over*compensation which will encourage too many traders to invest too much in the acquisition of information so as to gain an advantage over other traders. See Eugene F. Fama and Arthur B. Laffer, "Information and Capital Markets," 44 *Journal of Business* 289 (1971).

17. Cf. Harold Demsetz, "The Private Production of Public Goods," 13 *Journal of Law and Economics* 293 (1970). As Demsetz points out, the key feature of the public good is that "it is possible at no cost for additional persons to enjoy the same unit of a public good." Id. at 295. Why, then, is price not "an approximate public good"?

18. 456 N.E.2d 84 (Ill. 1983). For the connection between this case and the *INS* case, see Douglas Baird, "Common Law Intellectual Property and the Legacy of International News Service v. Associated Press," 50 *Chicago Law Review* 411 (1983).

19. Alternatively, the solution could be some form of state tax and transfer scheme to accomplish the same ends. This "commodification" solution may seem to run against the conventional wisdom that public or collective goods are those from which others "cannot be excluded." If the good can be commodified, one might ask, surely that means that it was never a public good in the first place? From my perspective, this definition

seems to depend on a certain confusion over baseline assumptions about legally protected interests, a confusion that is relatively common in the writing of nonlegally trained economists. Economists tend to think of an undifferentiated property concept as having resolved many of the questions of internalization and externality; to make no clear distinction between the possibility of physical, and legal, exclusion of users of public goods; to underestimate the extent to which property rights can be fragmented; and to insist on a somewhat naive separation between public and private law. The real problem with public goods is that a failure by their users to internalize their full costs will lead to underproduction (although some economists believe that in some cases, it may actually lead to *over*production; Hirshleifer, "The Private and Social Value of Information"). Demsetz makes a similar point. "Frequently there is confusion between the public good concept as I understand it, which states that it is possible at no additional cost for an additional person to enjoy the same unit of a public good, and a different concept that might be identified as a collective good, which imposes the stronger condition that it is *impossible* to exclude nonpurchasers from consuming the good." Demsetz, "The Private Production of Public Goods," 295. A central idea behind much of the law and economics literature since Coase is that many of the problems traditionally solved by recourse to the state taxation system can be just as well served by a system of limited property rights such as those found in copyright or patent.

20. For example, consider the following. "It is true that under a patent system there will, in general, be some shortfall in the return to the inventor, due to costs and risks in acquiring and enforcing his rights, their limited duration in time, and the infeasibility of a perfectly discriminatory fee policy. On the other side are the recognized disadvantages of patents: the social costs of the administrative-judicial process, the possible anticompetitive impact, and restriction of output due to the marginal burden of patent fees. As a second best kind of judgment, some degree of patent protection has seemed a reasonable compromise among the objectives sought. But recognition of the unique position of the innovator for forecasting and consequently capturing portions of the *pecuniary* effects— the wealth transfers due to price revaluations—may put matters in a different light. The 'ideal' case of the perfectly discriminating patent holder earning the entire technological benefit is no longer so ideal. For, the same inventor is in a position to reap speculative profits, too; counting these as well, he would clearly be over-compensated . . . Do we have reason to believe that the potential speculative profits to the inventor, from the pecuniary effects that will follow release of the information at his unique disposal, will be so great that society need take no care to

reserve for him any portion of the technological benefit of his innovation? The answer here is indeterminate." Hirshleifer, "The Private and Social Value of Information," 571–572.

21. 111 S. Ct. 1282 (1991).

22. John Shepard Wiley Jr., "Copyright at the School of Patent," 58 *University of Chicago Law Review* 119 (1991).

23. Frank H. Easterbrook, "Insider Trading, Secret Agents, Evidentiary Privileges, and the Production of Information," 1981 *Supreme Court Review* 309; Saul Levmore, "Securities and Secrets: Insider Trading and the Law of Contracts," 68 *Virginia Law Review* 117, 133 (1982). Cf. Anthony T. Kronman, "Mistake, Disclosure, Information, and the Law of Contracts," 7 *Journal of Legal Studies* 1 (1978).

24. Kenneth Arrow, "Economic Welfare and the Allocation of Resources for Invention," in *Rate and Direction of Inventive Activity: Economic and Social Factors,* 609, 617 (National Bureau of Economic Research ed., 1962). The Arrow article itself offers some lovely examples of the tensions between efficiency and anticompetitive provision of incentives. It is interesting to note that Arrow, writing for the RAND Corporation, believes that even with intellectual property rights it is unlikely that sufficient knowledge will be produced. He therefore suggests that "for optimal allocation to invention it would be necessary for the government or some other agency not governed by profit and loss criteria to finance research and invention." Id. at 623. Arrow uses this idea to offer a partial defense of the "cost-plus" method of developing weaponry for the military: "This arrangement seems to fly in the face of principles for encouraging efficiency and doubtless it leads to abuses, but closer examination shows both mitigating factors and some explanation of its inevitability." Id. at 624. Michael Perelman, most emphatically *not* writing for the RAND Corporation, uses a similar logic to reach a conclusion sufficiently indicated by his title, "High Technology, Intellectual Property, and Public Goods: The Rationality of Socialism," 20 *Review of Radical Political Economy* 277–282 (1988).

25. Fama and Laffer, "Information and Capital Markets."

26. Hirshleifer, "The Private and Social Value of Information," 571–572.

27. The problem is further compounded by the fact that many professional economists seem to have a naive, pre-realist understanding of law. (Comparing the confident assertions of the Chicago School to the carefully guarded conclusions of economists, I assume that the converse also holds.) In particular, I found the following recurrent mistakes. Professional economists often talk as though there were a natural suite of property rights which automatically accompanied a free market. They make strong and unexplained assumptions that certain types of activities (for

example, trading on a superior information position) would "naturally" be allowed, but that certain others (for example, trading on superior physical strength) would not be. This kind of error also creeps into the work of some lawyer-economists such as Easterbrook and Levmore (see Chapter 8). To the extent that they do use the concept of property, economists tend to assume that "absolute" property rights are the default position. The debates between Laffer and Arrow show the results of these shortcomings. For example, both Arrow and Laffer seem to assume that the "natural," unregulated position is that one would have "privileges" but not "rights" to trade in information. But if there is no such thing as a natural, unregulated market, we would have to compare the efficiency of *all* the possible legal positions—particularly since the legal system actually uses the full suite of Wesley Hohfeld's jural correlates in its regulation of different kinds of information. (For an excellent description of the many different legal relationships surrounding valuable information, see Easterbrook, "Insider Trading," 313–314.)

28. Pablo Challú et al., "The Consequences of Pharmaceutical Product Patenting," 15 *World Competition* 65, 115 (1991).

29. Id. at 68, 70.

30. Edwin Mansfield, "Patents and Innovation: An Empirical Study," 32 *Management Science* 173, 174–175 (1986).

31. To my knowledge, copyrights and patents are the only types of property that have an explicitly utilitarian Constitutional basis. Congress is empowered "to promote the Progress of Science and useful Arts, by securing for limited Times to Authors and Inventors the exclusive Right to their respective Writings and Discoveries." U.S. Constitution, art. I, §8, cl. 8. The clause demonstrates two important characteristics of intellectual property. First, intellectual property seems more *chosen*—more of a social artifact—than other types of property, though in fact it is not. Second, partly because of this, intellectual property is almost always discussed in terms of the social benefits it will bring. The person who is asked why she should have the right to pile his flax by the tracks regardless of the inconvenience to the railroad company is likely to say "because it's *my* land." The author who is asked why she should have some legally protected interest in a work after it has been conveyed through the marketplace cannot appeal so easily to any naturalistic or physicalist notion of property. This phenomenon is evidenced also in respect for different types of property rights; "nice" people, who would not steal a record from a record store even if they were sure they were unobserved, nonetheless tape albums they did not buy. For all of these reasons, intellectual property intuitively seems a fit subject for a utilitarian calculus of social interests. What better language than economics

in which to discuss "the way in which the incentive to produce information and the demands of current use conflict"? Easterbrook, "Insider Trading," 314. As a result, intellectual property in particular was subject to economic analysis long before other doctrinal areas. See, e.g., Arnold Plant, "The Economic Aspects of Copyright in Books," 1 *Economica* 167 (1934). Interestingly, this 1934 article argues for *diminished* copyright protection. Id. at 194–195.

32. "My preferences, as I earlier said, would be for complete protection of intellectual property. And so the higher the protection, the more I think it benefits the developing countries, who thereby then attract the transfer technology, investment, and creative endeavor. And of course, the more you protect intellectual property, those established firms are willing to pour more into research and development to try to address mankind's problems, whether they be disease or constructive building of agricultural crops or what have you, all for the benefit of peoples wherever they may be located." News Briefing by U.S. Trade Representative, *Fed. News Service*, Jan. 17, 1992, available in LEXIS, NEWS Library, FEDNEW File (Carla Hills, Remarks on the Signing of a Bilateral Memorandum of Understanding with the People's Republic of China).

33. There may also be a more indirect relationship between the exaltation of individuality, creative innovation, and utilitarianism. Joseph Schumpeter thought there was: "The typical entrepreneur is more self-centered than other types, because he relies less than they do on tradition and connection and because his characteristic task—theoretically as well as historically—consists precisely in breaking up old, and creating new, tradition. Although this applies primarily to his economic action, it also extends to the moral, cultural, and social consequences of it. It is, of course, no mere coincidence that the period of the rise of the entrepreneur type also gave birth to Utilitarianism." *The Theory of Economic Development*, 91–92 (1949). The reader may notice the similarity between Schumpeter's vision of the entrepreneur and the idea of authorship described here. I will explore this connection in my discussion of insider trading in Chapter 8.

34. I do not mean this as an insult, necessarily. *All* theoretical schemes function like blinders, focusing attention on certain phenomena while ignoring others. In its current incarnation, the economic analysis of law tends to ignore wealth effects, structural ("irrational") oppression, the possibility of manufacturing needs as well as products, and so on. To the extent that a more or less sophisticated version of economic analysis becomes the discourse of power in the regulation of information, such issues will *tend* to be ignored or at least marginalized. From my perspective, these seem to be exactly the issues that deserve our attention.

35. My friend Bob Gordon offers the following definition of "economist": "An economist is a person who believes that advertising is a means of conveying information."

5. Intellectual Property and the Liberal State

1. See Frances Philbrick, "Changing Conceptions of Property in Law," 86 *University of Pennsylvania Law Review* 691 (1938); Joseph W. Singer, "The Legal Rights Debate in Analytical Jurisprudence from Bentham to Hohfeld," 1982 *Wisconsin Law Review* 975; Kenneth Vandevelde, "The New Property of the Nineteenth Century: The Development of the Modern Concept of Property," 29 *Buffalo Law Review* 325 (1980).

2. To put it in the simplest terms possible, property is a strong barrier against potentially dangerous other people but, at least since the decline of classical legal thought, a weaker barrier against the state. See also Poletown Neighborhood Council v. Detroit, 304 N.W.2d 455 (Mich. 1981); Hawaii Housing Authority v. Midkiff, 467 U.S. 229 (1984). Constitutional rights, by contrast, are generally a stronger barrier against the state but a weak barrier against "private" parties. Or, as one of my colleagues puts it, the full panoply of Constitutional restraints applies to the actions of the dogcatcher in Gary, Indiana, but not to Exxon or General Motors. The best explanation of property as a mediator between freedom and security comes from Singer, "The Legal Rights Debate," and I am indebted to his analysis.

3. See Thomas Hobbes, *Leviathan*, 189–190 (C. B. McPherson ed., 1976); John Stuart Mill, *On Liberty*, 70–85 (1975); James Boyle, "Thomas Hobbes and the Invented Tradition of Positivism: Reflections on Language, Power, and Essentialism," 135 *University of Pennsylvania Law Review* 383 (1987); Duncan Kennedy, "The Structure of Blackstone's Commentaries," 28 *Buffalo Law Review* 205, 209–221 (1979).

4. Singer, "The Legal Rights Debate," 980.

5. Vandevelde, "The New Property," 328–329.

6. 232 U.S. 340 (1914).

7. If the railroad had a duty not to cause the destruction of only that property kept at a reasonably safe distance from the track, where was the wrong? To put it another way, why isn't the majority venturing a solecism by allowing the "wrong" of the flax stacker (in stacking the flax by the tracks) to limit the "rights" of the railroad company to operate its property?

8. Rust v. Sullivan, 500 U.S. 354 (1991).

6. Copyright and the Invention of Authorship

1. Christian S. Krause, "Uber den Buchernachdruck," 1 *Deutsches Museum* 415–417 (1783), quoted in and translated by Martha Woodmansee, "The Genius and the Copyright: Economic and Legal Conditions of the Emergence of the 'Author,' " 17 *Eighteenth-Century Studies* 425, 443–444 (1984) (emphasis added).
2. Ernst P. Goldschmidt, *Medieval Texts and Their First Appearance in Print*, 112 (1943) (emphasis added).
3. Georg H. Zinck, *Allgemeines Oeconomisches Lexicon* col. 442 (3d ed. n.p. 1753), quoted in Woodmansee, "The Genius and the Copyright," 425.
4. See James Boyle, "The Search for an Author: Shakespeare and the Framers," 37 *American University Law Review* 625, 628–633 (1988).
5. A view which persisted for some time: "Nevertheless, I had to be told about authors. My grandfather told me, tactfully, calmly. He taught the names of those illustrious men. I would recite the list to myself, from Hesiod to Hugo, without a mistake. They were the Saints and Prophets. Charles Schweitzer said he worshipped them. Yet they bothered him. Their obtrusive presence prevented him from attributing the works of Man directly to the Holy Ghost. He therefore felt a secret preference for the anonymous, for the builders who had had the modesty to keep in the background of their cathedrals, for the countless authors of popular songs. He did not mind Shakespeare, whose identity was not established. Nor Homer, for the same reason. Nor a few others, about whom there was no certainty they had existed. As for those who had not wished or who had been unable to efface the traces of their life, he found excuses, provided they were dead." Jean-Paul Sartre, *The Words*, 61–62 (1964).
6. I use the male form deliberately. It is true, that, despite the obstacles placed in their way, a number of women authors established themselves on the literary scene. To say, however, that they participated in the "invention" of romantic authorship, or to claim that such a notion accurately reflected the parts of their own creative practices which they thought most valuable, seems to me to be going too far. In this historical analysis, gender-neutral language might actually obscure understanding. See Sandra M. Gilbert and Susan Gubar, *The Madwoman in the Attic: The Woman Writer and the Nineteenth Century Literary Imagination* (1988); see also Ann Ruggles Gere, *Common Properties of Pleasure: Texts in Nineteenth Century Women's Clubs* 647 (1992); Marlon B. Ross, *The Contours of Masculine Desire: Romanticism and the Rise of Women's Poetry* (1989); Martha Woodmansee, "On the Author Effect: Recovering Collectivity," 10 *Cardozo Arts and Entertainment Law Journal* 279 (1992).
7. For an early but more comprehensive development of these ideas see

Boyle, "Search for an Author." The original hints for this line of thought can be traced back to Michel Foucault, "What Is an Author?" in *Textual Strategies: Perspectives in Post-Structuralist Criticism* (J. Harari ed., 1979). Woodmansee, "The Genius and the Copyright," provided the paradigm for actual research, and her article gives a marvelous account of the "rise" of intellectual property in Germany. For the linkage between romantic authorship and intellectual property in England see Mark Rose, "The Author as Proprietor: Donaldson v. Becket and the Genealogy of Modern Authorship," 23 *Representations* 51 (1988); see also Mark Rose's *Authors and Owners: The Invention of Copyright* (1993). But see John Feather, "Publishers and Politicians: The Remaking of the Law of Copyright in Britain, 1775–1842; Part II: The Rights of Authors," 25 *Publishing History* 45 (1989). For the same linkage in France, see Carla Hesse, "Enlightenment Epistemology and the Laws of Authorship in Revolutionary France, 1777–1793," 30 *Representations* 109 (1990). And for the United States, see Peter Jaszi, "Toward a Theory of Copyright: The Metamorphoses of 'Authorship,' " 41 *Duke Law Journal* 455 (1991).

8. Woodmansee, "The Genius and the Copyright," 427.
9. Harold O. White, *Plagiarism and Imitation during the English Renaissance*, 120, 202 (1935).
10. Johann G. Fichte, "Proof of the Illegality of Reprinting: A Rationale and a Parable" (1793), quoted in Woodmansee, "The Genius and the Copyright," 445.
11. 188 U.S. 239 (1903).
12. In fact, of course, Shakespeare engaged regularly in activity that we would call plagiarism but that Elizabethan playwrights saw as perfectly harmless, perhaps even complimentary. Not only does this show the historical contingency of the romantic idea of authorship, but it may even help to explain some of the "heretical" claims that Shakespeare did not write Shakespeare. Most of the heretics use the fact of this supposed plagiarism and their knowledge of the timeless truth of the romantic vision of authorship to prove that someone else, preferably the author of the borrowed lines, must have written the plays. After all, the Immortal Bard would never stoop to copy the works of another. Once again, originality becomes the key.
13. *Bleistein*, at 249–250 (emphasis added).
14. In the language of romantic authorship, uniqueness is by no means the only characteristic of the author. Originality may imply iconoclasm. The romantic author is going beyond the last accepted style, breaking out of the old forms. This introduces an almost Faustian element into the discussion. The author is the maker and destroyer of worlds, the irrepressible spirit of inventiveness whose restless creativity throws off inven-

tion after invention. Intellectual property is merely the token awarded to the author by a grateful society.

15. Jessica Litman, "The Public Domain," 39 *Emory Law Journal* 965, 999 (1990) (footnotes omitted); see also David Lange, "Recognizing the Public Domain," 44 *Law and Contemporary Problems* 147 (1981).

16. By focusing on the truly exceptional work one can even ignore the conceptual deflation that occurs in a case like *Bleistein.*

17. Paul Goldstein, "Copyright," 38 *Journal of the Copyright Society of the U.S.A.* 109, 110 (1991) (emphasis added).

18. Northrop Frye, *Anatomy of Criticism*, 96–97 (1957).

19. John Shepard Wiley Jr., "Copyright at the School of Patent," 58 *University of Chicago Law Review* 119 (1991).

7. Blackmail

1. By far the best survey comes from James Lindgren, "Unraveling the Paradox of Blackmail," 84 *Columbia Law Review* 670 (1984). Though I disagree with Lindgren's own explanation of blackmail, his article is an excellent introduction to the field—one to which I am indebted.

2. Lindgren formulates the problem in this way: "I have a legal right to expose or threaten to expose [a] crime or affair, and I have a legal right to seek a job or money, but if I combine these rights it is blackmail." Lindgren, "Unraveling the Paradox," 670–671. Although this is clearly an advance on other formulations, it tends to gloss over the variety of the legally protected interests involved. The legal relationships involved are not actually all "rights," but a mixture of privileges, powers, and immunities. This tendency to reduce all legal relationships to a single "right" concept appears to play a role in undermining Lindgren's own theory. Later in the book, I will argue that there are other cases in which the legal system makes it illegal to commodify various privileges and powers—for example, parents may arrange private adoptions but they may not sell babies to adoptive parents—and that it is in this context that blackmail should be understood.

3. This idea of the tasks of jurisprudence is rendered problematic by the essentialist vision of language on which it rests. See James D. A. Boyle, "Thomas Hobbes and the Invented Tradition of Positivism: Reflections on Language, Power, and Essentialism," 135 *University of Pennsylvania Law Review* 383 (1987); James Boyle, "Ideals and Things: International Legal Scholarship and the Prison House of Language," 26 *Harvard International Law Journal* 327 (1985). I will argue here that a related problem besets the analysis of blackmail.

4. William M. Landes and Richard A. Posner, "The Private Enforcement of Law," 4 *Journal of Legal Studies* 1, 42 (1975).
5. Cf. Dennis C. Mueller, *Public Choice* (1979) (surveying legislator and voter behavior from an economic point of view); Jack M. Beermann, "Interest Group Politics and Judicial Behavior: Macey's Public Choice," 67 *Notre Dame Law Review* 183 (1991); Jonathan R. Macey, "Special Interest Groups Legislation and the Judicial Function: The Dilemma of Glass-Steagall," 33 *Emory Law Journal* 1 (1984).
6. Landes and Posner, "The Private Enforcement of Law," 42.
7. Id. at 43.
8. Id.
9. Lindgren also makes much of these points in his critique of Posner. At the same time, however, he makes what I consider to be an error—at least tactically—in his criticisms of Posner and other economic theorists such as Douglas Ginsburg. In both cases, he criticizes theories that focus on the inefficiency of investing resources in acquiring "blackmailable" information, because they cannot explain the prohibition of blackmail based on accidentally acquired information. To this, I think Posner et al. would simply respond that problems of formal realizability and difficulties of proof would more than justify drawing the rule so as to include the person who accidentally learns of some scandalous behavior as well as the person who waits, night after night, with camera in hand. In the following discussion of Coase and Ginsburg, I reformulate this criticism in a way that does not appear to be countered by the formal realizability argument.
10. Douglas Ginsburg, "Blackmail: An Economic Analysis of the Law" (n.d.) (unpublished manuscript, on file at the offices of the *Columbia Law Review*); Ronald H. Coase, "Blackmail," 74 *Virginia Law Review* 655 (1988).
11. Coase, "Blackmail," 674.
12. Lindgren, "Unraveling the Paradox," 695 n.125.
13. Coase, "Blackmail," 675–676.
14. See Walter Block, *Defending the Undefendable*, 53–54 (1976), and Murray N. Rothbard, *The Ethics of Liberty*, 124–127 (1982).
15. Richard Epstein, "Blackmail, Inc.," 50 *University of Chicago Law Review* 565 (1983).
16. Lindgren, "Unraveling the Paradox," 704.
17. An economic concept about which Chicago School economists (and econo-libertarians such as Epstein) maintain an intriguing silence.
18. Epstein, "Blackmail, Inc.," 565, 566.
19. Robert Nozick, *Anarchy, State, and Utopia*, 85 et seq. (1974).
20. Rothbard, *The Ethics of Liberty*, 241–243.

21. James Lindgren, "More Blackmail Ink: A Critique of 'Blackmail, Inc.,' Epstein's Theory of Blackmail," 16 *Connecticut Law Review* 909, 923 (1984). Lindgren's full explanation of his theory is given in "Unraveling the Paradox."

22. Wesley N. Hohfeld, *Fundamental Legal Conceptions as Applied in Judicial Reasoning and Other Legal Essays* (Walter W. Cook ed., 1923); see also Hitchman Coal & Coke Co. v. Mitchell, 245 U.S. 229 (1917); Morton Horwitz, *The Transformation of American Law, 1870–1960*, 151–156, 193–206 (1992); Walter W. Cook, "Privileges of Labor Unions in the Struggle for Life," 27 *Yale Law Journal* 779 (1918).

23. The baseball example, like many cases of blackmail, involves a situation close to a bilateral monopoly. Obviously, there are limits—e.g., substitute goods (other baseball teams, other activities, other foods)—but the ability to sell the privilege still gives considerable power to the party possessing it.

24. Lindgren, "More Blackmail Ink," 923.

25. Robert L. Hale, "Bargaining, Duress, and Economic Liberty," 43 *Columbia Law Review* 603 (1943).

26. Duncan Kennedy, "Distributive and Paternalist Motives in Contract and Tort Law, with Special Reference to Compulsory Terms and Unequal Bargaining Power," 41 *Maryland Law Review* 563 (1982).

27. To say this is *not* to say that since societal institutions have nonrational elements we must give up the tools of reason (although my claim is that those tools are less powerful than is often assumed). But it does offer an interesting insight into that kind of theorizing which assumes the correctness of a strongly held social belief and works to fashion a principled justification for it—rather like putting a slipcover onto an existing chair. Looking at issues in the way I suggest here also helps us to understand the *connections* between apparently diverse questions. The will theory of contracts, the doctrine of no duty to act, and the continued constitutional challenges to punitive damages, for example, all share certain premises about the role of private law vis-à-vis the distribution of wealth. Attacks on one of these will, therefore, often be perceived as attacks on them all.

28. There are many other examples. In wrongful birth cases, the refusal of many courts to include the costs of raising a child as part of the "damage" attributable to a negligently imposed sterilization operation stems partly from the desire to keep the market out of the realm of home and hearth. Courts produce a whole set of arguments ranging from the ineffable benefit of extra children to the difficulty of quantification, the duty to mitigate damages, and the impossibility of tracing the chain of

causation. Yet a moment's analysis of each of these reasons reveals that the problems posed are, in fact, far less different than those posed in other tort issues involving these problems. In the end, one is hard put not to conclude that the court is really imposing a particular belief about those areas that should not be subject to market quantification—no matter how real the loss.

8. Insider Trading and the Romantic Entrepreneur

1. S.E.C. v. Materia, 745 F.2d 197, 198 (2nd Cir. 1984) (per Kaufman, J.), *cert. denied,* 471 U.S. 1053 (1985).
2. Id. at 199.
3. Chiarella v. U.S., 588 F.2d 1358, 1365 (2nd Cir. 1978), *rev'd* 445 U.S. 222 (1980) (emphasis in original).
4. Chiarella v. United States, 445 U.S. 222, 231 (1980) (quoting *Chiarella* 588 F.2d at 1365).
5. Id. at 233 (footnote omitted). The majority seemed to feel that some degree of inequality inheres in the very idea of a market. Thus "not every instance of financial unfairness constitutes fraudulent activity under 10 (b)." Id. at 232. In the later case of Dirks v. S.E.C., 463 U.S. 646 (1983), the court amplified its acceptance of the idea that certain participants in the marketplace could be allowed to exploit their position of informational advantage as a form of compensation for some real or imagined public function. "Congress has expressly exempted many market professionals from the general statutory prohibition set forth in 11(a)(1) of the Securities Exchange Act 15 U.S.C. 78k(a)(1) . . . We observed in *Chiarella* that 'the exception is based upon Congress' recognition that [market professionals] contribute to a fair and orderly marketplace at the same time they exploit the informational advantage that comes from their possession of [nonpublic information].'" Dirks, 463 U.S. at 657 n.16 (quoting Chiarella v. United States, 233 n.16). Market professionals are private actors who perform a public function and are given license to exploit the information that comes their way, as a payoff. The private right secures the public role. Again, the parallel to copyright is striking.
6. This theory had been suggested in the *Chiarella* case, but since it was never submitted to the jury, Chiarella's conviction had been overturned and the resolution of the issue left "for another day." Id. at 238 (Stevens, J., concurring).
7. S.E.C. v. Materia, 203.
8. The court was understandably vague in explaining the idea of misappropriation. Was the information property, and if so, whose? If it was not property, could it be misappropriated? Would a third party, overhearing

the same information in an elevator, have been "misappropriating" it? Or is the court merely saying that Materia's contractual fiduciary duties authoritatively allocate opportunities for information gathering, thus conditioning the offense on the breach of a private agreement?

9. Materia v. S.E.C., 471 U.S. 1053 (1985), *cert. denied.*

10. This is a conflict that also split the Supreme Court. Whereas the majority in *Chiarella* sees disparities of information as an inevitable part of a market, the dissent believes that the mere fact of disparate access is crucial to a 10b-5 case. Thus, in the view of Justices Harry Blackmun and Thurgood Marshall, an earlier Supreme Court case—Affiliated Ute Citizens of Utah v. United States, 436 U.S. 903 (1978)—"lends strong support to the principle that a structural disparity in access to material nonpublic information is a critical factor under Rule 10b-5 in establishing a duty either to disclose the information or abstain from trading." Chiarella v. United States, 251. On the multiple confusions of the case law, see Alan R. Bromberg and Lewis D. Lowenfels, *Securities Fraud and Commodities Fraud,* §7.5(510)-7.5(513) (1991). For scholarly reactions to the misappropriation theory, see Manning G. Warren III, "Who's Suing Who? A Commentary on Investment Bankers and the Misappropriation Theory," 46 *Maryland Law Review* 1222 (1987); Elliot Brecher, "The Misappropriation Theory: Rule 10b-5 Insider Liability for Nonfiduciary Breach," 15 *Fordham Urban Law Journal* 1049 (1987); Karen A. Fischer, "The Misappropriation Theory: The Wrong Answer to the Chiarella Questions," 32 *New York Law School Law Review* 701 (1987). Of course, as I tried to show earlier, the conflict goes far beyond insider trading. For an application to intellectual property of cognate principles derived from the *INS* case, see Chapter 4. For a discussion of the countervailing desire to promote competition, see Leo J. Raskind, "The Misappropriation Doctrine as a Competitive Norm of Intellectual Property Law," 75 *Minnesota Law Review* 875 (1991).

11. James D. Cox, "Insider Trading and Contracting: A Critical Response to the 'Chicago School,'" 1986 *Duke Law Journal* 628 (1986) (emphasis added).

12. J. A. C. Hetherington, "Insider Trading and the Logic of the Law," 1967 *Wisconsin Law Review* 720.

13. "Insiders' profits are not outsider's losses but evidence of more efficient resource allocation." Michael Moran, "Insider Trading in the Stock Market: An Empirical Test of Damages to Outsiders" (Center for the Study of American Business, Washington University Working Paper no. 89, July 1984).

14. "The SEC first should recognize that in an efficient market, where prices are by definition 'fair,' it is impossible for investors to be cheated by

paying more for securities that their true worth." Christopher P. Saari, Note, "The Efficient Capital Market Hypothesis, Economic Theory, and the Regulation of the Securities Industry," 29 *Stanford Law Review* 1031, 1069 (1977) (footnote omitted). See also Harold Demsetz, "Perfect Competition, Regulation, and the Stock Market," in *Economic Policy and the Regulation of Corporate Securities*, 11–16 (Henry Manne ed., 1968).

15. Michael Dooley, "Enforcement of Insider Trading Restrictions," 66 *Virginia Law Rewiew* 37–44 (1980). See generally Dennis W. Carlton and Daniel R. Fischel, "The Regulation of Insider Trading," 35 *Stanford Law Review* 857 (1983).

16. Kim Scheppele's work is particularly good at pointing out the way in which economic analysis fails to explain the concern of fraud cases with issues of power and inequality—exactly the types of issues that a more egalitarian (or, in her case, Rawls-influenced contractarian) vision of the law of "legal secrecy" would concentrate on. Kim Scheppele, *Legal Secrets: Equality and Efficiency in the Common Law* (1988). See also Anthony T. Kronman, "Mistake, Disclosure, Information, and the Law of Contracts," 7 *Journal of Legal Studies* 1, 1–34 (1978).

17. See Friedrich A. Hayek, *The Constitution of Liberty*, 81–102 (1960); Friedrich A. Hayek, *Law, Legislation, and Liberty* (1979); Friedrich A. Hayek, *The Road to Serfdom* (1944); Ayn Rand, *The Virtue of Selfishness* (1964). Sanford Grossman and Joseph Stiglitz, "On the Impossibility of Informationally Efficient Markets," 70 *American Economic Review* 393 (1980).

18. With the exception of Ronald Gilson and Reinier Kraakman, very few scholars have attempted to integrate the literature dealing with the efficient capital markets hypothesis with the actual mechanisms of market efficiency and the associated problems of incentives and transaction costs. Ronald J. Gilson and Reinier H. Kraakman, "The Mechanisms of Market Efficiency," 70 *Virginia Law Review* 549 (1984). Gilson and Kraakman argue that (in at least two market mechanisms) the limited temporal monopoly on information will allow the first party to develop it to reap a reward, while subsequent imitation or learning by other traders will move the market toward an efficient equilibrium, thus harmonizing the "incentive" and the "efficiency" sides of the information debate. I am skeptical about this idea—or at least about its more general implications—for the reasons given in the discussion of information economics. Gilson and Kraakman propose the legalization of (certain kinds of) insider trading together with a requirement that insiders identify themselves and the size of their trade at the time of the trade. I believe that such a proposal must be based on a firm empirical analysis of the costs and benefits of allowing insider trading (including the incentives that result from existing disparities in information; see Jack Hirshleifer, "The

Private and Social Value of Information and the Reward to Inventive Activity," 61 *American Economic Review* 561 [1975]) versus the costs and benefits of prohibiting insider trading (including lessened incentives to produce the information that would otherwise be traded; see Eugene F. Fama and Arthur B. Laffer, "Information and Capital Markets," 44 *Journal of Business* 289, 297–298 [1971]). Gilson and Kraakman explicitly acknowledge this problem, but do not consider it to be a fatal flaw: "To be sure, any increase in informational efficiency from insider trading may alter the incentives to create the information because it reduces the opportunity to exploit informational disparities through trading. Because the derivatively informed trading mechanism does not disclose the information itself, however, it will not reduce the returns to information creators who exploit their information through production rather than trading, and concern over an impact on allocation is thereby minimized." Gilson and Kraakman, "The Mechanisms of Market Efficiency," 632 n.218.

This claim would depend, presumably, on two things: first, that there is the opportunity to exploit the information through production rather than trading and, second, that the trading mechanism informs traders sufficiently to make the market move toward an efficient equilibrium but insufficiently to permit others to guess the information, thereby nullifying the information creator's trading advantage. Imagine an insider under the old rules who invests time and money to deduce that one of Polaroid's rivals has developed a newer and better instant camera. That person could trade on the knowledge through production or by selling Polaroid shares short. Because some insider trading rules allow delay in reporting the trade or disclosing the information, the trader could benefit from the time lag—again, either in production or through trading. Now imagine the same trader under the new rules. Gilson and Kraakman seem to argue that while the incentives offered by trading have been changed, the returns offered by production have not. I am not sure why this is the case. Under a regime of instant disclosure of the identity and size of the sale, many traders might draw negative conclusions about Polaroid from short sales by industry insiders. There would certainly be less incentive to invest in information creation for trading. Why would investment in production be any different? What difference would it make if the trader buys the Polaroid license cheaply and floods the market with cut-price Polaroids before the new camera arrives on the scene, rather than, say, selling Polaroid short? It seems dubious to assume that because this is classed as "production" the returns would not be diminished—"production," too, is a datum, and other traders and consumers might draw similarly negative inferences. There seems to be no reason to assume that, as a general matter, production decisions can benefit more from *precise* knowledge (in other words, that a new camera is coming out, rather than just that the stock price is going down). The important distinction is not so much between production and trading as between the creation of information that is and that is not socially valuable. Actually, we might benefit from prohibiting traders from investing in this kind of information creation, although to say so for sure we would need to know more about the frequency of serendipitous, socially valuable discoveries occurring in searches originally designed to yield a trading advantage.

Perhaps when Gilson and Kraakman talk about "production" they have in mind something like the production of the Polaroid camera in the first place, and thus the incentives they are talking about are incentives to engage in fundamental research and development, not distributionally advantageous market research. In that case, the conclusion seems more intuitively convincing. Part of the reason that it is convincing, however, might be that the creator of the information would have some kind of intellectual property right to exploit through production, rather than having a mere privilege to trade. Yet, as I argued in the discussion of information economics, to identify those "creators" who should be the beneficiaries of property rights, we must first resolve exactly the tension that Gilson and Kraakman are dealing with: the tension between incentive and efficiency.

19. "As a general rule, neither party to an arm's length business transaction has an obligation to disclose information to the other unless the parties stand in some confidential or fiduciary relation. This rule permits a businessman to capitalize on his experience and skill in securing and evaluating relevant information; it provides an incentive for hard work, careful analysis, and astute forecasting. But the policies that underlie the rule should also limit its scope. *In particular, the rule should give way when an informational advantage is obtained, not by superior experience, foresight, or industry, but by some unlawful means.*" Chiarella v. United States, 239–240 (1980) (Burger, C.J., dissenting). Since the definition of insider trading defines exactly what *are* "unlawful means," to use "unlawful means" to define insider trading is an underwhelming analytic technique.

20. Saul Levmore, "Securities and Secrets: Insider Trading and the Law of Contracts," 68 *Virginia Law Review* 140 (1982). Cf. Kronman, "Mistake."

21. The same problem bedevils many other analyses. For example, Dooley's thesis (in "Enforcement of Insider Trading Restrictions") that if insider trading was harmful, companies would prohibit it themselves seems dramatically to underestimate the importance of the fact that under the current rules, insider trading *is already illegal*. Henry Manne's argument

in *Insider Trading and the Stock Market* (1966)—that entrepreneurs will seek employment inside firms so as to engage in insider trading—is subject to the same difficulties.

22. Frank H. Easterbrook, "Insider Trading, Secret Agents, Evidentiary Privileges, and the Production of Information," 1981 *Supreme Court Review* 309, 324.

23. Id. at 330.

24. An analysis that avoids most of these pitfalls is Steven Shavell, "Acquisition and Disclosure of Information prior to Economic Exchange," Harvard Law School Program in Law and Economics, Discussion Paper no. 91 (April 1991). Limiting his conclusions to the world of his model, Shavell argues that if sellers are not to be given unduly high incentives to acquire information, they should be required to disclose, but that buyers should sometimes be allowed to conceal their information. Briefly stated, the argument is that we must distinguish between information that has social value and that which has no social value. We want to encourage production only of the former. Shavell takes as a definition of "socially valuable information" "that which allows an activity to be taken that raises the value of the good to the party who possesses it." Id. at 4, n.6. Shavell wishes to avoid rules that would simply achieve a different distributive effect with no impact on allocative efficiency. We do not wish to give incentives to acquire information that will merely make one party or other richer, but we do wish to give incentives to produce information if it will help in moving resources to their use-value. Under a rule of compulsory disclosure for sellers, sellers will only invest in information gathering when the chances of the information's revealing something positive, multiplied by the amount of the increase in value the information would allow the seller to recoup, would be greater than the chance of the information revealing something that would *decrease* the value of the property, multiplied by the amount of the decrease in value.

Shavell is careful not to generalize his approach to other issues of information inequality. Interested by his method, I have tried to imagine how one might do so. One difficulty would be that once we go beyond the model, we can contemplate situations in which the seller can profit by "selling short" (as in insider trading)—offsetting the losses involved in the sale of his current portfolio by trading on the knowledge that the price of similar goods is likely to fall. This raises some problems for the baseline measurement for socially valuable information. In certain kinds of markets, the seller will be able to "raise the value" of his property whether the information is positive or negative. But the raise in value is at least partly contingent on the possibility of silence. A basic problem appears to arise here. The decision whether or not we want individuals to invest in information, depends on the effect of the research on the asset's price, but the asset "price" depends on the postulated rules of disclosure. In the concrete example given, the rule of compulsory disclosure would tend to undermine the possibility of selling short. Therefore, sellers would not invest in acquiring information when they knew it was likely to be of this kind. (Since the "seller" is also a "buyer" with respect to other units of the fungible good, the possibility of trading advantageously would appear to depend on the relative *inefficiency* of informational market mechanisms similar to those discussed by Gilson and Kraakman in "The Mechanisms of Market Efficiency.") Factoring in the empirical uncertainties of information costs, we might find that a compulsory disclosure rule produced underinvestment by sellers in information likely to be negative, or that the absence of a compulsory disclosure rule would lead to inefficient investment in information gathering merely to gain an advantage over other traders, thus yielding distributional changes but no increase in allocative efficiency. (See Fama and Laffer, "Information and Capital Markets.") Once again, the efficiency claims seem to be in tension with the incentive claims (see Grossman and Stiglitz, "Impossibility of Informationally Efficient Markets"), while the baseline price measure appears both to decide and to depend upon the regime of information disclosure. I am unsure whether a similar point could be made about the Capital Asset Pricing Model used to determine the existence of efficient markets. See Gilson and Kraakman, "The Mechanisms of Market Efficiency."

25. Levmore, "Securities and Secrets," 135 (emphasis added).

26. Cf. Hirshleifer, "The Private and Social Value of Information."

27. And these failings are made even more disturbing by the fact that many of these analyses use a persistent rhetoric of scientific certainty to cover up their extreme judgmental moralism. Here is Levmore excoriating a farmer who is nasty enough to ask the mineral company *questions* about what it is doing. He begins by comparing the farmer to a house owner who holds out against (and holds up) a development: "The owner of the 3001st tract of land who demands a high price is really the despicable character. Similarly the seller who, to preserve a fraud claim, asks specific questions *about activities he would otherwise never engage in* is really the contemptible party. Like eminent domain, optimal dishonesty operates to deny a windfall to a passive party when to do otherwise might lead to a net social loss." Levmore, "Securities and Secrets," 142 (emphasis added). Of course, the question of whether the farmer would engage in the activities *himself* is irrelevant. (Wasn't that Adam Smith's basic point?) And to call the farmer "passive" strikes me as judgemental labeling rather than economic science. It also seems to go against every-

thing Coase ever taught us about joint activities. If, however, the ideology being reflected by these statements was that of the romantic author, then we might expect that the parties that get the rights are those whose life plans seem congenial to the analyst, or those who can most readily be portrayed as active romantic innovators, rather than passive, unoriginal sources. *That* picture seems to fit fairly well.

28. Saari, "The Efficient Capital Market Hypothesis."
29. Kenneth Arrow, "Economic Welfare and the Allocation of Resources for Invention," in *Rate and Direction of Inventive Activity*, 609, 617 (1962), cited in Saari, "The Efficient Capital Market Hypothesis," 1068 n.190.
30. Fama and Laffer, "Information and Capital Markets"; Hirshleifer, "The Private and Social Value of Information," cited in Saari, "The Efficient Capital Market Hypothesis," 1031, 1068 n.197.
31. Harold Demsetz, "Information and Efficiency: Another Viewpoint," 12 *Journal of Law and Economics* 1 (1969), cited in Saari, "The Efficient Capital Market Hypothesis," 1031, 1068 n.197.
32. See Easterbrook, "Insider Trading."
33. See Robert L. Hale, "Bargaining and Economic Liberty," 43 *Columbia Law Review* 603 (1943).
34. Richard A. Epstein, *Takings: Private Property and the Power of Eminent Domain* (1985).
35. See Wards Cove Packing v. Atonio, 490 U.S. 642 (1989).
36. Of course, the transaction costs involved make this simplistic assumption extremely problematic; earlier I showed some of the other possible conclusions one could draw. In one sense, I see this issue as a playing out of the "paradox" I proposed in Chapter 4.
37. If this hypothesis is right, one would expect to see a diverging pattern of treatment of informational inequalities and (other kinds of) wealth inequalities—particularly after the abandonment of the most Lochneresque visions of laissez-faire. In the late nineteenth century, courts would seldom allow plaintiffs to get out of bargains by showing evidence of *either* wealth inequalities or information inequalities. (There is, though, certainly a convincing story in American legal history which claims that classical legal thinkers had to work quite hard to ignore older doctrines such as "just price." These were the doctrines that allowed juries to inquire into the relative wealth and power of the parties—was this particular merchant "grinding the faces of the poor"? As such, they were anathema to a legal consciousness built on the faith that Marx described—the idea that the inequalities of civil society were taboo as far as the state was concerned.) In any event, under the influence of a will theory of contract and a caveat emptor theory of bargaining, it was hard even to explain why there should be contractual redress for disparities

in information or power. But look at the relative changes of these doctrines since the early part of the twentieth century. Courts are still uneasy about striking down bargains merely because of disparities in wealth or power between the parties. Yet they seem much more comfortable imposing disclosure requirements, extensive and non-derogable "duties to warn," and even requirements that the particular class and educational requirements of potential purchasers be taken into account in constructing warnings. Informational egalitarianism is clearly not as threatening as economic egalitarianism—hardly an unimportant fact to understand as we enter the information age.

38. Manne, *Insider Trading and the Stock Market*, 1 (1966).
39. William J. Carney, "Signalling and Causation in Insider Trading," 36 *Catholic University Law Review* 863 (1987).
40. Manne, *Insider Trading and the Stock Market*, 1, 110.
41. Manne has to tread carefully here. As Schumpeter describes the entrepreneur, he is the enemy of tradition whose "conduct and motive are 'rational' in no other sense. And in *no* sense is his characteristic motivation of the hedonist kind." Joseph A. Schumpeter, *The Theory of Economic Development*, 92 (Redvers. Opic trans., 1961) (1934). This tends to fit the idea that routinization and bureaucracy will undermine the opportunities for entrepreneurship. But when Manne goes on to argue that entrepreneurs need more profits if they are to be motivated, the entrepreneur suddenly switches from the nonrational creator and destroyer to the economically rational actor who, presumably, would find a modern corporation entirely congenial.
42. Schumpeter, *The Theory of Economic Development*; Paul Samuelson and William D. Nordhaus, *Economics*, 858, 871 (13th ed. 1989).
43. Schumpeter's "psychology of the entrepreneur" lists as principal motivations, "the dream and will to found a private kingdom . . . the will to conquer . . . the impulse to fight, to prove oneself superior to others, to succeed for the sake . . . of success itself . . . Finally there is the joy of creating, of getting things done, or simply of exercising one's energy and ingenuity." Schumpeter, *The Theory of Economic Development*, 93. Dream, will, success for the sake of success, nonrational imperatives, and, above all, the joy of creating and transforming—it sounds as if Schumpeter is painting the picture of the romantic author-genius, particularly when he claims that the entrepreneur comes from that portion of society distinguished by "super-normal qualities of intellect and will." Id. at 82. His analysis is certainly an interesting answer to a wider question: To whom do we attribute the growth of civilization, of culture, of capital—to the individual who makes the change, or to the society, culture, public domain, and workforce that makes that change possible?

Schumpeter's book is a premier (and unusually convincing) example of the style of argument that attributes growth to the iconoclastic individual. The argument takes the form of "but for" causation: "but for the entrepreneur . . ." Manne goes one step further; he concludes from the "but for" argument that the entrepreneur is entitled to some share of the proceeds, both because it is his just desert and because society needs to encourage further production. This style of argument is of course exactly the style of argument that justifies property rights for the (great) author and then, by analogy, for all authors—provided only that they make something original. Originality and individuality become the central qualities we look for in conferring property rights. It should be noted, however, that Schumpeter thinks that economic reward to the entrepreneur is not central to entrepreneurship, precisely because the motivations of the iconoclast are not "rational," money-grubbing ones. This tension between romaticizing the author and making utilitarian arguments about the need to encourage authorship reappears throughout his book. In the English edition, Schumpeter denied the charge that he was glorifying the entrepreneur: "Our analysis of the role of the entrepreneur does not involve any 'glorification' of the type, as some readers of the first edition of this book seemed to think. We do hold that entrepreneurs have an economic function, as distinguished from, say, robbers. But we neither style every entrepreneur a genius or a benefactor to humanity, nor do we wish to express any opinion about the comparative merits of the social organization in which he plays his role, or about the question whether what he does could not be effected more cheaply in other ways." Id. at 90 n.1. To my mind, Schumpeter's adjectives speak for themselves.

44. Manne, *Insider Trading and the Stock Market*, 116. At another point Manne describes the entrepreneur in decidedly Faustian terms: "this upsetter of societies, this creator of disruptive forces." Id. at 119.

45. "The typical entrepreneur is more self-centered than other types, because he relies less than they do on tradition and connection and because his characteristic task—theoretically as well as practically—consists in breaking up old and creating new tradition." Schumpeter, *The Theory of Economic Development*, 91–92.

46. Schumpeter makes explicit the point that, although he views the entrepreneur as the engine of capitalist development, economic gain is not a vital motivation for the entrepreneur. Two out of three of the goals of the entrepreneur could in principle be taken care of by social arrangements other than the profit motive. Id. at 94.

47. Manne, *Insider Trading and the Stock Market*, 123. However, given Manne's own thesis, this would imply that at present either few entrepeneurs exist in large companies or that they are there, and are trading illegally.

48. Id.
49. Id. at 55.
50. Indeed, for the reasons given above, it is only through innovation that capital accumulation will continue.
51. Manne, *Insider Trading and the Stock Market*, 156–157.
52. Id. at 110.
53. Drawing on the ideas advanced in the chapter on information economics, one might ask other critics of insider trading regulation the extent to which their ideas achieve apparent determinacy without recourse to such romantic notions only by underplaying the kinds of paradoxes discussed by Grossman and Stiglitz, "Impossibility of Informationally Efficient Markets."

9. Spleens

1. This is certainly a theory which reappears time and again in the regulation of information; see International News Service v. Associated Press, 248 U.S. 215 (1918). But it is also frequently denounced; see Feist Publications, Inc. v. Rural Telephone Service Co., Inc., 111 S. Ct. 1282 (1991).
2. The two most impressive examples of such a combined moral-utilitarian analysis in the field of copyright are provided by Wendy Gordon and William Fisher. See particularly Wendy J. Gordon, "An Inquiry into the Merits of Copyright: The Challenges of Consistency, Consent, and Encouragement Theory," 41 *Stanford Law Review* 1343 (1989); William Fisher, "Reconstructing the Fair Use Doctrine," 101 *Harvard Law Review* 1659 (1988). In their prudential analysis of the optimum level of property rights, however, both articles concentrate more on the amount of property necessary to encourage authors to produce than on the countervailing need to keep a large amount of information free from property rights so that authors and creators will have the necessary raw materials with which to work. To put it in the terms I use in this book, the private property component of the prerequisites of information production gets more attention than the public domain. See Jessica Litman, "Public Domain," 39 *Emory Law Journal* 965 (1990). One explanation of this emphasis, even in the best and most sophisticated copyright literature, might be the power of the vision of authorship I have described in this book. The romantic vision of authorship emphasizes creativity and originality and deemphasizes the importance of sources, genre, and conventions of language and plot. Thus when economists and legal scholars come to do their analysis, most of them see the issue as the extent of property necessary to motivate and reward the creative spirit, rather than the extent of the public domain necessary to give the magpie genius the raw

material she needs. William Landes and Richard Posner's work on copyright offers a significant exception, though they themselves point out that the role of the public domain is a "neglected consideration." William Landes and Richard Posner, "An Economic Analysis of Copyright Law," 18 *Journal of Legal Studies* 332 (1989).

3. 8 F. Cas. 615, 619 (C.C.D. Mass. 1845). See also the discussion of Emerson v. Davies, in Chapter 2.

4. 793 P.2d 479 (Cal. 1990), *cert. denied,* 111 S. Ct. 1388 (1991).

5. Id. at 492.

6. Christian Sigmund Krause, "Uber den Buchernachdruck," 1 *Deutsches Museum* 415–417 (1783), quoted in and translated by Martha Woodmansee, "The Genius and the Copyright: Economic and Legal Conditions of the Emergence of the Author," 17 *Eighteenth Century Studies*, 425, 443–444 (1984).

7. Thanks to David Seipp for this example.

8. Moore v. Regents, 488. It is interesting to contrast this view with the majority's equally strong opinion that the "important policy concerns" worrying the dissent should be handled elsewhere: "Shedding no light on the Legislature's intent, philosophical issues about 'scientists bec[oming] entrepreneurs' are best debated in another forum." Id. at 492 n.34 (quoting id. at 514) (Mosk, J. dissenting)).

9. Id. at 495.

10. The classic examples are provided by juxtaposing International News Service v. Associated Press and Feist Publications, Inc. v. Rural Telephone Service Co., Inc. INS copied news from AP's newspapers and bulletin boards, thus enabling itself to produce a newspaper without having to pay quite as much for its news. "Facts" are not copyrightable, being merely the raw material from which the author manufactures an original creation. Yet the court felt that it had to give AP a quasi–property right in its news, because—among other reasons—it believed that any other decision would take away the incentive to operate costly news-gathering services and thus lead to an underinvestment in news collection. The court thus treated news as a qualified public good—like lighthouse keeping or national defense. In this case, the solution to the public goods problem was a qualified property right. In *Feist,* where the issue was the copyrightability of a white pages telephone directory, Justice O'Connor takes exactly the opposite line. The AP decision stresses the importance of securing to producers of information the fruits of their labor, in order to encourage further production. Justice O'Connor describes this as the outmoded "sweat of the brow" theory and rejects it as inconsistent with the structure of copyright.

11. Moore v. Regents, 495.

12. Lugosi v. Universal Pictures, 25 Cal.3d 813 (1979); Motschenbacher v. R. J. Reynolds Tobacco Company, 498 F.2d 821 (9th Cir. 1974), cited in Moore v. Regents, 490.

13. Moore v. Regents, 490.

14. See generally Ludwig Wittgenstein, *Philosophical Investigations* (1958): "This [philosophical error] is connected with the conception of naming as, so to speak, an occult process. Naming appears as a *queer* connexion of a word with an object. And you really get such a queer connexion when the philosopher tries to bring out *the* relation between name and thing by staring at an object in front of him and repeating a name or even the word 'this' innumerable times. For philosophical problems arise when language *goes on a holiday.* And *here* we may indeed fancy naming to be some remarkable act of mind, as it were a baptism of an object. And we can also say the word 'this' *to* the object, as it were *address* the object as 'this'—a queer use of this word, which doubtless only occurs in doing philosophy." Id. at 19 (emphasis in original).

15. Moore v. Regents, 490.

16. Louis Brandeis and Samuel Warren, "The Right to Privacy," 4 *Harvard Law Review* 193 (1890).

17. Motschenbacher v. R. J. Reynolds Tobacco Co. (arguing that the tobacco company misappropriated, in an advertisement for cigarettes, the distinctive narrow white pinstripe that appears on the leading edges of Lothar Motschenbacher's race car and the oval background to his racing number "11").

18. Hirsch v. S. C. Johnson & Son, Inc., 280 N.W. 2d 129, 130 (1979).

19. Lugosi v. Universal Pictures (affirming the trial court's decision that Lugosi had a protectable property right "in his facial characterisitics and the individual manner of his likeness and appearance as Count Dracula").

20. But of course most labor theories of property have as their most basic postulate the ownership of one's own body. It is from this *a priori* naturalistic property right that labor theorists deduce the case for one's ownership of the fruits of that body's work.

21. Moore v. Regents, 490.

22. Id. at 490 n.30.

23. Of course, this distinction breaks down fairly quickly. For one thing, there is no such thing as a "theory-free" description of facts, and thus all natural facts are really social facts if only one picks the right "society." Thus, more precisely, we could say that the ordinary language notion of privacy starts from the protection of the individual's subjectively defined "personal information" from the gaze of the peer group the individual chooses to recognize, given the common knowledge which that peer

group possesses. The more the revealing party seems to profit by the information, the more we allow the "victim" to define the sphere of privacy. Thus a butcher would probably not be found to have violated George Bernard Shaw's privacy rights if he revealed in a letter to *The Times* that Shaw secretly violated his vegetarian principles by eating pork pies. But if the butcher demanded £100 on pain of disclosure, we call that demand "blackmail," this actually *prohibiting* the commodification of the information.

24. Moore v. Regents, 492–493 (citations and footnote omitted) (emphasis added in part). It should be noted that although the court can justifiably say that the themes of originality, inventive effort and functional use are appropriate to a discussion of patent law, these are in fact the themes that organise the entire opinion, and not merely the section on patent law. The mention of artistry—largely irrelevant in the patent law context—is further support for my thesis.

25. There is a parallel here to Saul Levmore's discussion of farmers who own land that, unbeknownst to them, contains valuable mineral deposits. If a mineral company seeks to buy the land, should it be able to respond dishonestly to the farmer's inquiry about possible mineral deposits? Levmore is convinced the answer is yes, and goes on to say that any attempt by the farmer to find out the full value of his land is "despicable" because he has no intention of mining the land himself. Saul Levmore, "Securities and Secrets: Insider Trading and the Law of Contracts," 68 *Virginia Law Review* 117 (1982).

10. Stereotyping Information and Searching for an Author

1. Frank H. Easterbrook, "Insider Trading, Secret Agents, Evidentiary Privileges, and the Production of Information," 1981 *Supreme Court Review* 314.

2. For a discussion of the relevance of the assumption that social institutions are subject to critique by reason, and an analysis of the *conservative* objections to such an idea, see James Boyle, "A Process of Denial: Bork and Post-Modern Conservatism," 3 *Yale Journal of Law and Human Rights* 263, 299–314 (1991).

3. See, e.g., Whalen v. Roe, 429 U.S. 589 (1976) (defining privacy in terms of "the individual interest in avoiding disclosure of personal matters, and the interest in independence in making certain kinds of important decisions") Id. at 599–600. The focus is on retention and control of information to protect the person and the life plan. One interpretation of this idea is that information is the only *resource,* or form of wealth, the need for which can be convincingly derived from the liberal theory of

personhood. This may be one reason that Rust v. Sullivan 500 U.S. 173 (1991)—a case which allowed the state to prohibit government-funded doctors from revealing the *possibility* of abortion to pregnant women—disturbs people who would find a government refusal to *fund* abortion unexceptionable. For an interesting analysis in the light of current Supreme Court doctrine see Francis S. Chlapowski, Note, "The Constitutional Protection of Informational Privacy," 71 *Buffalo University Law Review* 133 (1991).

4. An inexact analogy may help to demonstrate the profoundly contingent, socially constructed nature of our notion of "public sphere" and "privacy." Imagine a society in which everyone lived in communal dormitories, with socialized child-rearing, limited taboos about public displays of sexual behavior, and so on. Imagine also that universal access to excellent health care was seen as a defining, essential quality of the society. Then imagine a person in that society who offered permanently to give up her right to health care, in return for some release from communal obligations. Such a transaction might well be seen as no more legitimate than an attempt by a citizen in this society permanently to renounce his vote, or his right to counsel, perhaps even to sell himself into slavery. That transaction might seem to violate the "logic" of the public sphere in a way that for us, in our society, it does not. Conversely, imagine the way that "privacy" would be seen in such a society. Certainly, an individual whose neighbor in the dormitory threatened to reveal some unpleasant fact would be unhappy, but would that society necessarily have thought "control of information about oneself" to be an important principle of social organization, as opposed to, say, "policing those who shirk their social duties"?

My point is not that certain forms of social organization *necessarily* produce certain principled normative concerns. Quite the contrary. Rather, a process by which we imagine changes in fundamental aspects of our social life makes it easier to grasp the contingency of our own beliefs. In fact, the relationship of social form to normative structure is highly contingent—perhaps a dormitory-based social system would be *more* concerned with privacy than we are—but its contingency is concealed precisely by the fact that, within any given society, the normative structure is widely shared. Thus it seems that our particular association of individuality with control over information, and our belief that inequalities of information in market transactions raise concerns that inequalities of wealth do not, are both "rational," or even inevitable, principles potentially explicable by rights theory or economic analysis.

5. I use the word to mean that as a society we project onto an institution or set of actions an emotional and intellectual charge—in this case a positive

one—and that we then perceive that charge as always already being contained *within* the romanticized object. See Peter L. Berger and Thomas Luckmann, *The Social Construction of Reality* (1980), and James Boyle, "The Politics of Reason," 133 *University of Pennsylvania Law Review* 685 (1985).

6. Felix Cohen, "Transcendental Nonsense and the Functional Approach," 35 *Columbia Law Review* 1 (1935).

7. See Barnaby J. Feder, "Toward Defining Free Speech in the Computer Age," *New York Times*, sec. 4, p. 5 (November 3, 1991); Barnaby J. Feder, "Computer Concern Assailed on Anti-Semitic Notes," *New York Times*, A21 (October 24, 1991); Barnaby J. Feder, "Computer Speech—Also Free," *New York Times*, A24 (October 30, 1991); Michael W. Miller, "Prodigy Computer Network Bans Bias Notes from Bulletin Board," *Wall Street Journal*, B1, B6 (October 24, 1991).

8. Barton Crockett, "DA Probes Practices at Prodigy," *Network World*, 4 (April 15, 1991) (emphasis added).

9. Jerry Berman and Marc Rotenberg, "Free Speech in an Electronic Age," *New York Times*, sec. 3, p. 13 (January 6, 1991). Civil libertarian groups have tried to get the Supreme Court to recognize that some of the classic "public spaces" of the nineteenth century no longer function in contemporary society; the contemporary equivalent of the speaker in Hyde Park may be the leafleteer in the enclosed shopping mall. The Supreme Court has proven remarkably resistant to analogy on this topic.

10. "CompuServe's CIS product is in essence an electronic, for-profit library that carries a vast number of publications and collects usage and membership fees from its subscribers in return for access to the publications." Cubby, Inc. v. Compuserve, Inc., 776 F. Supp. 135, 140 (1991) (per Leisure, J).

11. Peter H. Lewis, "The Executive Computer: On Electronic Bulletin Boards, What Rights Are at Stake?" *New York Times*, sec. 3, p. 8 (December 23, 1990).

12. The best summation of the Prodigy debate itself may have come at the end of a *Boston Globe* article. "Industry analyst Gary Arlen has a different view. What may have happened, he says, is that Prodigy unwittingly attracted people looking for a real communications network instead of consumers eager to spend money in an electronic shopping mall. Citing a computer magazine editorial, he says, 'Prodigy's message to its subscribers seems to be "Shut up and shop." ' " Chris Reidy, "Computer Flap: Is Speech Free on Prodigy?" *Boston Globe*, 35 (January 30, 1991).

13. This is one of my disagreements with the economic analysts of information issues. Easterbrook, for example, believes that the problem with intellectual property issues is that abstract (and I would say, metaphoric)

terms conceal from the court the *real* functional requisites of the information market. Yet to engage in economic analysis is (at least as Easterbrook does it) to abstract certain aspects of a complex social situation—whether of blackmailing, baby selling, book writing, or boat covering—and to declare that this is *really* a market. And that, of course, is a metaphoric, analogical process.

14. Steven Shavell suggested to me that when professional economists talk about "public goods" they do *not* mean that there are a general category of goods that share the same economic characteristics, manifest the same dysfunctions, and that may thus benefit from pretty similar corrective solutions. Most economists, he argued, would agree that there is no such thing as "public goods"; there is merely an infinite series of particular problems (some of overproduction, some of underproduction, and so on), each with a particular solution that cannot be deduced from the theory, but that instead would depend on local empirical factors. If this is what economists think, I would be happy to agree with it. Certainly, lawyer-economists often seem to have more expansive ideas. See Landes and Posner, "An Economic Analysis of Copyright Law," 18 *Journal of Legal Studies* 325, 326 (1989) (a distinguishing characteristic of intellectual property is its 'public good' aspect). See also Demsetz, "The Private Protection of Public Goods"; Easterbrook, "Insider Trading"; Edmund W. Kitch, "The Law and Economics of Rights in Valuable Information," 9 *Journal of Legal Studies* 683 (1980). Economics texts also make more general claims. James M. Buchanan, *The Demand and Supply of Public Goods* (1968); Paul Samuelson, "Contrast Welfare Conditions for Joint Supply and for Public Goods," 51 *Review of Economics and Statistics* 26 (1969); Earl Thompson, "The Perfectly Competitive Production of Collective Goods," 50 *Review of Economics and Statistics* 1 (1968). This tendency to make more general claims seems to be true of economists of all political opinions and theoretical types. See Michael Perelman, "High Technology, Intellectual Property, and Public Goods: The Rationality of Socialism," 20 *Review of Radical Political Economy* 277 (1988); David Hemenway, *Prices and Choices: Microeconomic Vignettes* (2nd ed. 1988). Finally, detailed articles *by* economists often make the same mistakes that one would expect of someone working with an overgeneral and reified "public good" vision of information. Kenneth Arrow, "Economic Welfare and the Allocation of Resources for Invention," in *The Rate and Direction of Inventive Activity: Economic and Social Factors* (National Bureau Committee for Economic Research ed. 1962). Nevertheless, there are articles putting forward ideas consistent with Shavell's point of view (Jack Hirshleifer, "The Private and Social Value of Information, and the Reward to Inventive Activity," 61 *American Economic Review* 561 [1971]), although

it is noticeable that these articles generally adopt the tone of a protestant dissenter, rather than that of normal science. In the end, my conclusion has to be that Shavell is committing the entirely laudable error of being too kind to his colleagues.

15. In other words, the argument on behalf of the doctors, that we must secure to producers the fruits of their labors in order to encourage research, has an equal and opposite counterpart. The opposing argument identifies Moore as a co-producer in terms of desert and argues that unless individuals are rewarded for allowing their genetic material to be used for research, too little genetic material will be made available to researchers. The California Supreme Court avoids, suppresses, or counters these arguments by appealing to its audience's reverence for the original, creative laborer, the transformer of the environment, whose property rights are appropriately limited by their very function. The ideal of authorship first *identifies* the researchers as the relevant parties and then *justifies* their property rights.

16. Saul Levmore, "Securities and Secrets: Insider Trading and the Law of Contracts," 68 *Virginia Law Review* 142 (1982).

11. The International Political Economy of Authorship

1. "Nimbus Announces Breakthrough Holographic Labelling Technology for Compact Discs," *PR Newswire* (September 11, 1995).
2. Annual Report of the Recording Industry Association of America (1993).
3. "Nimbus Announces Breakthrough Holographic Labelling Technology for Compact Discs."
4. "Industry Presses U.S. to Act against Thirty-six Countries for Copyright Piracy," *BNA Patent, Trademark, and Copyright Law Daily* (Feb. 22, 1994).
5. "Bill Would Amend Trade Act to Take Account of GATT-TRIPS Implementation," *BNA Patent, Trademark, and Copyright Law Daily* (June 22, 1994).
6. Dorothy Schrader, "Intellectual Property Provisions of the GATT, 1994: 'The TRIPS Agreement,'" *Congressional Research Service for Congress* (March 16, 1994); Uruguay Round Agreement Act, Pub. L. No. 103–465, 1994 U.S.C.C.A.N. (108 Stat) (to be codified at 19 U.S.C. 2411(c)).
7. Pete Engardio et al., "Yankee Traders Breathe a Sigh of Relief," *Business Week*, 39 (February 3, 1992).
8. See David Gantz, "A Post-Uruguay Round Introduction to International Trade Law in the United States," 12 *Arizona Journal of International and Comparative Law* 7, 13 (1995).
9. Warlike metaphors abound. In a Senate Hearing, the chief executive officers of the Motion Picture Association compared the battle over TRIPs

to the Cold War, and unauthorized copying to thermonuclear weapons. His analogies were all the more striking since they were being used to describe piracy of Snow White videocassettes. *Hearing of the International Trade Subcommittee of the Senate Finance Committee,* 102 Cong., 2nd Sess. (Remarks of Jack Valenti, President and CEO, Motion Picture Association of America).

10. "You feel the importance and necessity of defending property today. Well, begin by recognising the first and most sacred of all properties, the one which is neither a transmission nor an acquisition but a *creation,* namely literary property . . . reconcile the artists with society by means of property." Victor Hugo, speech to the Conseil d'Etat, September 30, 1849, quoted in B. Edelman, *Ownership of the Image* (1979).

11. Harold Demsetz, "The Private Protection of Public Goods," 13 *Journal of Law and Economics* 293, 295 (1970).

12. Eric Wolfhard, "International Trade in Intellectual Property: The Emerging GATT Regime," 49 *University of Toronto Faculty Law Review* 106 (1991).

13. Statement of Carla Hills on the signing of a bilateral Memorandum of Understanding with the People's Republic of China, *Federal News Service On-Line* (January 17, 1992).

14. David Judson, "Lawmaker Urges U.S. to Come Clean on 'Seed Ripoffs,' " *Gannett News Service* (July 19, 1990).

15. Michael D. Lemonick, "Seeds of Conflict," *Time,* 50 (September 25, 1995).

16. Darrell Posey and Graham Dutfield, *Beyond Intellectual Property Rights: Towards Traditional Resource Rights for Indigenous and Local Communities* (1995). See also J. R. Kloppenberg, *First the Seed: The Political Economy of Plant Biotechnology, 1492–2000* (1988); Darrell Posey, "Intellectual Property Rights: What Is the Position of Ethnobiology?" 10 *Journal of Ethnobiology* 93–98 (1990); *Intellectual Property Rights for Indigenous Peoples: A Sourcebook* (T. Greaves ed., 1994).

17. Daniel Goleman, "Shamans and Their Lore May Vanish with the Forest," *New York Times,* C1 (June 11, 1991).

18. The example is actually a more complex one. When tested as a drug to ameliorate the symptoms of diabetes, the alkaloids derived from the periwinkle did not perform well. Subsequent testing showed that the drug had other, equally valuable uses. How, then, should we value the contribution of Madagascar's flora and indigenous medical lore? At zero? If we do, how are we to avoid public goods problems, or the tragedy of the commons problems that I discuss?

19. Fred Pearce, "Science and Technology: Bargaining for the Life of the Forest—Poor Nations Want Drug and Food Companies to Pay for the Plants They Plunder," *The Independent,* 37 (March 17, 1991).

20. Goleman, "Shamans and Their Lore," C6.

21. Id.
22. Pearce, "Science and Technology."
23. Basic Books, Inc., et al. v. Kinko's Graphics 758 F. Supp. 1522 (1991).
24. Id.
25. Campbell v. Acuff-Rose Music, Inc., 114 S. Ct. 1164 (1994).
26. Kinko's, 1530 (emphasis added).
27. Claire Whitmer, "Industry Divided over Software Patents; Patent and Trademark Office Weighs Protecting vs. Stifling Innovation," *InfoWorld*, 20 (February 28, 1994).
28. Id.
29. Bruce Rubenstein, "Billion Dollar Win for Intel Corporation: Courtroom Victory Creates Huge Competitive Edge," *Corporate Legal Times* 1 (January 1993).
30. Lawrence M. Fisher, "Patents: Aggressive Defender Branches Out," *New York Times*, A38 (January 25, 1992); Edmund L. Andrews, "Patents: There's Cash in Mining the Courts," *New York Times*, D2 (November 9, 1992).
31. For a discussion of the intersection of patent and antitrust see Louis Kaplow, "Patent-Antitrust Intersection: A Reappraisal," 97 *Harvard Law Review* 1813 (1984).
32. Federal Courts Improvement Act, Pub. L. No. 97–164, 96 Stat. 25 (1982).
33. Lawrence Baum, "The Federal Courts and Patent Validity: An Analysis of the Record," 56 *Journal of the Patent Office Society* 758, 760 (1974).
34. Robert P. Merges, "Commercial Success and Patent Standards," 76 *California Law Review* 805, 822–823 (1988).
35. Rubenstein, "Billion Dollar Win for Intel Corporation," 1.
36. Elizabeth Corcoran, "Microsoft Settles Case with Justice: Software Giant Accused of Boosting Prices, Thwarting Competitors," *New York Times*, A1 (July 17, 1994); Proposed Final Judgment in United States of America v. Microsoft Corp., 59 Fed. Reg. 42,845 (proposed August 19, 1994).
37. Harsh reactions to criticisms of the current system show the extent to which the author-inventor vision becomes an article of religious faith, rather than a construct to balance efficiency against incentives, the vibrancy of the public domain against the motivation of future creators. When Pamela Samuelson, a prominent intellectual property scholar, offered some mild criticisms of the expansiveness of the current system— suggesting a sui generis regime for software—she was accused of being a Marxist in the pay of the Japanese who envied the creative genius of the programmers and wanted to take away their rights as a consequence. As she pointed out at the time, the final accusation is particularly ironic, because those within the software engineering community who are protesting the current expansiveness of intellectual property, fit the creative genius model very well.

38. "Intellectual Property and the National Information Infrastructure," *The Report of the Working Group on Intellectual Property Rights* (September 1995) (hereinafter White Paper).
39. Id. at 71, 90–95.
40. Pamela Samuelson, "Legally Speaking: The NII Intellectual Property Report," *Communications of the ACM*, 21 (December 1994).
41. White Paper, 84.
42. Id. at 84 n.266.
43. Elizabeth Rosenthal, "Research, Promotion, and Profits: Spotlight Is on the Drug Industry," *New York Times*, A1 (February 21, 1993).

12. Private Censors, Transgenic Slavery, and Electronic Indenture

1. I have argued elsewhere that it is not: "Modernist Social Thought: Roberto Unger's Passion," 98 *Harvard Law Review* 1066 (1985); "The Politics of Reason," 133 *University of Pennsylvania Law Review* 685 (1985); "Legal Fiction: *Law's Empire* by Ronald Dworkin" (book review), 38 *Hastings Law Journal* 401 (1987); "Is Subjectivity Possible? The Post-Modern Subject in Legal Theory," 62 *University of Colorado Law Review* 489 (1991).
2. The first time I was able to find the phrase "private censorship" was in Justice Bright's opinion in Hughes Tool Co. v. Motion Picture Ass'n of America, Inc., 66 F. Supp. 1006, 1009 (S.D. N.Y. 1946) ("under economic threat of finding more than 90% of the theatres barred to them; producers, distributors, and exhibitors are compelled to conform their advertising to defendant's arbitrary, discriminatory, and preconceived notions of public propriety; a private censorship is imposed upon the industry, by which defendant has assumed quasi-governmental functions and police powers which may properly be exercised only by governmental agencies"). The phrase is best known from Red Lion Broadcasting Co., Inc., v. FCC, 395 U.S. 367 (1969) ("The First Amendment does not protect private censorship by broadcasters who are licensed by the Government to use a scarce resource which is denied to others"). It also formed the title of Wendy Gordon's memorable article, "Toward a Jurisprudence of Benefits: The Norms of Copyright and the Problem of Private Censorship," 57 *University of Chicago Law Review* 1009 (1990).
3. San Francisco Arts & Athletics, Inc., et al. v. United States Olympic Committee, 483 U.S. 522, 532–533 (Powell, J., quoting Zacchini v. Scripps-Howard Broadcasting Co., 433 U.S. 562, 575 [1977]). I may be a griping skeptic, but I would venture to believe that if Congress thought that the word "Olympic" held a positive connotation and a "commercial and promotional value" because of the work that the *United States* Olympic

Committee has done, then Congress is anything but reasonable. There was this whole thing in Greece, see . . .

4. Felix S. Cohen, "Transcendental Nonsense and the Functional Approach," 35 *Columbia Law Review* 35 (1935).
5. Id. at 532.
6. Texas v. Johnson 491 U.S. 397, 429–430 (1989).
7. David Streitfeld, "Whose Life Is It Anyhow?" *Washington Post*, X15 (September 12, 1993). Leavitt also said that he had initially contemplated acknowledging Spender, but had decided not to do so under advice from the publisher's lawyers. Later, apparently after talking to the lawyers again, Leavitt was to change his story, something that did not make his behavior more morally attractive.
8. "Spender Fury after Book Ban Is Flouted," *Evening Standard*, 8 (June 27, 1995).
9. Streitfeld, "Whose Life Is It Anyhow?" X15.
10. There would still have been the possibility of asserting a variety of tort claims—that Spender was somehow presented in a "false light," intrusion upon seclusion, and so on. The first could be defeated if the portrayal was truthful, the latter if the biographical material was a matter of public knowledge or record. Both claims are made additionally problematic because Leavitt's book is a novel, not a biography—the main character is not named as Sir Steven Spender.
11. John Ezard, "Spender Wins Right to Suppress Novel," *The Guardian Home Page*, 10 (February 18, 1994).
12. If it was science fiction, that would not necessarily be a bad thing. One of the humbling realizations involved in writing this book was that science fiction writers are doing considerably better than academics in producing thoughtful and provocative social-theoretical commentary on the information society.
13. Samuel Butler, *Erewhon*, 182–183 (Hans-Peter Breuer and Daniel F. Howard eds., 1981) (1872). There is a certain appropriate irony to the use of this passage in a book commenting on the control of property and meaning by authors. Butler originally published the "Book of Machines" chapters in an essay called *Darwin among the Machines*. This was initially taken to be a satire of Darwin's work—by showing that on the same evidence one could argue that machines were "evolving." Yet Butler himself wrote to Darwin claiming that the opposite was true; the "Book of Machines" was meant to defend Darwinism by mocking exaggerated *religious* arguments, such that those which claimed to find proof of divine purpose in every aspect of the material world. Then again, Butler made notes in his diary which indicate that he was not entirely honest in offering this reassurance. Finally, there are entries in Butler's notebooks

that convince me he may well have half-believed his own arguments about the possibility of machine development and, like many a utopian architect before him, was taking refuge in irony and sarcasm in order to have it both ways. Breuer and Howard quote the following interesting excerpt, paralleling explicitly the efforts of contemporary behaviorists and cognitive psychologists to explain how mental consciousness can arise from—*ex hypothesi*—nonconscious biological building blocks: "This element of free-will which comes from the unseen kingdom in which the writs of our thoughts run not, must be carried to the most tenuous atoms, whose action is supposed most purely chemical and mechanical." Samuel Butler, *Notebooks*, 197 (1889), quoted in Erewhon, 187. It is precisely such a reflection on the difficulty of explaining human consciousness as an assemblage of individually nonconscious elements that has made some philosophers more open to the possibility of machine consciousness, similarly assembled from nonconscious elements.

14. It was precisely to cash in on this feeling of revulsion that Marxists referred to wage labor as wage slavery.
15. Robert Nozick, *Anarchy, State, and Utopia*, 85 et seq. (1974).

13. Proposals and Objections

1. Sadly the line is François de La Rochefoucauld's and not my own.
2. One response is to say that it must be in the interest of companies to insist on strong intellectual property protection, otherwise they would not have done so. At this point, the argument has become circular.
3. Very briefly, my theoretical objections are as follows. First, functionalist arguments are often overdeterminative. They can be used to explain any outcome, and thus nothing at all. Both the repression and the encouragement of infantile sexuality, a free press, mini skirts, and anything else for that matter, can be portrayed as deeply necessary to the current stage of monopoly capitalism. Second, such arguments tend to move in circles, something like this: "The legal regime is a functional response to the problems of the time. Despite its apparent alternatives, and its apparently nonfunctional features, this *must* be the functionally appropriate system because it is the one we ended up with." Third, these arguments often ignore important historical and geographical differences of development—such as the quite different historical development of copyright in Germany, France, England, and the United States—particularly those differences which would lead us to doubt their overweening determinism. For instance, Carla Hesse has shown fascinating differences between the French and the English treatments of the public domain. Carla Hesse, *Publishing and Cultural Politics in Revolutionary Paris, 1789–1810,*

122–125 (1991). For the best general critique of these errors see Robert Gordon, "Critical Legal Histories" in *Critical Legal Studies*, 93 (James Boyle ed., 1992).

4. But even here I would want to cavil slightly at the general form of the proposition. It seems possible that, in some intellectual property fields, ease of copying might be associated with the very technological developments that made it feasible to be rewarded for innovation or for information production, simply by being "the first to market." Thus technology might make copy-right both possible and unnecessary at the same moment.

5. One answer is that the system cannot have been functional; otherwise it would not have been changed. Not only is this argument obviously circular, but it also manifestly contradicts the evidence of the significant geographical and historical differences in the actual development of European copyright regimes. See Hesse, *Publishing and Cultural Politics*.

6. One response to this kind of argument is to say that obviously there were no functional alternatives, because otherwise we would not have ended up with the system we in fact have. At this point, of course, the functionalist argument has again become circular and thus both irrefutable and meaningless.

7. Bleistein v. Donaldson Lithographing Co., 188 U.S. 239, 249–250 (1903) (emphasis added).

8. Marc Rotenberg, "Communications Privacy: Implications for Network Design," 36 *Communications of the ACM* 17 (1993).

Conclusion

1. In this context, the ambiguity between the two uses of the word "supposed" seems entirely appropriate.

2. This is not to say that I am arguing in favor of the labor theory of value. One of the achievements of marginalism in economics and legal realism in property law was to point out the flaws of both the Marxist labor theory of value and the conventional vision of property which it opposed.

3. This, I think, is a point that Foucault would have agreed to, even as he would have insisted (again rightly in my view) that the method that grand theory offers to *find* and criticize this "discourse" is exactly the wrong one.

4. See Jaques H. Drèze, "A Paradox in Information Theory," in Drèze, *Essays in Economic Decisions under Uncertainty*, 105 (1987).

5. I have to say that I like the irony of saying this near the end of a book whose myriad footnotes are the fruit of every electronic research service the world has to offer.

6. Cf. D. M. Lamberton, "The Emergence of Information Economics," in *Communication and Information Economics: New Perspectives*, 7–22 (M. Jussawalla and H. Ebenfield eds., 1984): "The emergence of information economics can be seen as response to the deficiencies of economic theory based on perfect knowledge, the failures of policy, or the spectacular advent of intelligent electronics with greatly enhanced capacity for communication, computation, and control. Whichever is the preferred interpretation, it remains a personal judgment whether the battle for recognition and respectability has only just been joined, is well advanced, has been won, or perhaps been lost." Id. at 7.

7. Because of the "infinite" vision of information I discussed earlier, we do not tend to see information as a good, the maximization of which is not always a good thing. A moment's reflection should confirm the fact that there are occasions when the unbridled growth of information may actually be hurtful. Some decisions become *harder* with more information. See Drèze, "A Paradox in Information." When we think of information not as a good, but as the life blood of the public sphere of debate, or the perfect information of a market model, we ignore the *constraints* produced by overproduction. To use a simple example, given a retrieval system of a limited capacity, I will prefer to have a smaller database which will give me answers 50 percent of the time rather than a larger, more complex database which theoretically would give answers 100 percent of the time but which so overwhelms my abilities to retrieve and process data that I can only find answers 40 percent of the time. In neoclassical price theory, these kinds of trade-offs are exactly the ones that market decisions make so well. Yet the double quality of information— its being both part of the model and a good to be traded under the model—may prevent the operation of economic feedback mechanisms on the level of market behavior, and make questions of microeconomic analysis undecidable on the level of scholarship. As the case of the polluting factory shows, the parallel to welfare economics operates at both levels, the practical and the theoretical.

8. Of course, as I tried to show earlier, the author ideal often does appear in that particular issue, especially when analyzed by Henry Manne.

9. I admit that these are abstractions that do not resolve concrete cases, that they frequently contradict each other, and so on, and so on.

10. Rust v. Sullivan, 500 U.S. 173 (1991).

11. "For of all sad words of tongue or pen / the saddest are these: 'It might have been!' " (John Greenleaf Whittier).

Appendix B

1. There are different ways to explain the nature and protection of authors' rights, which are based on various historical and cultural differences. We

honor those differences, and we attempt to find common language to express our concerns and aspirations for the international intellectual property system.

2. The way of thinking which this exclusive idea of "authorship" supports also has consequences beyond the realm of law. To a greater or lesser extent, we tend to enact this exclusive understanding of the "author" in our practices: for example, as scholars, scientists, teachers, writers, and business people. That effect, however, is beyond the immediate scope of this declaration.

Acknowledgments

This project has consumed me for five years. I have pursued it under the auspices of four excellent law schools, involving myself in at least three disciplines where I had only the most dubious of credentials. Everywhere I went, both geographically and conceptually, I have profited from the kindness of strangers who have guided me through libraries and terminologies, corrected at least some of my errors, and been generous with advice and encouragement. I find, as I sit down to write the acknowledgments, that the useful self-protective phrase "intellectual debts too numerous to mention" is literal truth in my case. Out of this tidal wave of kindness, I must single out the special contributions of Keith Aoki, David Gray Carlson, Terry Fisher, Bob Gordon, Margreta de Grazia, Darrell Posey, Jamie Raskin, Mark Rose, William van Alstyne, Martha Woodmansee, and the organizers of the "Frontiers of Legal Thought Conference" at Duke Law School. My colleague Peter Jaszi bears a disproportionate share of the blame for this book, having first inspired and then instructed me. His blend of literary erudition and doctrinal sophistication is without peer. I received invaluable benefit from David Lange's writing on the public domain as well as from his frequently expressed skepticism about this work (and its author). I would also like to recognize the generous financial support of the Washington College of Law, Duke Law School, Harvard Law School, and Boston University Law School. I have particularly benefited from the excellent research assistance provided by Gail Brashers-Krug, Jeff Dobbins, Sarah Marchesi, and Michael O'Connor. Finally, I would like to thank my two children, David and Alison, and my wife, Lauren, for making life worth living.

Washington, D.C., September 1995

Index

Adorno, Theodor, 213n14
Affiliated Ute Citizens of Utah v. U.S., 235n10
AIDS, 128
American Civil Liberties Union, Privacy Project, 203n3
Andersen, Torben M., 216n4
Aporia, definition of, 218n6
Apple Computer, Inc. v. Microsoft Corp., 208n6
Arrow, Kenneth, 41–42, 225n24, 225n24, 226n27, 241n29, 250n14; on information production and unregulated markets, 88–89
Artificial intelligence: as assemblage of nonconscious elements, 256n13; and Samuel Butler, 255–256; and ownership of intelligent beings, 151–153
Association for Computing Machinery(ACM), Code of Ethics, 165
Audio Home Recording Act, 205n11
Authorship: and construction of self-interest, 159–161; and craft, 54; current regime as impediment to, 165; defense of, 16; and definition of "book," 53; and Divine inspiration, 54; and effects on free speech, 145–150; and genetic information, 106; history of concept of, 53; and iconoclasm, 230n14; idea/expression distinction in, 56–57; inevitability of idea of, 158; and inspiration, 54; and intellectual property, 113; and international effects of author-centered regime, 119–143; and invention of plagiarism, 54; as a liberating ideal, 59–60; and literary criticism, 59; medieval ideas of, 53; and originality, 54–55; and patents, 206n13; as premise for an intellectual property system, 175–176; as a problem-solving method, 116; as Procrustean concept, 117–118; and recombination of prior elements, 53; as rhetoric, 157–158; scholarship on, 205n9; and Shakespeare, 54; as a solution to ideological problems, 60; as a technological by-product, 161–163; and tensions between utilitarianism and romance, 243n43; and undervaluation of sources, 160; Woodmansee's theories of, 54

Baird, Douglas, 223n18
Baker, Edwin C., 220n9
Barlow, John Perry, 201n4
Basic Books Inc., et al. v. Kinko's Graphics, 130–132, 253n23
Bellagio Conference, 143
Bellagio Declaration, 143, 169; text of, 192–200
Berger, Peter L., 249n5

Berman, Jerry, 112
Bio-informatics, 2, 8
Biological Information Theory and Chowder Society, 2
Biotechnology. *See* Genetic information
Bittlingmayer, George, 215n23
Blackmail: and the accidental blackmailer, 66; and baseline for measuring harm, 71; as a cause of other forms of crime, 69–70; Coase's analysis of, 66–67; and commodification, 109; compared to insider trading, 78; and constitutional coercion, 74; and economic explanations, 62; Epstein's analysis of, 68–71; and false consciousness, 68; Ginsburg's analysis of, 66; and Hohfeldian analysis, 73; compared to insider trading; Landes and Posner's work on, 62–66; libertarian analysis of, 68; Lindgren's analysis of, 72–73, 231nn1,2; Nozick's analysis of, 68, 70–72; and paternalism, 75; and the private realm, 77; and prohibition of mutually beneficial transactions, 66; and the public-private distinction, 77, 79; as a puzzle, 61; and the rejection of consumer sovereignty, 74; and the sale of information to the media, 78; the sale of silence distinguished from the sale of information, 78, 110; and the search for a general principle, 75; social meaning of, 75; and typing information issues, 109
Blackmun, Harry, 235n10
Bleistein v. Donaldson Lithographing Company, 55–56, 91–92, 94–95, 257n7
Block, Walter, 232n14
Board of Trade of City of Chicago v. Dow Jones & Co., Inc., 40
Bolter, David, 202n8
Boyle, James, 202n7, 205n9, 212n4, 228n3, 229n4, 230n7, 231n3, 247n2, 249n5
Braudel, Fernand, 190
Brandeis, Louis. *See* Warren and Brandeis
Branscomb, Anne W., 201n5
Brecher, Elliot, 235n10
Breyer, Stephen, 219n7
British Society of Authors, 150
Bromberg and Lowenfels, 235n10
Buchanan, James M., 250n14
Business Software Alliance, 121
Butler, Samuel, 255n13; on machine consciousness, 152

Campbell v. Acuff-Rose Music, Inc., 253n25
Carlton, Dennis W., 236n15
Carney, William J., 215n24, 242n39
Carson v. Here's Johnny Portable Toilets, Inc., 103, 104, 211n21
Censorship. *See* Private censorship
Challú, Pablo, 226n28
Chiarella v. U.S. , 82–83, 234n4,6, 238n19
Civil liberties, and the electronic frontier, 249n9
Clay, Jason, 129
Coase, Ronald H., 20, 66, 67, 68, 69, 71, 74, 125, 209n11, 215n25
Codes, electronic and genetic, 8
Cohen, Felix S., 249n6, 255n4
Conservation International. *See* Plotkin, Mark
Cook, Walter W., 233n22
Copyright, 16, 18–20; and authorship, 57; and basic constellation of ideas, 114; and creation *ex nihilo*, 57; definition of, 18; fact works, 208n5; fair use doctrine, 130, 208n7; history of, in Germany, 52; and idea/expression distinction, 56–58; moral justification for, 53; and negative effects on free speech, 18–19; notions of property in, 18; and originality of the author's spirit, 55; and romantic vision of authorship, 56; strangeness of, 18; structure of the doctrine, 19, 207n1; technological obsolescence of, 162–163; and telephone directories, 245n10
Copyright Act (1988), 149
Cox, James D., 210n13, 215n24, 235n11
Cubby, Inc. v. CompuServe, Inc., 249n10
Cultural Survival, 129
Curare. *See* Ethnobotany
Cyberspace. *See* Internet
Cyberpunk, 1

Darwin, Charles, 255n13
Databases. *See* Intellectual property
David, Paul, 206–207n15
Definitionalism, as a moral method, 144
Demsetz, Harold, 88, 210n13, 223n17, 224n19, 236n14, 241n31, 250n14, 252n11
Diamond, Peter A., 216n1
Diamond v. Chakrabarty, 203n5
Dickens, Charles, 123, 202n1
Dirks v. S.E.C., 234n5
Disclosure: and authorship, 117; duty of mining companies regarding, 85; Easter-

brook's analysis of, 85; and financial markets, 90; Levmore's analysis of, 117

DNA, 4; definition of, 203n4. *See also* Human Genome Project

Drèze, Jacques H., 216n4, 257n4, 258n7

Dutfield, Graham. *See* Posey and Dutfield

Easterbrook, Frank H., 117, 204n9, 213n10, 215n23, 220n9, 225nn23, 27, 239n22, 247n1; and baseline errors, 85; on insider trading, 85–86, 108

Economic development, and the role of the entrepreneur, 92

Economics of information: and ad hoc claims about behavior, 87; and analysis of information disparities, 84; and aporias in, 218n6; and balancing rhetoric, 218n7; and baseline errors, 84–87, 223–224n19; and baseline fallacies in the White Paper, 138–139; category errors, 86; and choice between incentives and efficiency, 37; and class structure, 176–179; and coalition politics, 168; combining multiple errors, 88; compared to Godel's Theorem, 36; and compulsory disclosure, 239–240n24; and conflicts between efficiency and incentives, 237n18; and "cost-plus" weapons procurement, 225n24; and debate over commodification, 217n5; and democratic debate, 157; and definition of a perfect market, 215n1; determinacy of, 95; and disparate access, 235n10; and economic effects of the patent regime, 43; and errors of professional economists, 225–226n27; and fair use as an example, 38–39; and fallacy of the "natural market," 89; and fears about 176–182; and GATT, 44; and Grossman and Stiglitz's self-destructing market, 39–40; and impossibility of efficient markets, 222n16; and liberalism, 44; as a mask for political dogma, 88; and news gathering as an example, 37; and originality, 4; and oscillation between perfect and actual markets, 218n5; and overproduction of information, 42; and paradoxical structure, 36, 39, 115, 216n4; and price as a public good, 40; and problems with consumer sovereignty, 45; and production of information in unregulated markets, 88; and production of telephone directo-

ries, 41; and public goods problem, 38; reified "property" concept in, 224n19; and reliance on natural rights, 86; rhetorical certainty in, 219n7; and rights in market indices, 40; and rule changes; 86; and the time value of information, 217n5; typical mistakes in, 80; and underproduction of information, 42; and undervaluation of sources, 129; value of, 46

Edelman, Bernard, 204–205n9, 210n16

Einstein, Albert, 164

Electronic bulletin boards, 112–113

Electronic democracy, 1

Emerson v. Davies, 209n8

Entrepreneurs: and creative innovation, 227n33; lawyers as, 95; Schumpeter's analysis of, 92–95, 227n33, 242–243n43; and tradition, 243n45

Epstein, Richard A., 20, 68–71, 74, 209n11, 215n25, 232n15; on blackmail, 90

Equality, formal or substantive, 212n7

Ethnobotany: and the authorship regime, 126; and bio-prosperity of indigenous peoples, 128–130; curare, 129; Madagascar, 128–129; and the neem tree, 126–127; and pharmaceutical research, 128–130; and the rosy periwinkle, 128

Fair use doctrine: and authorship, 244n2; and classroom copying, 131–132; Fisher's analysis of, 244n2; as method of providing raw materials to creators, 139; and public domain, 244n2; as "subsidy," 139; as a "tax" on right-holders, 138; and transformative value, 13

Fama, Eugene F., 42; economic analysis of information regime, 223n16. *See also* Fama and Laffer

Fama and Laffer, 42, 223n16, 225n25, 237n18, 241n30

Feather, John, 230n7

Feder, Barnaby J., 249n7

Feist Publications, Inc. v. Rural Telephone Service Co., 41, 208n2, 244n1, 245n10

Fichte, Johann G., 55, 230n10

First Amendment. *See* U.S. Constitution

Fischel, Daniel R., 236n15

Fisher, William W., III, 208–209n7, 215n22, 221n12, 244n2

Foucault, Michel, 57, 202n8, 230n7

Free speech. *See* Authorship; Private censorship

Frontier: metaphor of, 9
Frye, Northrop, 57, 156, 231n18
Functionalism, problems with, 256n3
Futurism, 5

Gaines, Jane, 202n8
Gates, Bill, 7,8
Gay Olympics. *See* Private censorship
General Accounting Office, 172
General Agreement on Tariffs and Trade,
   13–14, 44, 126, 127, 132, 141, 148; and
   effect on intellectual property world-
   wide, 121–125; and Trade Related As-
   pects of Intellectual Property (TRIPS),
   251–252n9
Genetic information, 4; and developing
   countries, 128; and effects of ownership
   on research, 101; and ethnobotany, 128;
   and *Moore* case, 22–24, 99–107; property
   rights in 8, 9, 99
Gere, Ann Ruggles, 229n6
Gideon v. Wainwright, 212nn6,7
Gilbert, Sandra M., 229n6
Gilbert, Walter, 10
Gilder, George, 133
Gilson, Ronald J. *See* Kraakman and Gil-
   son
Ginsburg, Douglas, 66, 232n10
Goldschmidt, Ernst P., 229n2
Goldstein, Paul, 57, 156, 231n17
Goleman, Daniel, 252n17
Goodhart, Arthur L., 209n11
Gordon, Robert W., 205n11, 228n35, 257n3
Gordon, Wendy J., 208n4, 219n7, 244n2,
   254n2
Gore, Albert, 10, 135
Gorinsky, Conrad, 129
Grace, W. R., 126–127
Grossman, Sanford J. *See* Grossman and
   Stiglitz
Grossman and Stiglitz, 39–40, 216nn1, 4,
   219nn7,8, 222n16, 236n17, 244n53
Gross National Product, 120, 125
Gubar, Susan, 229n6

Hale, Robert L., 233n25, 241n33
Harper and Row, Publishers, Inc. v. Nation
   Enterprises et. al., 213n12
Hawaii Housing Authority v. Midkiff,
   228n2
Hawking, Steven, 164
Hayek, Friedrich A., 83, 236n17
Hayes, David L., 208n6

Hemenway, David, 250n14
Hesse, Carla, 230n7, 256–257n3
Hetherington, J. A. C., 210n13, 235n12
Hills, Carla, 124, 227n32, 252n13
Hirsch v. S. C. Johnson & Son, Inc., 103,
   246n18
Hirshleifer, Jack, 219n7, 220n9, 223n16,
   224nn19,20, 225n26, 236–237n18,
   250n14; and economic analysis of patent
   regime, 41
Hitchman Coal & Coke Co. v. Mitchell,
   233n22
Hobbes, Thomas, 228n3
Hohfeld, Wesley N., 233n22
Hollings, Ernest, 33
Holmes, Oliver Wendell: on property
   rights and "originality," 55–56; on the
   relativism of the property concept,
   48–49
Horkheimer, Max, 213n14
Horwitz, Morton J., 212n4, 233n22
Howard, John J., 210n16
Hughes, Justin, 208n3
Hughes Tool Co. v. Motion Picture Associ-
   ation of America, Inc., 254n2
Hugo, Victor, 123, 252n10
Human Genome Project, 4, 7–12; and in-
   tellectual property, 10–11. *See also* Ge-
   netic information
Hunter, Ian, 205n9

Indigenous peoples. *See* Ethnobotany
Information: conflicting roles of, 30; and
   diminishing cost of the medium relative
   to the message, 7; disparaties in, 90; distinguished from innovation, 16; egalitarian conceptions of, 91, 166; and equality,
   241–242n37; as externality, 180; as "finite" and "infinite," 30–32; and formal
   equality, 181; as gift that enriches, 30–
   31; and the idea of choice, 166–167; and
   insider trading law, 82; and liberal theory of personhood, 247–248n3; liquidity
   of, 7; and the logic of the information
   relation, 7; mandatory transfers of, 31;
   and norms of market behavior, 83; as an
   organizing concept, 2; overload of, 179,
   258n7; as a puzzle, 83; as a resource,
   247n3; and rhetoric of entitlements to,
   177; and solving problems by drawing
   lines, 32–33; and theft, 83; and typing
   information issues, 30
Information age, role of law in under-

standing, 12; skepticism about, 5. *See also* Economics of information

Information economics. *See* Economics of information

Information society: skepticism about, 5–12; role of law in understanding, 12

Information Super Highway. *See* Internet

Innovation, economic history of, 206n15

Insider trading; and circular arguments, 238n19; and confusion in case law, 235n10; and efficient markets, 235–236n14; and egalitarianism, 90; and idea of equal access, 82; and incentives, 216n5; and information age, 81; and information disclosure, 87; by lawyers, 95; Levmore's analysis of, 84–85, 86–88; Manne's analysis of, 92–96; and market professionals, 234n5; and misappropriation, 234–235n8; and perfect information, 217n5; production distinguished from trading, 237–238n18; and profits as evidence of efficiency, 235n13; reasons for prohibition of, 20–21; and romantic authorship, 91–96; by secretaries, 95; and selling short, 94; and typing information issues, 110–111

Intellectual property: absolute conceptions of, 49, 138–139; basic tensions in, 156; and benefit to developing countries, 141–142; as competitive edge of Western companies, 134; and constitutional basis for, 31; and databases, 169–170; defense of current system, 139–141, 158; difficulty of, 49; and elevation of the romantic author, 54–55; functionalist explanations of, 162; inevitability of the current regime, 158; and international distributive effect, 124–127; and international effect on innovation, 124, 127–130; international importance of, 121, 125; international protection of, 2–3, 121; and labor-based property scheme, 97–98; as legal form of the information age, 13–14, 143; and legitimacy, 50; and liberalism, 49; as method for ensuring political loyalty of artists, 252n10; as monopoly, 179, 220n9; moral and utilitarian arguments for protection of, 133; and "more is better" fallacy, 227n32; as most sacred form of property, 252n10; and the physicalist notion of property, 226n31; and poverty of current systems, 175; proposals for reform, 155; and pro-

tection of liberal views, 49–50; and protection of research and innovation, 42–43; and public goods problem, 8–9; response to the expansion of, 135; and slavery, 150–153; sui generis systems, 170–171; technological dependency of the legal regime, 161; and underprotection of sources, 127; and worldwide expansion, 14

International News Service v. Associated Press, 37, 41, 244n1, 245n10

International trade, and intellectual property, 2–3, 12

International Trade Commission, 3

Internet: 6, 10; and intellectual property rights, 136–139; where "information wants to be free," 6–7; "White Paper" on intellectual property rights on, 135–137

Jaszi, Peter, 143, 202n8, 208n5, 230n7; and Bellagio Declaration, 192

John, Oliver P., 11

Joyce, Craig, 208n2

Kantian anthropology, 75–76, 233n27

Kaplow, Louis, 215n23, 253n31

Kapor, Mitchell, 201n2

Katsh, Ethan M., 202n7

Kennedy, Duncan, 104, 212n4, 220n9, 221n9, 228n3, 233n26

Kiraly, Karch, 104

Kitch, Edmund W., 204n9, 215n23, 250n14

Kloppenberg, J. R., 252n16

Kraakman, Reinier H. *See* Kraakman and Gilson

Kraakman and Gilson, 39, 89, 94; on the conflict between efficiency and incentives, 237n18; and insider trading, 236–237n18; and mechanisms of market efficiency, 222–223n16; and production versus insider trading, 237–238n18

Krause, Christian S., 52, 100, 116, 229n1, 245n6

Kronman, Anthony T., 213n13, 225n23, 236n16

Laffer, Arthur B., 42, 88, 223n17, 226n27. *See also* Fama and Laffer

Lamberton, D. M., 258n6

Landes, William M., 20, 38, 62–65, 67; on blackmail, 62–65; on information economics, 38. *See also* Landes and Posner

war, 252n9; and U.S. foreign policy, 122; by the United States, 3

Plotkin, Mark, 129

Poletown Neighborhood Council v. Detroit, 228n2

Posey, Darrell. *See* Posey and Dutfield

Posey and Dutfield, 127, 252n16

Posner, Richard A., 20, 67, 74, 89; on blackmail, 62–65; and economic fantasies, 221n14. *See also* Landes and Posner

Poster, Mark, 202n8

Priest, George L., 219n7

Privacy: and genetic information, 10; and information as a resource, 182; and information technology, 4; and intellectual property, 121–122; and "natural" facts and "social" facts, 105, 246–247n23; social construction of, 248n4; and supermarket scanners, 3–4

Private censorship: and flag burning, 147–148; and the Gay Olympics, 145–148; and on-line services, 112; origin of phrase, 254n2

Prodigy, Inc., 112; and free speech, 249n12

Property: absolute conception of, 100; apparent conceptual coherence of physical compared to intellectual property, 52; and bundle of rights, 48; compared with constitutional civil rights, 228n2; decline of absolute vision of, 48–49; disaggregation of, 218n18; and Oliver Wendell Holmes, 48; and *LeRoy Fibre*, 48; limitations on, 99–100; and "originality," 5; and reciprocal causation, 228n7; rights of publicity as, 101–102; and utilitarian justification for, 100–101; as weak barrier against the state and others, 228n2

Property rights, 220–221n9. *See also* Intellectual property

Proposals for reform: on protection of databases, 169; on protection of public domain, 168; sui generis systems, 170–171. *See also* Bellagio Declaration

Public domain, 209n8; in France and England, 256n3

Public goods, 223n17; expansive use of the idea, 250–251n14; Shavell's analysis of, 250–251n14; and socialism, 225n24

Publicity, right of, 23, 101–103;

Public-private distinction, 28, 211–212n4, 214n20; and blackmail, 78–80; and differing moral realms, 27; and equality, 26;

and formal equality, 212n5; and insider trading, 91; and the market, 29; Marx on, 25, 212n5; and politics, 29; and the role of information, 28–29; and the role of law, 26; and solving problems by drawing lines, 27–28; and typing of information issues, 32–33, 78–80, 109–111

Rand, Ayn, 83, 236n17

Reagan, Ronald, 134

Red Lion Broadcasting Co., Inc. v. FCC, 254n2

Reform. *See* Proposals for reform

Rehnquist, William H.: on private censorship, 147–148

Rose, Mark, 205n9, 230n7

Rosy periwinkle. *See* Ethnobotany

Rotenberg, Marc, 249n9, 257n8

Rothbard, Murray N., 232n14

Rubenstein, Bruce, 253n29

Russell, Bertrand, 36

Rust v. Sullivan, 181, 213n9, 228n8, 248n3

Saari, Christopher P., 88, 215n24, 236n14

Sakaiya, Taichi, 201n4

"Sampling," of musical works, 206n11

Samuelson, Pamela, 136, 253n37, 254n40

Samuelson, Paul, 250n14

San Francisco Arts and Athletics, Inc., et al. v. U.S. Olympic Committee, 145–148, 254n3

Sanjek, David, 206n11

Sartre, Jean-Paul: on authorship, 229n5

Saunders, David, 205n9

Scheppele, Kim L., 204n9, 214n21; on power differentials in fraud cases, 236n16

Schrader, Dorothy, 251n6

Schrage, Michael, 203n8

Schumpeter, Joseph A., 16, 206n14, 242–243nn41,46; on entrepreneurship, 92–95, 242–243nn41,46

Science fiction, 255n12

Scottish Enlightenment, 32

Securities and Exchange Commission, 90

S.E.C. v. Materia, 81–83, 234n1

Seed varieties, and indigenous peoples, 126–127

Shakespeare, William, 163–164; and plagiarism, 230n12

Shamans, 128

Shavell, Steven, 250n14; inefficient information-gathering incentives, 239–240n24
Singer, Joseph W., 228nn1,2,4
Slavery, 150–153; and intellectual property, 5
Social theory, 187–191; and functionalism in the law, 205n11; and the idea of stages in history, 190; and the positive role of moral indeterminacy, 190
Software: and free-market conservatives, 133; and League for Programming Freedom, 132–133; and opposition to patents, 165; and patent law, 132–133; and Stallman's critique, 132–133
Spender, Sir Stephen: and plagiarism, 148; and privacy, 148–149
Spleens. See Genetic information; Moore v. Regents of the University of California
Stallman, Richard, 132–133, 165, 201n2
Stationers Company, 162
Sterling, Bruce, 201n6
Stewart, Susan, 204n9
Stigler, George J., 216n4
Stiglitz, Joseph E. See Grossman and Stiglitz
Streeter, Thomas, 202n8
Streitfeld, David, 148, 255n7

Telemarketing, 33
Texas v. Johnson, 255n6
Thirteenth Amendment. See U.S. Constitution
Thompson, Earl, 250n14, 255n6
Thompson, Larry, 203n7
Toffler, Alvin, 201n4
Trade Related Aspects of Intellectual Prop-

erty. See General Agreement on Tariffs and Trade
Transgenic species: and the Declaration of Independence, 154; and intellectual property, 150; and patenting human beings, 150–153
United States Trade Act of 1988, 122
U.S. Constitution: "copyright clause" of, 226n31; First Amendment, 30, 154, 182; Thirteenth Amendment, 150–151, 159, 160

Vandevelde, Kenneth, 47–48, 228nn1,5
Ventner, Craig, 8–9

Wards Cove Packing v. Atonio, 241n35
Warren, Manning, III, 235n10
Warren, Samuel. See Warren and Brandeis
Warren and Brandeis, on privacy, 102, 182, 246n16
Whalen v. Roe, 247n3
White, Harold O., 230n9
Whitehead, Alfred North, 36
"White Paper." See Internet
Whittier, John Greenleaf, 258n11
Wiley, John Shepard, Jr., 225n22, 231n19
Wittgenstein, Ludwig, and linguistic essentialism, 246n14
Wolfhard, Eric, 252n12
Woodmansee, Martha, 52–53, 143, 205n9, 229n6, 230nn7, 8; and Bellagio Declaration, 192; on the elevation of the romantic author, 54
Wordsworth, William, 16, 116, 206n14
World Wide Fund for Nature, 128
World Wide Web. See Internet
Wrongful birth, cases 233n28

Yen, Alfred, 208n3